The Social Life of Busyness

The Social Life of Busyness

BY

CLARE HOLDSWORTH
Keele University, UK

emerald
PUBLISHING

United Kingdom – North America – Japan – India – Malaysia – China

Emerald Publishing Limited
Emerald Publishing, Floor 5, Northspring, 21-23 Wellington Street, Leeds LS1 4DL.

First edition 2021

Reprints and permissions service
Contact: www.copyright.com

British Library Cataloguing in Publication Data
A catalogue record for this book is available from the British Library

ISBN: 978-1-78743-699-2 (Print)
ISBN: 978-1-78743-698-5 (Online)
ISBN: 978-1-78754-511-3 (Epub)
ISBN: 978-1-78756-306-3 (Paperback)

INVESTOR IN PEOPLE

In memory of my father, David Becket, and my mentor, David Morgan. Both Davids exemplified the benefits of leading a busy and fulfilling life.

Contents

List of Figures

List of Tables

Acknowledgements

My time to research and write this book was facilitated by a Leverhulme Trust Major Research Fellowship, *The Social Life of Busyness in an Age of Deceleration* (MRF-2017-044). I am extremely grateful to the Leverhulme Trust for this unique opportunity to be able to dedicate time to this project. I would like to thank Reena Mistry from the Leverhulme Trust for her assistance in managing the fellowship. I would also like to thank Jonathan Wastling, Dean of the Faculty of Natural Sciences, and Chris Fogwill, Head of the School of Geography, Geology, and the Environment, at Keele University for approving and supporting this research fellowship. My time spent teaching crochet was also supported by a Collaborative Investigator Grant, *Putting self-care into practice: a creative learning approach*, awarded by Methods North West, part of the Economic and Social Research Council North West Social Science Doctoral Training Partnership.

I would like to thank Pete Adey, David Bissell, Graham Crow and David Morgan for their support and encouragement of my original Leverhulme application. Special thanks to David Bissell for suggesting the title. David Morgan's enthusiasm for this project has been extremely encouraging in shaping my ideas. His ability to think tangentially about family life and weave together diverse literature has always been inspirational. David very sadly died in July 2020 and his loss to sociology is shared by many researchers who, like me, had the privilege to work with him.

In writing this book, I have benefitted from conversations and suggestions from current and former colleagues and PhD students at Keele University and the Morgan Centre for Research into Everyday Lives, University of Manchester. These include Daniel Allen, David Amigoni, Laura Brennan, Alison Briggs, Sarah Briggs, Stephen Cropper, Mark Featherstone, Janet Finch, Emma Head, Sue Heath, Mark Lucherini, Vanessa May, Marina Mendonça, Ceri Morgan, Kat Mycock, Alex Nobajas, Emma Randall, Paul Simpson (who introduced me to the work of Roberto Esposito), Simon Pemberton and Richard Waller. I would also like to thank Rich Burgess, Stef Everill and Elaine McFarlane for technical and administrative support at Keele. Further afield I would like to acknowledge Jennifer Whillans who commissioned the Mass Observation diaries and made these available electronically for other researchers to use. Jennifer also kindly shared her initial analysis with me. Beverley Sykes copy-edited the manuscript and the text is much improved by her careful observations.

Special thanks to Lisa Dikomitis, Tamsin Fisher and Sarah Hall who collaborated on the *Putting self-care into practice* project. We are all very grateful to

Charlotte Burke for initiating and organising the Keele Student Union *Crafternoons*. Sarah Hall, along with Mark Lucherini, also very generously took the time to read and comment on a draft of the manuscript and I am very grateful for their insightful comments. I have greatly enjoyed my many virtual chats with Sarah and Mark that have been welcome distractions during Covid-19 lockdowns.

I would like to acknowledge the help and support of staff at the Mass Observation Archive at The Keep, University of Sussex. Material from the archive is reproduced with permission of Curtis Brown Group Ltd, London on behalf of The Trustees of the Mass Observation Archive © The Trustees of the Mass Observation Archive.

Kathryn Hughes at the Timescapes Archive, University of Leeds generously assisted in access to the Work and Family Lives dataset. These data are kindly provided with the consent of Sarah Cunningham-Burley, Lynn Jamieson, and Jeni Harden and the Timescapes archive, administered by University of Leeds, sponsored by the Economic and Social Research Council.

A previous version of Table 4.1 was published in Holdsworth (2020b). Three of the case studies of working busyness discussed in Chapter 5 were originally published in Holdsworth (2020a). These materials are reproduced with kind permission of Taylor Francis.

At Emerald, I have had the pleasure of working with a number of editors. Phillipa Grand originally encouraged me to write the book and subsequently to apply for the Leverhulme Trust fellowship. Helen Beddow supported the writing stage and shared her enthusiasm for sewing and fabric craft. Kathy Mathers has overseen the production of the book.

Writing about busyness necessarily touches on all aspects of everyday life and my family have contributed to this book is many different ways. This is especially the case as I wrote most of this book during the isolation of Covid-19 lockdowns. My partner Marty has been an invaluable and patient sounding board for my ideas. My daughter Bethan Holdsworth, my sister Janet Curran, and my mother Anne Becket have all encouraged and inspired me to remain busy and not be too pre-occupied with writing. Bethan especially learnt not to disturb and kept me going with a plentiful supply of cake. Janet very kindly read a draft of the manuscript and provided professional advice on time management. As a family, we have all supported each other following my father's death in April 2020. My father was an active, busy person and his tireless commitment to supporting his family and local community has inspired my ambition to identify the positive benefits of keeping busy.

Chapter 1

Being Busy

White Rabbits

This book is about the social life of busyness, the busyness that we experience and encounter in our everyday lives that makes us weary or elated and that pushes us towards and away from other people. Busyness can validate everyday life or be an excuse for not doing something. It is not an exact thing or practice; if we are busy, it is because of a sense of fulfilment or of being overwhelmed. As an excuse, it is simultaneously watertight and vague. If someone says they are too busy to do something, this is their final decision, though the precise details of busyness need not be revealed. Busyness can be a default position we assume about other people, especially if we require something from them. Acknowledging busyness is often interspersed within the requests of others: 'I know you are busy, but could you....?'.

By framing this account of busyness through its social life, this book addresses how busyness organises the social and simultaneously is of the social.[1] I am interested in how busyness frames relationships but equally in how its prominence may be explained through the economic and social contexts of relational work. Busyness is manifest in 'the effort of establishing, maintaining, negotiating, transforming, and terminating interpersonal relations'.[2] How this relational work is valued and who values it may also explain the popularity of busyness. Investment in relational work or collaboration can lead to tensions between doing stuff for other people and getting on with our own work or practices of self-care. Busyness is, therefore, of the social because it condenses the tensions of interpersonal relations. These tensions can be found at different scales, from those of intimate and family relations to those of corporate organisations, and are shaped by the uneven politics of time.[3] Busyness can be draining but it can also engender feelings of worthiness. These experiences depend on how it is valued by others as well as its relationship to feelings of self-identification. However, while busyness might be experienced as relational, our attempts to nullify it are increasingly individual.

---

[1]Bastian, Baraitser, Flexer, Hom, and Salisbury (2020, pp. 289-296).
[2]Zelizer (2012, p. 147).
[3]Sharma (2014).

The Social Life of Busyness, 1–10
Copyright © 2021 by Clare Holdsworth
Published under exclusive licence by Emerald Publishing Limited
doi:10.1108/978-1-78743-698-520211002

It is up to us to maximise time independent of others, whether we use time management strategies or implement a work–life balance to do so.[4]

My own interest in busyness was initially sparked by overhearing colleagues' declarations about busyness. As I was working in my office in a British university, halfway down a long corridor, I became aware of crescendoing complaints about the busyness of working life: colleagues running late for meetings, protesting that they had too much to do and complaining about the overwhelming stress of being busy. Details concerning what needed to be done and whether particular activities had been completed were more muted. In these overheard statements, there was little recognition of the virtue of keeping busy. The temporal quality of busyness that I especially overheard was not in the declarations of busy people saying they were getting things done; it was found in the anxiety concerning what needed to be done. Busyness did not mean synthesising the present with the past or the future; instead, it unsettled the flow of time. The intensity of disruption corresponds with the temporal condition that Ivor Southwood describes as 'non-stop inertia'.[5] This is the overwhelming sense of being trapped by frenetic inactivity and, as a consequence, feeling that it is not possible to experience the satisfaction of getting things done.[6] My initial curiosity about busyness did not align with the need to quantify busyness or peruse strategies for its amelioration. Instead, I was intrigued by why there was so much talk of busyness and what this chatter inferred about colleagues' fulfilment or neglect of their responsibilities and their anxieties about time. Busyness puzzled me because it is paradoxical, and paradoxes are the imaginative fuel of social inquiry.[7]

These paradoxical qualities of busyness have often meant that my own attempts to explain this temporal phenomenon have ended up with me chasing my tail or being stuck in cul-de-sacs. My reaction to colleagues' comments about their busyness initially took me in the wrong direction. Overhearing their complaints reminded me of the White Rabbit in Lewis Carroll's 1865 fantasy novel *Alice's Adventures in Wonderland*; he is obsessed with time and cannot move beyond this obsession.[8] So I started my study of busyness by revisiting Carroll's White Rabbit to see what I could learn about busyness from his fixations with time. I was familiar with the White Rabbit's comments about time, such as 'The hurrier I go, the behinder I get', and his reply to Alice's question 'How long is forever' – 'sometimes just one second'. These quotations are provided when 'White Rabbit quotes' is searched for online and adorn arty-crafty home decorations. Even the physicist Carlos Rovelli quotes the White Rabbit's explanation of forever in his

---

[4]Melissa Gregg details how time management strategies isolate workers from each other: Gregg (2018).

[5]Southwood (2011).

[6]See Rosa (2017).

[7]Holdsworth (2020a).

[8]Carroll (1865). The sociologist Dale Southerton also begins his recent book about time squeeze with a reference to the White Rabbit: Southerton (2020).

2017 book *The Order of Time*.[9] I had assumed that the character of the White Rabbit was obsessed with time and was a pioneer of the twenty-first century busyness. Curiously, when I sat down to reread *Alice's Adventures in Wonderland*, I did not find these quotations in the original text. Carroll's White Rabbit is not a busy rabbit. He is obsessed with time and his pocket watch simply because he is late for a meeting with the Duchess. We do not learn why he is late or the purpose of the meeting he is rushing to get to. The White Rabbit is a plot device.[10] Alice pursues him into and through Wonderland, but he has little to do or say until he reappears with the royal entourage as the King of Heart's herald. At Alice's trial, the White Rabbit is deferential and nervous, and is anxious that things should be done properly and corrects the King of Hearts about procedure. Carroll wrote that he intended the White Rabbit to be the opposite of Alice; the elderly, timid and feeble rabbit that wears spectacles contrasts with Alice's youth.[11]

Curious about where my interpretation of the busy White Rabbit came from and the source of the much-quoted aphorisms, I turned to Walt Disney's 1951 animated version of Carroll's book. Disney's White Rabbit is old and wears spectacles, as Carroll described him, but lacks the original's fastidiousness. The cartoon White Rabbit is rotund with a matching outsize pocket watch that is always falling out of his pocket. His watch carries him along; he is literally moved by time. Disney develops the White Rabbit's circular fascination with time. He joins the Mad Hatter and the March Hare at their tea party, where the Mad Hatter declares the rabbit's watch to be 'two days late' and, encouraged by the March Hare, destroys this 'mad watch'. Disney's White Rabbit, like Carroll's, is perpetually late and does nothing to resolve this. Disney exaggerates the White Rabbit's character and his contribution to the storyline, but this rabbit is also not the source of the quotations found online and elsewhere allegedly by the White Rabbit.

My pursuit of these White Rabbits and their musings about time and busyness proved to be a plot device that led me in the wrong direction.[12] Neither of these White Rabbits are the source of the much-quoted musings about time; the words are simply figurative expressions of the worry that surrounds not getting things done. While Disney's White Rabbit comes closer to the popular image of the time-obsessed leporid, the popularity of the quotes attributed falsely to the White Rabbit transcends both Carroll's original characterisation and Disney's interpretation. Falsely accrediting these aphorisms to Lewis Carroll is convincing because they appeal to popular obsessions with time-related problems. The misquotes also update the White Rabbit's fastidiousness about being 'on time' to more modern

---

[9]Rovelli (2018, p. 52).

[10]It has been pointed out to me that the film *The Matrix* also uses the White Rabbit as a plot device.

[11]This description is taken from Alice-in-Wonderland.net (n.d.).

[12]For completeness, I have also checked the White Rabbit character in the Tim Burton movies *Alice in Wonderland* and *Through the Looking Glass*. Neither of these films are the source of the quotes.

sensibilities concerning experiencing time. It is easy to turn the original White Rabbit's obsession with being late into musings about the misuse of time.

The lesson I learnt from this initial wrong turn was how easy it is to make judgements and convince ourselves about the certainty of time, or at least what is written about it, even though the temporal frustratingly remains just beyond our conceptual grasp. By perpetually being busy, we segue between having some sense of certainty about what we have to do, and feeling being overwhelmed because we have too much to do. Writing about busyness is similarly frustrating; at the moment that a precise conceptual interpretation comes into view, it very quickly falls away. Busyness defies an exact definition, but this does not imply that it is immune to interpretation.

My starting point is to offer a definition of busyness as the intersection of what others expect or request us to do and what we need to or want to get done. This account of the social life of busyness does not seek to define, remedy or perfect busy uses of time. Instead, my purpose is to interrogate how being busy oscillates around intersections of multiple and tangled responsibilities. I am intrigued by busyness because of how it is essentially relational yet at the same time uniquely individual. I am interested in how busyness articulates the acceptance and rejection of interdependencies. If, as Rovelli writes, 'the study of time does nothing but return us to ourselves',[13] studying busyness does more than reveal us to ourselves; it also exposes our relationships with and responsibilities to others.

By framing this account of busyness through its social life, I am deliberately opening up a consideration of busyness beyond the realm of work and time management. Although my curiosity about busyness originated at work, I do not intend to suggest that busyness is exclusive to organisational cultures. While contemporary critiques of busyness are aligned with the relationship between busyness and productivity, the problem with including busyness in the more defined constraints of time management is that doing so makes an assumption about who is busy and in what ways. Busyness becomes the specific condition of workers doing some form of managerial or bureaucratic work. These workers may be lured into having the status of busyness as a badge of honour, as the time use researcher Jay Gershuny suggests.[14] Equating self-worth with busyness also permeates other forms of employment, such as the 'Bullshit' jobs described by David Graeber that serve to maintain the status of middle management.[15] This honour of being busy does not necessarily equate with being productive. If busyness is recognised as a fault, it is one to be put right through the application of productivity techniques.[16] However, busyness is found beyond the closed world of professional time management. We cannot ignore the busyness of workers employed beyond a restrictive interpretation of professional work. Many such employees were classified as essential workers during the Covid-19 pandemic, thus, revealing

---

[13]Rovelli (2018, p. 147).
[14]Gershuny (2005, pp. 287-314).
[15]Graeber (2019).
[16]See, for example, Gregg (2018).

the necessity of their labour, such as health and social care workers, cleaners, retail assistants, delivery drivers and transport workers. Moreover, a relational approach does not prioritise the economic sphere over other domains of everyday life; instead, it interrogates the interrelationships between diverse responsibilities. The busyness of parents and carers, retirees, students, the unemployed and the under-employed is also equally valid. Extending the reach of busyness to consider diverse forms of work, the temporal demands of care and the experiences of people not in work opens up a diverse interpretation of busyness beyond understanding it as a failure of time management or productivity.

A final introductory note acknowledges the spatial and temporal limitations of this book. The data that I have collated, which I introduce below, and the social theories that I discuss in the next chapter are located within an Anglo-American economic, political and cultural location. However, cultural diversity is one of time's most intriguing attributes, and this will be equally relevant to studies of busyness. How we speak about time and its linguistic variations (e.g. the construction of tenses and temporal vocabulary), temporal cultural and social norms (e.g. when shared activities happen, judgements about being 'on time' and customs concerning waiting) and differential interpretations of time over the life-course (e.g. expectations of generational solidarity versus generational change) will have an impact on busyness. However, a consideration of the cultural variations in the concept of busyness is beyond the scope of this text because of the enormous amount of research data and various analytical techniques that this would require. My examination of busyness has, therefore, remained within a specific sociocultural location.

Busy Methodologies

Studying busyness can take the researcher in numerous directions. It can be examined as a symptom of sociocultural trends, quantified through detailed empirical examination or interrogated through philosophical inquiry. The almost infinite possibilities of busyness make it an equally irritating and intriguing topic for research, and it is necessary to define a framework to work within. This study of the social life of busyness prioritises the diversity of experiences within assemblages of time–space and intimate and public relationships. I am not seeking to either refute or confirm broad theoretical narratives of sociocultural change. For the most part, this study holds grand narratives in the background to bring to the fore the subjectivity of busyness and to consider the ongoing synthesis of thought and talk of busyness within social practices and habits. At times, this synthesis is illuminated by considering it in parallel with theorisations of temporality and how busyness evokes slippage between past, present and future. This orientation also requires examination not just of individuals but also of people in the social contexts of work, family, community, etc. If a study of busyness can add to an understanding of the social conditions of the twenty-first century society, it is through unpicking the relational context of everyday life and how we navigate responsibilities to ourselves and others. In other words, I am interested in how busyness is experienced in different spaces rather than assuming it is a universal temporal expression.

Prioritising an empirical examination raises the question of how busyness can be studied. Given its multiple and normative nature, busyness does not lend itself to the methods of conventional social science inquiry such as interviews or social surveys. However, at the same time, it is possible to find busyness in multiple sources. Rather than me designing a specific methodology to study busyness, I have based the research for this book on narratives about busyness that I found when looking for busyness elements in existing data. This method of repurposing data – using data for a different purpose to that which it might have been collected for – facilitates studying busyness in different domains rather than restricting it to specific experiences or contexts (such as those of a particular type of worker).[17] To write this book, I, therefore, collected a bricolage of data on time in everyday contexts and examined these for narratives of busyness.

The decision not to collect primary data was as much an ethical decision as a practical one. My own collection of primary data sources would have been limited to a restrictive range of participants, and using secondary data also eschews the busyness of conventional social science inquiry. Busyness cannot be external to this study, by which I mean that it cannot be studied in isolation; it permeates the very research itself. I have not excluded my own practices from my study of busyness, and I outline below the autoethnographic techniques that I used as part of the bricolage of data. However, a study of busyness provides more than an opportunity to engage in autoethnographic practices; it allows an examination of the time-intensive practices of research itself. Collecting primary data makes temporal demands on researchers and participants and unavoidably involves collecting data that remain unused. I propose that an examination of busyness provides an ideal case study of how repurposing data can slow down the temporal intensity of research. My reuse of data that have been collected for purposes that are different to the use I have for the data, responds to a growing debate about the acceleration that universities expect regarding both teaching and research and the possibility of slow study.[18]

The primary data sources that I used are as follows:

- 134 one-day time diaries from the UK Mass Observation Archive (MOA)[19] on the theme of time pressure that were written in the autumn/winter of 2017/2018.

---

[17]I borrow the term repurposing from big data research that explicitly uses data for a different purpose from that for which it was collected, such as the analysis of administrative data. See Woodall (2017). Repurposing has a different meaning from the more conventional term, secondary analysis; in particular, it captures the possibility of finding accounts of busyness in data that were not collected for this specific purpose.

[18]See, for example, Berg and Seeber (2016).

[19]The Mass Observation Archive (MOA) was established in 1937 to record everyday life in the UK by volunteer writers. It ceased collecting observations in the mid-1960s and was subsequently revived in 1981. The MOA issues three directives a year inviting correspondents to write about their experiences of a particular theme. One-day diaries are often requested in these directives. See http://www.massobs.org.uk/ for further information about the MOA.

- A longitudinal study of Work and Family Time carried out with 13 families in southern Scotland between 2007 and 2010 which forms part of the UK Economic and Social Research Council Timescapes study.[20]
- A sample of 15 self-help text books on time use and busyness published between 2004 and 2019.
- A scoping review of 41 published journal articles detailing longitudinal analysis of time use data.
- 87 short accounts of a writer's day collated by *The Guardian*, a UK-based national newspaper, between 2016 and 2018.
- Observations from teaching crochet in a series of 11 informal 'crafternoons' run by Keele University Student Union from October 2019 to March 2020.

Although I have attempted to identify data that do not restrict busyness to specific practices, such as particular types of work, as I have already noted, these data are constrained within a particular geographical location. All the primary data that were either collected in the UK or written in a transatlantic Anglo-American cultural space and my interpretation of busyness are necessarily constrained within these spaces. Moreover, the data selection and analyses come with the usual caveat about not being representative. I have had to use data sets that I could access and whose participants were selected by others. However, for the study of busyness, a requirement for representation is perhaps a red herring because it would imply that it is a discernible, objective thing that happens to us because of our socio-economic characteristics. Rather than using representation as a benchmark, I have prioritised different types of busyness.

I introduce the details of each data set because I use these to study different aspects of busyness in subsequent chapters of this book. To analyse this data, I used both quantitative content analysis and narrative methods. Because of the disparate, messy nature of the data, I found simple counting techniques a useful first stage in making sense of the data. Although initially this might appear to be at odds with my reluctance to try and quantify busyness, the technique of counting and deciphering numerical patterns in the data has proved to be an insightful and concise way of revealing the timing of busyness and the significance of numbers in the stories that are told about being busy. Narrative analysis investigates stories of busyness in more depth, though the approach I use varies between the data sets. The one-day diaries (from both the MOA and *The Guardian*) are ideally suited to a narrative approach that distinguishes between the structure, emotion, substance and function of each account.[21] In other words, how the writer writes about a particular day, the emotional tone they use, what they have to say about time and busyness, and how the dairies reveal the relational qualities of being

---

[20]The Timescapes archive was funded by the UK Economic and Social Research Council to archive qualitative longitudinal data on personal and family relationships. For further information about the archive, see https://timescapes-archive .leeds.ac.uk/timescapes/
[21]Riessman (1993).

busy. In the family interviews, the narrative analysis follows the conversation between the interviewer and the interviewee to reveal the distinction between the symbolic busyness that families live by and the busyness they actually live with. Finally, regarding the analysis of self-help books, I am intrigued by the busyness of these texts and the different ways in which they tell stories of busyness as well as suggest strategies for making the most of our time.

The final element of this research is autoethnographic. Reflecting on my own experiences of busyness was unavoidable rather than a deliberate strategy.[22] Rovelli's claim that studying time tells us more about ourselves than anything else cannot be denied when writing about busyness. Taking an autoethnographic approach also resists any attempt to rely on disembodied accounts of busyness. At the same time, I do not want to exaggerate my own busyness; it is no more exceptional than anyone else's. Indeed, as an academic who has the privilege of being awarded a fellowship, I have less reason to be busy than most. I have used autoethnography to examine how we can reflect on our use of time rather than to add to the stories of busyness. While I was writing this book, I kept a detailed time use diary to reflect on how keeping track of time is a valuable tactic of self-care. My reflections on this process lean towards what I have learnt from the discipline of tracking time, not what I have learnt about how I spend time. I have also been involved in teaching therapeutic busyness through working with a university student union to teach craft to students and staff (mostly, but not exclusively, crochet). While teaching crochet, I have learnt to adapt my expectations of what can be achieved through teaching craft as self-care and to assess how I use craft as a therapeutic practice for myself. This self-examination of how and when I craft develops a counter-narrative of busyness as an expression of frenetic inactivity to consider how the busyness of craft can be a therapeutic practice of actively stilling the body.

Chapter Overviews

This account of busyness starts with an overview of theoretical accounts of time. My intention is not to refute or confirm broad theoretical temporal narratives, but what theory can do is hold a researcher to task regarding resisting the appeal of normative accounts of busyness, and the review is organised for this purpose. Of particular interest are explanations of temporal change that make the case for individualism and/or social acceleration and how these accounts are challenged by empirical research that identifies the diversity of temporal experiences and the obduracy of uneven politics of time. I also consider the limitations of historical comparisons for making the case for the uniqueness of the twenty-first century busyness. Key ideas that are useful for interpreting busyness include moving beyond mind/body dualism so as not to differentiate between thinking and doing busyness and developing a temporal examination of this mental chatter and activity that focusses on the synthesis of past, present and future.

---

[22]Lucherini (2017, pp. 429–435).

My empirical examination of the social lives of busyness begins in Chapter 3 with an examination of clock time that is based on analysis of published longitudinal analyses of time use data and analysis of the temporal references in the MOA one-day diaries. Inspired by Christian Marclay's video installation *The Clock*, I consider how these data on time reveal the tensions between individualised and collective co-ordinations of time and timing. The scoping review of time use unsettles the expectation of universal temporal trends and upholds the significance of social diversity in relation to how time is used, particularly in relation to gender. This analysis of inequality in time use contrasts with the findings from the MOA data that reveal the shared significance of timing. In other words, we are busy in different ways, but different linear rhythms of time coalesce at the same temporal pinch points. This chapter concludes with a brief reflection on my own experiences of tracking time and how these reveal the ongoing tensions between making the most of one's own time and the pull of external commitments.

Chapter 4 develops this theme of the duality of individual and collective experiences of time through an analysis of self-help books on time management and busyness. These texts necessarily assume that busyness is everyone's responsibility, although the methods that they promote tend to exaggerate the social distances between people. This analysis of self-help books is carried out in two parts. The first collective analysis of all 15 texts explores what these books say about busyness and identifies the temporal norms that these texts reproduce. The second part considers what these texts have to say about time itself and about how successful time management routines, as developed by the time management guru David Allen in the bestselling text *Getting Things Done*, necessarily depend on the ongoing synthesis of past, present and future. The overall conclusion of my analysis is that the notion of time management is perhaps misleading, as these techniques are more directly concerned with the management of space and other people than with managing time.

The theme of managing space and other people is developed in Chapter 5, which considers the busyness of work. The empirical data for this analysis concern the diverse experiences of time pressure (or lack of time pressure) of workers employed in different types of organisations that require specific assemblages of time, space and organisational structure. These case studies are selected from the MOA one-day diaries. This analysis underscores my observation that busyness is not a specific thing that can be related to social and cultural trends in work organisation, as workers have differential experiences of these changes. Some people work in organisations that are at the vanguard of social changes (and I discuss the director Ken Loach's depiction of the temporalities of the gig economy in his 2019 film *Sorry We Missed You*), but not everyone does. In this analysis, I am particularly interested in how the busyness at work is expressed through relationships with colleagues and employees' assimilations of responsibilities. This observation about the relational qualities of working time are explored further through an examination of working on one's own, using *The Guardian*'s series 'My writing day'. This series considers how the isolation of an author is dependent on assemblages of space, technologies and other people. Even authors cannot escape busyness and worries about productivity.

Chapter 6 investigates the necessary busyness of family time. In this chapter, I adapt the historian John Gillis's distinction between the family we live by (the family that does the symbolic work that represent us as the people we like to think we are) and the family we live with (the more self-interested and often disruptive family that is fragmented and indeterminate) to interrogate discussions of time squeeze and busyness in an empirical study of work and family life. My analysis of the temporality of family life contrasts narratives of busyness and balance and how the everyday family we live by is explained through accounts of balancing time and responsibilities. The families we live with, in contrast, reveal the impossibility of achieving balance in the present moment. Balance is necessarily a retrospective or hopeful condition of busy family lives.

Throughout all of these empirical chapters, the tension between resolving the responsibilities one has to oneself and those one has to others is a recurrent theme of busyness. In the final empirical chapter on free time (Chapter 7), I consider this dilemma in more detail. My starting point is the impossibility of me-time being the negation of relationships with others. I draw on the work of the philosopher Roberto Esposito to consider how yearnings for me-time assimilate both the necessity of community and the desire to shut this out. I am particularly interested in the therapeutic benefits of me-time and the possibility of achieving flow by being immersed in activities that only benefit oneself. Drawing on my experiences of doing and teaching craft using fabric and yarn, I consider how these therapeutic expressions of me-time are not about immunising the self against the outside world and can be achieved through recognising our obligations to others.

In the concluding chapter, I attempt to pull all of these diverse empirical threads together to consider the past, present and futures of busyness. This book was written in the summer of 2020, so it is impossible to ignore how our expectations and experiences of busyness have been radically altered by the Covid-19 pandemic. In this final chapter, I consider how narratives of busyness make sense of what has happened before, of what is happening in the present and of our orientations towards the future in the wake of societal responses to Covid-19.

Chapter 2

Busy Time

Busyness by Stealth

In his 2017 BBC radio programme, the social commentator Oliver Burkeman investigates modern-day obsessions with busyness.[1] Beginning his exploration in Times
Square in New York, a place that at least in pre-Covid-19 times epitomised the rush
of everyday life, Burkeman muses that 'somewhere when we weren't looking, it's
like busyness became a way of life'. Clearly busyness has not simply been unwit-
tingly imposed on us. We might be surprised and frustrated by the pace of everyday
life and concur with the sentiment that busyness has come upon us by stealth, but
there has to be an explanation of why busyness has become omnipresent.

Popular commentaries, such as Burkeman's, tend to develop explanations of
busyness by referring to psychological experimental research on time-perception
and timing. An examination of the social life of busyness requires a different
direction to consider social rather than psychological explanations. The multiple
causes of busyness might obscure a definitive explanation; at the same time, its
status as the zeitgeist of the twenty-first century temporality means that busyness is in tune with a broad spectrum of theoretical accounts of social order
and change. Busyness is the temporal expression of post-structuralism – the
body of theories that defies the credibility of grand theory and the status of
certainty. Busyness is adeptly suited to post-structuralism's requirement that it
should be theoretical without being exclusive. It condenses the multiplicity of
responsibilities with the retreat of structural forces and as such can be interpreted
through the lens of individualisation and the requirement in late modernity
for responsibility for the self; for the dispersal of authority through the interconnected networks of control; and for the social acceleration of everyday life
that has been brought about through an increasing pace of life and social and
technological change.

In this chapter, I develop this interpretation of busyness as a temporal expression of relational interdependencies that are not constrained to defined organisational spaces. This relational reading of busyness is developed with reference to
theoretical and empirical accounts of social and temporal change. The challenge

---

[1]Burkeman (2017).

The Social Life of Busyness, 11–27
Copyright © 2021 by Clare Holdsworth
Published under exclusive licence by Emerald Publishing Limited
doi:10.1108/978-1-78743-698-520211003

I have struggled with in writing about busyness is the impossibility of escaping from the fundamentals of being busy. Writing about busyness necessarily takes a writer in different directions, and as I have already highlighted in the previous chapter, not all of these directions are helpful. This review is necessarily selective, and my intention is to provide a theoretical and empirical account of a relational interrogation of busyness. I also use this account to consider the historical framing of being busy and the popular assumption that busyness is a particular quality of modern times. The final part of this review considers conceptualisations of temporality and timing that are necessary to move beyond a descriptive interpretation of busyness to a more analytical account.

Theorising Busyness

Individualisation and Control

The fetishising of busyness accords with theoretical accounts of individualisation in capturing the need to assimilate responsibilities that is required in the project of the self.[2] Individualisation is relevant for busyness in two possible ways. The first relates busyness to the decline of institutional timetables and the dominance of individual schedules. For example, Dale Southerton's empirical investigation of time squeeze links this phenomenon concerning the twenty-first century temporalities with a decline in the importance of institutionalised temporal events (e.g. divergence in the timing of the working week) and a decline in the need to coordinate individual routines within interconnected networks, especially family groups.[3] The second interpretation views busyness as an expression of a worthy, productive self. Michelle Shir-Wise develops the concept of conspicuous busyness to capture how busyness has become a sign of status; the busier we are, the more we have to do, indicates a greater depth and breadth of responsibility.[4] The mantras of choice and responsibility also promote expectations that people can become entrepreneurs of time when they make calculated decisions about how to prioritise and sequence activities.[5] These lines of thought are persuasive as they separately point towards a straightforward, linear interpretation of busyness that directly links the decline of structures and institutions with the rise of busyness. However, shared anxieties about busyness also reveal the limitations of how people act in this way. Rather than busyness being a mode of calculated action

---

[2]My writing about individualism follows the work of key theorists such as Ulrich and Elizabeth Beck, who do not equate individualism with a fetishising of the individual but with the expectation that responsibilities are assumed to be individual and the choices that individuals are required to make are navigated in lieu of defined structural constraints and pathways. Their classic explanation of these theories can be found in Beck and Beck-Gernsheim (2002).

[3]Southerton (2020).

[4]Shir-Wise (2019b).

[5]Erikson and Mazmanian (2017, pp. 152–168).

that is guided by entrepreneurial consideration of choices,[6] it is a default reaction to the proliferation of choice and the constraints of self-biography. The exhaustion resulting from busyness can be equated with overwhelming responsibilities and choices that are accepted and made respectively without the guidance of structural pathways that would reveal the outcome of these choices.[7] Busyness is not just about having too much to do but is also about the uncertainty of what happens if certain actions are not followed up. Instead of acting in a calculating entrepreneurial style, busyness keeps people to the mantra of keeping going and getting as much done as possible so not to restrict their choices.

The uncertainty of busyness can be equated with the temporal intensity of the dispersal of power. In his short and captivating essay 'Society of Control', Giles Deleuze writes of people being 'undulatory, in orbit, in a continuous network'.[8] His thesis that the structural regulation of discipline has given way to more nebulous, extensive and de-territorial distributions of power in control societies chimes with the sense that busyness has taken over by stealth. Interpreting busyness as being the sense of being pulled in different directions by responsibilities and obligations that compete rather than synchronise captures the essence of Deleuzian molecular lines.[9] These lines do not express what the body is as much as what it can do, and they are formed from a busy assemblage of diverse connections.[10] I suggest that busyness can usefully be interpreted as the temporal expression of these dense, vibrant and disruptive molecular lines. The added value of moving beyond a focussed conceptualisation of individualisation into the more fragmented and amorphous framing of control is that it places the messy and unfocussed quality of busyness at the heart of what we are trying to make sense of rather than seeking a rational, articulated explanation of why we are hooked on busyness. It also foregrounds a more heterogeneous conceptualisation of time–space that is not contained within organisations or places but is found in the interconnections between them. We can see how busyness has crept in through the bleeding that takes place between work and domestic life and that erodes the assumption that these are separate spheres.[11] This has less to do with the desire to curate a worthy,

---

[6]The centrality of enterprise does not imply that everyone should aspire to be an entrepreneur but rather that people need to develop entrepreneurial techniques to govern the self. This conceptualisation of the entrepreneurial self develops Foucault's later writings on biopower: Foucault (2008). For a discussion of how social relations are reformed around the centrality of enterprise, see Bröckling (2015), Davies (2014) and Rose (1999).

[7]Southerton (2020).

[8]Deleuze (1992, p. 6).

[9]Deleuze and Guattari (2004).

[10]This reading of molecular has engaged mobility scholars and led them to account for the movement that is 'vital, incessant, and unruly, operating below the threshold of perception and associated with becomings of innumerable kinds': Merriman (2019, p. 67).

[11]Gregg (2011).

productive self and is more about being overwhelmed by multiple, open-ended and (a)synchronous responsibilities.

Speed and Acceleration

Examining busyness is not simply a question of developing a theoretical framing to fit it; equally valid is considering how fetishising busyness, and its assumed universal qualities, has shaped social theory. Social theorists have been busy identifying new forms of time that emerged in the latter decades of the twentieth century. This theorisation has generated a proliferation of neologies that aim to express the novelty of temporal experiences, for example, instantaneous time,[12] timeless time[13] and chronoscopic time.[14] The temporal quality that these individual neologies share prioritises speed and acceleration.[15] Paul Virilio's foundational account of Dromocracy identifies speed as the foundation of power relations. Virilio observes that whatever moves at speed comes to dominates slower-moving forms.[16] David Harvey's comprehensive examination of the changing quality of relationships between space and time identifies this shifting duality as a key condition of late modernity.[17] Harvey's interrogation of time–space compression reveals how the acceleration of economic activities brings about the demolition of spatial barriers and distances. Hartmut Rosa's recent theorisation of social acceleration seeks to develop a distinctive account of the temporal structures of society. Rosa interprets acceleration as cultural formations of the unchecking of the forces of production rather than as the inevitable outcome of the expansion of circulation and consumption.[18] His examination of social acceleration identifies three categories of change in the tempo of social life: technological change, social change and change in the pace of life, with each three domains reinforcing each other. Rosa's account of the pace of life draws on Georg Simmel's early twentieth century account of technological change that frees up time to do more things – or rather to do things differently – and it is this capacity to do more or to do things differently that quickens the pace of everyday life.[19] Fundamentally, Rosa argues that the outcome of these parallel processes is the shrinking of the present and that the speeding

---

[12]Urry (2000).

[13]Castells (2010).

[14]Hassan (2009) and Virilio (2006).

[15]Speed is used as a verb (meaning to move quickly) rather than a noun: see, for example, Tomlinson (2007). The dominance of speed is also developed in more populist commentaries; see, for example, Colvile (2016). These commentaries include work from authors who argue for the necessity of resisting speed; see, for example, Honoré (2005).

[16]Virilio (2006).

[17]Harvey (1990).

[18]Rosa (2013).

[19]As Rosa writes, the tempo of life was a theme that Simmel returned to in different writings and is summarised in the final chapter of *The Philosophy of Money*. See Simmel (2004).

up of institutional, personal and social life means that individuals are constantly driven by expectations of the past that will propel them into the future.

The Uneven Politics of Time

The certainty with which social theorists write about new forms of time is persuasive, and describing new forms of time is necessary to develop overarching narratives of social change. The problem with following theoretical expositions is that while it is feasible to write about a uniform quality of time, these approaches can diminish the uncertainty, diversity and messiness which are the hallmarks of busyness. Although time might have a theoretical universal quality, this does not imply that temporal experiences are similar in the same way. Concomitant with the theoretical interrogation of time, empirical inquiries have persistently pointed to the evenness of temporal experiences. This unevenness can be found in diverse epistemological orientations ranging from quantitative analysis of time use data[20] to qualitative inquiries into relational time.[21] These studies reveal the diversity of time use and how this corresponds with social identities. One reason for the disjuncture between theoretical commitment to a discernible temporal quality and empirical interest in diversity is, as the sociologist Judy Wajcman observes, that the former is concerned with individual temporal experiences, while empirical studies are orientated towards the relational distribution of time and activities.[22] For example, a desire to examine how tasks are allocated is the rationale behind time use studies that analyse detailed national data sets to study the distribution of activities over 24-hour periods. Although the challenge of providing an empirical basis for assumptions about universal temporal change has not been ignored in time use research,[23] this analysis is more applicable to understanding inequalities in time use and how these are demarcated by social identities, particularly gender and class. The point to make here is that empirical analysis such as time use studies collate data which are inherently relational and as such are more orientated towards documenting the unevenness of temporal experiences. Synthesising these accounts with theoretical narratives of social change is not straightforward.[24]

---

[20]Examples of texts that develop an empirical interpretation of changing and diverse uses of time include Gershuny (2000), Gershuny and Sullivan (2019), Hammermesh (2018) and Robinson and Godbey (1997).

[21]Examples of qualitative studies include Nansen, Arnold, Gibbs, and Davis (2009) and Southerton and Tomlinson (2005).

[22]Wajcman (2008, pp. 59–77).

[23]See, for example, Gershuny (2000).

[24]Not surprisingly, there is a debate in the literature about the accuracy and relevance of different accounts. For example, Rosa discusses the limitations of objective analysis of time use data that cannot refute theories of acceleration as these are based on a different epistemological interpretation of how time can be studied. He defends his theory of social acceleration by claiming that subjective experiences of time pressure, which are intensifying (see Robinson & Godbey, 1997) are required to confirm acceleratory logics rather than objective data on time allocation: Rosa (2013, pp. 122–148).

It is easy to get caught in an epistemological trap between individual/collective and subjective/objective measures of time. One study that makes an important breakthrough in getting beyond debates about the direction of social change is Sarah Sharma's detailed ethnographic account of workers at different positions in the relentless pursuit of speed.[25] Sharma's examination of the uneven politics of time effectively demonstrates how the temporal is not a generalised experience but a form of 'social power and a type of social difference'.[26] Privileged workers have greater dominion over time and more opportunities for diverse temporal expressions, for example, acceleration at work versus slow leisure. This expectation that time should be both managed and 'meaningful' relies on people being able to exploit other people's time. In Sharma's account, the temporal narratives of the frequent business traveller cannot be lived without the implicit contribution of workers such as Uber drivers, hotel cleaners, baristas and airport staff. The temporal experiences of these workers uphold the temporal experiences of those with greater privilege. Sharma observes how individual solutions to being overwhelmed by busyness often depend on purchasing other people's time (e.g. babysitters, cleaners, personal assistants, drivers, odd-jobbers), and her analysis necessarily foregrounds the relational dimensions of busyness.[27] Her analysis also undermines the expectation of theoretical narratives that changes in the pace of time are unidirectional. The temporal relations that Sharma uncovers are defined by acceleration but they are equally shaped by temporal impasse and moments of waiting, such as a taxi driver waiting for a fare.[28]

Gender

The uneven politics of time are not just distributed within the spatial configuration of global capitalism but are also discernible at more intimate scales. A consistent finding of time use analysis is ongoing gender differences in the temporal

---

[25]Sharma (2014).

[26]Sharma (2014, p. 9). Sharma develops her theorisation of time through the concept of power-chronography. She offers power-chronography as a development of Doreen Massey's formulation of power-geometry; see Massey (1994). Sharma contends that whilst Massey's foundational writings about space as multiple and relational have inspired the intellectual project of the spatial turn, the temporal imaginary has received less attention. She argues that it is not enough to acknowledge the multiplicity of social time because an understanding of temporality needs to make the differential relations of power within time visible.

[27]Sharma (2017, pp. 131–151).

[28]Counter to the assumption about universal acceleration, the politics of waiting are receiving increasing attention. For example, waiting is an important theme in youth studies as a temporal impasse can take different forms for young people. These include a practice of resistance, such as young people hanging out; see Corrigan (2006, pp. 84–87). Periods of moratoria can take place as young people 'wait' for employment opportunities in overcrowded labour markets; see Cuzzocrea (2019, pp. 567–586) and Jeffrey (2010).

allocation of tasks at home and at work.[29] For feminist scholars, time is a key component of gender inequality.[30] Time remains an empirical and theoretical focus for feminist inquiry precisely because of the persistence of temporal inequality that masculinist theories of unidirectional temporal change overlook.[31] Indeed, there is an intriguing gender division of academic labour; male researchers dominate research involving theoretical accounts of temporal change, while female researchers direct their attention towards empirically detailing temporal inequality. Feminist inquiry does not just examine how time is differentially spent; it also subverts theoretical conventions about time.[32] In particular, the contribution of feminist theory to the study of temporality develops the concept of women's time, which is inherently relational.[33]

This tradition is augmented in Lisa Baraitser's examination of the relationships between care and time.[34] Her examination of the temporal trope of endurance develops feminist ethics of care that start from the idea that care is a necessity rather than a burden or something to be managed efficiently.[35] Approaching time through the lens of care rather than productivity unsettles preoccupations that involve perpetual motion and brings to the fore the temporal tropes of endurance: waiting, staying, delaying, enduring and returning. Thus, feminist contributions not only call attention to the differences in time use for men and women but also query the fascination with speed, transgression and vitality. As Baraitser writes, 'staying close to the lived experiences of time that appear neither eventful not vital' (p. 13) is about resisting the acceleration of global capitalism but it also uncovers practices that remain beyond its reach: the non-productive acts of care that make productivity possible. Studying busyness requires that fixations with speed and acceleration are abandoned and that recognition is given to the diversity of temporal experiences and the endurance of activities that are not preoccupied with productivity and outcomes. Baraitser's observations about the necessity of endurance have become especially relevant during Covid-19 lockdowns. Although being busy is about keeping up with the acceleration of everyday life, it also involves segueing between competing demands for stillness and speed.

---

[29]See Folbre and Bittman (2004).

[30]Nancy Fraser provides a foundational account of how time is a principal component of gender inequality; see Fraser (1994, pp. 591–618). More recent feminist contributions unsettle the linear assumptions about time that are developed in masculinist accounts. See, for example, Lahad (2017).

[31]Sullivan (2004, pp. 207–222).

[32]The theorisation and study of time are also confined within heteronormative practices; see Freeman (2010).

[33]Kristeva, Jardine, and Blake (1981).

[34]Baraitser (2017).

[35]Baraitser develops Judith Butler's feminist ethics of care that foregrounds dependency as being 'what fundamentally defines us'; Butler (2004, p. 33) and the 'inescapable troubles of interdependent existences' in de la Bellacasa (2012, p. 199).

Thinking-doing Busyness

What matters is not simply accounting for why we are busy; it is equally important to recognise and acknowledge that we are overwhelmed by expectations of
busyness when we attempt to assimilate interdependent responsibilities. Empirical and theoretical studies of time have emphasised this disjuncture between
subjective and objective experiences. Therefore, one explanation for the lack of
empirical evidence for social acceleration is that this process is revealed through
documenting what people feel rather than the detail of what people do. In other
words, there are two questions to consider: can busyness be explained by examining social practices or does it depend on what we think about what we have to do?
But these questions are not satisfactory because they rely on a division between
mind and body and prioritise what we think about busyness over what we do.
Being busy cannot be devolved to either activity or thought; it requires an explanation that concerns the fusion of mind and body rather than their separation.[36]
Busyness might be exaggerated in the fault lines between thought and action,
but interrogations of how it is experienced cannot rely on an artificial distinction
between the two.

I find David Bissell's interpretation of thinking habits[37] – the erratic mental
chatter that we are all susceptible to – particularly useful for seeing busyness as the
duality of thinking and doing.[38] Bissell's interrogation of thought as a habit takes
reflective thought beyond a Cartesian interpretation of orientation and coordination of a passive body towards thought being a 'potentially intransigent thinking
habit that does not necessarily orientate itself around utility and productivity and
is not enrolled into a project of individual self-styling'.[39] Bissell reminds us that
thought is varied and that identifying it as a habit does not exclude rational calculation or intuition. Instead, thought takes on different forms in response to the
intensity of being in the world. The busyness of mental chatter is not dissociated
from activity, but it does not coordinate what the body needs to do either.

The point I will make to wrap up this initial examination of theoretical
accounts that can anchor busyness is that we cannot exclusively interrogate busyness through what people say or what people do. My initial interest was sparked by
overhearing colleagues' frustrations and wondering how these captured what was
being done and the individual capacity to get things done. Rather than attempting to make sense of busyness through reconciling thought and action or focussing exclusively on studying either what people say and feel or what people do, I
suggest that what is fascinating about busyness is how it frames the dissonance
of thinking and doing. Thinking habits do not rationalise external demands; they

---

[36]See, for example, Elizabeth Olson's thoughtful discussion of urgency and waiting
that draws attention to the body 'both as a single unit and a plurality, as a legitimate
scale of normative priority and social care'. Olson (2015, p. 523).
[37]I discuss the relevance of Bissell's thinking habits for busyness in Holdsworth
(2020a).
[38]Bissell (2011, pp. 2649–2665).
[39]Bissell (2011, p. 2662).

hold the body in place by resisting external shocks. The paradox of busyness is that it is not just a condition imposed by speeded-up temporalities; it is also a tactic that is used to hold these demands at a distance.[40] From this perspective, Lewis Carroll's White Rabbit is busy: he is running around *not* getting to his meeting.

If busyness is about doing and not doing, it is not contradictory to suggest that both a Deleuzian explanation of perpetual motion and the necessity of what Baraister describes as the non-event – times when nothing purposively happens – are equally relevant to interrogating being busy. Rather than treating incessant busyness as a default response to the temporal demands of global capitalism, it can be considered a useful strategy for resisting external demands. Busyness is not just overwhelming but can also be therapeutic, and it is important to retain a distinction between busyness and burnout. According to the philosopher Byung-Chul Han, burnout is a result of excessive positivity and the universal availability of people and goods to prioritise the ascendancy of the imperative *can* over the hypothetical *should*.[41] Busyness can be understood as an alternative to these two positions to encapsulate the non-event of simply doing. Because we are obsessed with societal speeding up, we can overlook the fact that 'keeping busy' is equally important and that ensuring that we have things to do can be as challenging as being overwhelmed by external demands or possibilities. The one constant thread that runs through contradictory positions is that busyness cannot be distilled to individual thought and action; it is located at intersections of interdependencies. These locations can be formed through the spatial practices of global capitalism and within more intimate assemblages, especially family life.[42]

Busyness in Past Times

The Time We Live By

One important quality of busyness in the twenty-first century is the shared expectation that we are busier now than in the past. As I have already outlined, this assumption underlines theoretical interrogations of time as well as empirical analyses that attempt to document the validity of these claims. Yet the purpose of these convictions about social change is not to present a valid interpretation of social change but to make sense of the present. Stories about time and busyness can be usefully interpreted with reference to John Gillis's distinction between the families we live by and the families we live with.[43] Gillis's history of the family distinguishes between family traditions and practices to draw attention to how the ideal of families in past time (the symbolic families we live by) that is projected onto the present bears little resemblance to what we know about family life in the past. In particular, the distinctions that are drawn between family decline in the

---

[40]Holdsworth (2020a).
[41]Han (2015).
[42]Holdsworth (2019, pp. 155–176).
[43]Gillis (1997).

twentieth century (the everyday families we live with) and family solidarity in the past cannot be supported by the historical record.

This distinction between the past we live by and the present we live with is very relevant to busyness. Lay and academic accounts of time are replete with unverifiable descriptions of past times as quieter, slower and more relaxed than the intensity of the present-day pace of life. In the introduction to his 2016 book *Rest: Why You Get More Done When You Work Less*, the social commentator Alex Soojung-Kim Pang is not very subtle in drawing a line between how time is spent in the second decade of the twenty-first century compared with in earlier times.[44] Pang surmises that people led a simpler life a century ago, with less distraction, more 'forgiving' economies and respect for leisure.[45] Writing in 2020 during the intensity of the Covid-19 pandemic means that parallels with events that took place a hundred years ago are commonplace. Media reports are keen to report the similarities with and differences between the coronavirus pandemic and the Spanish influenza outbreak of 1918–1920 that took an estimated 50 million lives worldwide. However, difficult times are during the Covid-19 pandemic, it is inconceivable to claim that the decade that witnessed the carnage of World War I, the political rupture of the Russian Revolution, the savagery of the Armenian Genocide and the intensity of the flu pandemic as a time of respect and rest. And it is not just popular accounts that rely on rose-tinted representations of past time. Writing in 2017 in an essay about time pressure, Rosa identifies the twenty-first century temporal squeeze with individuals' inability to draw a line under getting things done, so nagging doubts about there being more things to do remain at the end of the day.[46] He contrasts this temporal frustration with the satisfaction of peasants and farmers in past times, who could experience a sense of finality regarding the demands placed on them 'quite regularly after dark, when the cattle (and kids) were taken care of'.[47]

Writing history backwards to make sense of the present can lead us to make false interpretations of the distinctive qualities of current and past times. The historical record does not reveal the peace and tranquillity that Pang and Rosa imagine. For example, Elizabeth Page Moch's detailed account of mobility in premodern Europe identifies the intensity of movement, particularly for the poor – staying put was a luxury that only the wealthy had – rather than the romanticised view of happy, satisfied peasants going gently to bed.[48] Similarly, in relation to the nineteenth century, Colin Pooley's examination of English diaries and court records reveals the intensity of movement experienced by men and women of all ages who could be found walking around at all times of day and night rather than a picture of immobility and quiet times.[49] Oral histories of women's paid

---

[44]Pang (2016).
[45]Pang (2016, p. 8).
[46]Rosa (2017).
[47]Rosa (2017, p. 28).
[48]Moch (2003).
[49]Pooley (2019) and Pooley (2017).

and unpaid work in the late nineteenth and early twentieth centuries confirm the sustained contribution that women's labour has made to household economies and that women's paid work should not be interpreted as a late twentieth century phenomenon.[50] Jacqueline Sarsby's oral history of women in the North Stafford-shire pottery towns of England during the first decades of the twentieth century emphasises the busyness of working women's everyday lives.[51] Women worked in the pottery factories but also had to be enterprising outside of formal work to find additional sources of income: taking in washing, cleaning, looking after other women's children and selling homemade products. Improvising multitask-ing was not about making time for restful leisure; it was done to provide basic household essentials.

Writing about time in the past as a unified experience means making universal assumptions that flatten inequalities, and this is limiting in terms of understanding both the past and the present. Yet this urge to write about past time with certainty is difficult to resist. One of the most celebrated historical accounts of past time is E. P. Thompson's essay on 'Time, Work-discipline and Industrial Capitalism'.[52] Thompson's essay is frequently referenced to support the argument that the onset of industrial capitalism brought about the discipline of clock time, and his essay is taken as the authoritative historical record of this social change. The simplicity of this interpretation does not stand up to closer inspection. It is efficiently dismantled in Paul Glennie and Nigel Thrift's detailed empirical history of clock time as an assemblage of concepts, devices and practices.[53] Their account draws attention to the diversity of clock time in the past, which unsettles its taken-for-granted quality in modern times. However, the simple appeal of Thompson's paper is reproduced through ubiquitous referencing rather than close reading. Thompson's assertion that the imposition of factory time was not a simple triumph of the external shap-ing of habit but fashioned through much broader cultural change seeks to ask questions of the past rather than answer them. He writes that examination of the discourse and practice of time and work-discipline reveals

> not that one way of life is better than the other, but this is a place
> of the most far-reaching conflict; that the historical record is not
> a simple one of neutral and inevitable technological change, but is
> also one of exploitation and of resistance to exploitation, and that
> values stood to be lost as well as gained.[54]

Thompson's account of the introduction of factory time aligns with Henri Lefebvre's description of the 'bitter and dark struggle around time and the use of time'.[55]

---

[50]See, for example, Alexander (1983).
[51]Sarsby (1988).
[52]Thompson (1967, pp. 56–97).
[53]Glennie and Thrift (2009).
[54]Thompson (1967, pp. 93–94).
[55]Lefebvre (2004, p. 74).

Technological Determinism

Thompson's observations that the examination of historical time use cannot be reduced to technological determinism are apposite for the study of twenty-first century busyness. The popular lament that reliance on technology facilitates busyness, particularly the adoption of portable devices such as the smartphone, is difficult to resist. The dangers of an over-reliance on technology for individual well-being, intimate relationships and social cohesion are repeated in popular and academic writings.[56] Yet, as with the ubiquitous assumption about the imposition of factory time in the nineteenth century, these claims require careful examination. Wajcman's analysis of lifestyles that are reliant on technology considers how these are created through individuals' priorities and their positions in complex social networks.[57] She cautions against relying on technological determinism to explain social and cultural change. Wajcman argues that the potential for everyday life to be experienced at a faster pace is not caused by technology but by how this technology is used.[58] Thus, we should not assume that technology determines the pace of everyday life; instead, speed is 'related to social norms that *evolve* as devices are integrated into daily life'.[59] Technologies are not made up of isolated things; they are assemblages of 'people, materials, equipment, components and institutions'.[60] The significance and meaning of specific technological innovations is produced through how they are used recurrently in these assemblages. Thus, Wajcman's empirical account of social and cultural change foregrounds the inherently relational and embedded qualities of being pressed for time. If we are looking for temporal differences between present and past times, we need to go beyond the obvious differences in access to technology and consider the social norms that are constructed around their use.

The stories that we tell about past time write a history that is intuitively appealing, but, as with Gillis's account of the family we live by, they do more to reveal the pinch points of present-day everyday life. Nostalgia is not a good basis for explaining the present, although it does reveal present uncertainties. Yearnings for a simpler past underscore concerns about the complexity of time in the present day. The pull of nostalgia and the restricted stories of past times underscore present-day anxieties about the coordination of responsibilities and the social norms and values that are enacted and produced through these interdependencies.

Phenomenology: Temporality and Timing

Synthesis of Past, Present and Future

Situating busyness as the fulcrum of responsibilities and timing does not resolve how it expresses time. Studies of time use, organisation or management often

---

[56]See, for example, Turkle (2011).
[57]Wajcman (2015).
[58]For an account of the role of technology in social temporalities, see May and Thrift (2001, pp. 1–46).
[59]Wajcman (2015, p. 31), italics in original.
[60]Wajcman (2015, p. 31).

make no attempt to engage with philosophical inquiry about the nature of time itself. Instead, time is taken-for-granted as an external resource to be managed and the problem is not seen to be time per se but the coordination, prioritisation and sequencing of activities.[61] Questions about time are reduced to measured time – when things happen and for how long. However, busyness does not fit with this specific use of time. It lies at the fault line of sequencing: busyness is about the impossibility of keeping to temporal order and is an undeniability phenomenological experience of time that gets in the way of its management. Therefore, if busyness is the subject of inquiry, we cannot deny the relevance of philosophical interpretations of the reality or ideality of time. To circumvent a necessarily long excursion into the history of philosophical thought, for the purposes of making sense of busyness, I propose that a phenomenological focus on temporality rather than time is appropriate for dismantling the assumptions made about temporal order to get to the essence of being busy.

Temporality is not a thing; it is a process which is unified by its three dimensions: the past, the present and the future. In his foundational development of phenomenology, Edmund Husserl rejects the conceptualisation of time as an empty vessel in which events happen to fix objects and as a linear measure of motion.[62] Instead, Husserl conceptualises the present 'as horizontality of the flowing present in which impressions and perceptions in the now are extended by retentions and protentions'.[63] This 'lived present' necessarily incorporates things that have happened and are yet to happen in a continuously changing now. It is from this perspective of the synthesis of past, present and future that Martin Heidegger can write that we are time.[64] While temporality might eschew the requirement to agree whether time is real or ideal, it does not do away with the question of the direction of travel of this synthesis, and different phenomenological interpretations do not agree on how this should be read.[65] We can broadly distinguish between Heidegger's future-orientated reading of temporality – in which the passing of time is that of the future coming into the present – and Henri Bergson's claim that the past is not distinct from but rather part of the present.[66] Bergson's conceptualisation is also subtly different from Husserl's – who prioritises synthesis to retain a sequenced reading of time – in that Bergson sees time as essentially simultaneous.[67]

---

[61]One example of the necessity of treating time as an external, linear resource is Julie Rose's exposition of a distributive justice defence of the value of free time as a resource that all citizens should have equal opportunities to so that they can pursue their own conception of good; see Rose (2016).

[62]Husserl (1964).

[63]Adam (2004, p. 57).

[64]Heidegger (1962).

[65]Hoy (2012).

[66]Bergson famously writes that 'the essence of time is that it goes by; time already gone by is the past, and we call the present the instant in which it goes by': Bergson (2004, p. 176).

[67]Hoy (2012, p. 129).

A phenomenological perspective does not provide a cohesive reading of temporality; it presents different strategies to interrogate its synthesis. As the philosopher David Couzens Hoy suggests, rather than attempting to distil these different strategies into a singular 'correct' reading, phenomenology provides a depth and versatility of interpretation. Hoy describes how

> [t]hese are different ways of dealing with different senses of the time of our lives. They are all possible strategies, even if ultimately each will fall short. The sting of time can never be taken away entirely, if we can reconcile ourselves to that fact, then we will have made a positive step toward living more completely.[68]

Substituting time with temporality orientates a study of busyness around the synthesis of past, present and future, though the direction of this synthesis does not need to be resolved. We can reasonably equate busyness with a present that is too occupied with the need to put things in the past (the insistence on getting things done) or with rushing too quickly into the future. This latter possibility is considered in Heidegger's writings on time and the self. His central concept of Dasein – being there – captures the kind of beings that we are, that is, beings in the world.[69] Dasein cannot be forcibly rushed through busyness; having time, he suggests, provides a far 'greater balance and thereby security of Dasein'[70] compared with not having time. For Heidegger, time is essential for authenticity; an inauthentic person is someone who never has enough, whereas an authentic person always has time.[71] Having time requires a strategy for the synthesis of present into future; an inauthentic strategy rushes into the future, but the future comes towards an authentic self.

This temporal reading of authenticity, as Pierre Bourdieu has argued, conveniently ignores the social temporalisation of individual temporality.[72] The capacity to be authentic depends on the uneven politics of power. It is inconceivable to conclude that social conditions are not relevant to the authenticity of time. The temporal experiences of incarceration, whether as a convict, a political detainee, a refugee or a medical patient, might give one time, but cannot be compared with the temporal opportunities of an academic, writer or artist. If they were not overwhelmed by care, debt, home schooling and/or essential work, many people experienced an opening up of time during the Covid-19 pandemic lockdowns, though this was not equivalent to having time in 'normal' social conditions. As I previously discussed in relation to Sharma's account of the uneven politics of time, we cannot ignore the economic and social relations of time or the fact that the social lives of busyness exist in the social conditions of temporality as much

---

[68]Hoy (2012, p. 186).
[69]Heidegger (1962).
[70]Heidegger, 1962, quoted in Wittmann (2016, p. 115).
[71]Hoy (2012, p. 115).
[72]Bourdieu (1992). See Hoy (2012, pp. 114–116).

as in individual synthesis. Sociological studies necessarily consider social, cultural and economic variations in social time[73] and the relationship between time and social structures.[74] Yet keeping to a consistent interpretation of temporality that equally acknowledges social structures is no easy task. The social study of temporality is riddled with ambiguity, segueing between the interdependencies of temporal and social structures.[75] I keep coming back to the recurrent interpretation that studying busyness has to simultaneously engage with individual temporal experiences within social structures, which in turn are constituted by and through time. Busyness cannot exclusively be studied as a mediator of temporality or as a component of social time.

Timing

One possible way to make sense of these multiple interpretations is to consider busyness not simply as a temporal experience but more as a matter of timing. When we think about busyness, it seems to revolve around questions of when, where and with whom? In other words, the social temporal structure that co-constitutes busyness is the spatial–temporal coordination of activity and how this is conditioned by the uneven politics of time.[76] Locating the social lives of busyness within the domain of timing is a useful fix and it opens up a sociological analysis of how the temporal organisation of relational activities unevenly distributes power and resources and of the sense of grievance and anxiety that the tensions of timing engender. Moreover, locating the social lives of busyness in timing does not shut out the relevance of phenomenological concepts of temporality and how the resolution of timing requires a synthesis of past, present and future.

Engaging with timing rather than exclusively referring to time versus temporality provides a way of thinking through busyness in relation to externalised time that resonates with it as a moral institution rather than a method of spatialised demarcation.[77] Shifting the emphasis from time to timing gives rise to questions not just about when and where activities should take place but how long they should take and also about the normative expectation in management literature that timing should be precise and short.[78] Timing captures the impartial, relational and uneven qualities of time amongst its external, spatialised forms and subjective experiences. The critical time scholar Michelle Bastian has written about the potential for critical horology to unsettle the dualism between objective, spatialised clock time and experiential time by acknowledging that clocks are not apolitical; a clock does not simply represent time because it is read within a particular social,

---

[73]See, for example, Nowotny (1994) and Griffiths (2004).
[74]Adam (1990).
[75]Bergmann (1992, pp. 81–134).
[76]Southerton (2020).
[77]Snyder (2013, pp. 243–266).
[78]Du Gay (2017, pp. 86–101).

cultural and economic context.[79] Timing could be a component of this commitment to transcending conventional philosophical dualisms. However, developing a conceptual and indeed an empirical framework to achieve this is quite difficult. It is easier to write that timing is more relevant to understanding the twenty-first century social issues than either time or temporality than to conceive a study that would consider how this can be captured. At this initial point of an exploration of the social life of busyness, timing offers a reminder that busyness as the zeitgeist of the twenty-first century temporality revolves around the disunity of objectivity and subjectivity and, equally, around the interdependencies between the self and others. Timing effectively captures the idea that it is not just our time that matters but also how it synchronises with that of other people.

Summary

Although it might be assumed that everyone nowadays is busy, the ubiquitousness of busyness does not infer that it can be interpreted through a neatly defined theoretical lens. Indeed, the persuasiveness of busyness is caused because it eludes an exact definition and is open to numerous interpretations; even during 2020/2021 Covid-19 lockdowns, busyness has been reinvented through the intensity of Zoom meetings and the increased popularity of crafting/DIY. Busyness, thus, provides both an academic challenge and an opportunity. My theoretical exploration of busyness started with accounts of individualisation because performances of busyness centre on what individuals need to do. However, the resolution of multiple responsibilities through busyness does not equate to assumptions about calculation and choice. The feeling of being pulled in different directions and constantly keeping going is effectively captured in Deleuze's theory of control society. Equally, busyness cannot be reduced to the fetishising of speed. The problem with theorisations of speed and acceleration is that they originate in social and economic accounts of the self rather than social relations. Empirical investigations that do consider the relational distribution of time unsettle assumptions about ubiquitous temporal change. We need to consider not just unevenness in expressions of busyness but the connectivity between individual actions that constitute busyness. Many people's solution to busyness, if one is needed, is to outsource activities to others. The differential pull of busyness cannot be separated from the uneven politics of time.

One important dimension of the multiple expressions of busyness is that it cannot be separated into what people do or feel. It is not just a question of whether busyness is about having lots of things to do or feeling that one is overwhelmed. The mental chatter about busyness can be interpreted as an expression of multiple responsibilities but also as a justification of and/or a resistance to these. We need to be equally alert to what people say and do about busyness and

---

[79]Bastian (2017, pp. 41–55). Bastian contrasts philosophical suspicion of clocks with the imaginary appeal of maps, making the point that maps can be envisaged as transformative even though they are equal to clocks as technologies of domination.

should not prioritise one over the other. It is valid, though, to consider what responsibilities are voiced through busyness; in other words, what activities or requests are resisted and which ones are uncontested. When trying to make sense of busyness, it is tempting to make comparisons over time and place. Indeed, one of the important qualitative dimensions of busyness is the sense that others are not pulling their weight equally, either at home or work. These comparative accounts can also be applied over longer time frames and this can lead to the temptation to interpret past times as more restful and leisurely. These accounts do not stand up to closer empirical inspection and they are used to make sense of the present rather than explain the past. One important dimension that needs to be resisted, though it is easy to fall into, is the expectation that the twenty-first century busyness is technologically determined. It is easy to convince ourselves that technology both frees up and intensifies time: we can do more things quicker because of technology. Rather than reducing busyness to technological determinism, it is more useful to explore how norms of busyness and expectations of productivity or multitasking are created through the use of technology.

A final theoretical dimension, though also the most elusive, is the interpretation of busyness through philosophical readings of time. Busyness lends itself to phenomenological interpretations of temporality as the synthesis of past, present and future. Time can either pull us forward from the present into the future or push us from the past into the present. Busyness can be interpreted as the stickiness of this synthesis: the difficulty of getting things done (synthesis into the past) or the inability to move forward into the future. Moreover, the relational qualities of busyness (doing things with and for other people) require the synthesis of individual temporality, and timing, as well as time, are important.

The following chapters follow this theoretical synthesis by exploring different empirical locations of busyness, starting with the synchronisation of clock time and time organisation before moving on to consider busyness at work, in families and during free time. While these accounts draw on different dimensions of time, what is common throughout the analysis is a commitment to busyness as a relational expression of responsibilities. To echo Rovelli, from examining busyness, we can learn more about ourselves and our relationships with others, rather than simply how to interpret and manage time.

Chapter 3

Clock Time

The Clock

Christian Marclay's brilliant 2010 video installation *The Clock* has captivated audiences and received universal critical acclaim.[1] *The Clock* is both an artwork and a functional timepiece. It is a 24-hour montage of clips of time from films and television programmes. These clips capture people saying what the time is or images of timepieces showing the time. These clips are edited in real time. When *The Clock* is shown, it is synchronised to the viewer's local time; if you are watching *The Clock* at 3.05 p.m., the video will show a clock showing that time, or someone stating the time. *The Clock* took three years to make and Marclay employed six research assistants on the project.[2] It was first shown at the White Cube Gallery in London and has subsequently been purchased by six galleries. By the summer of 2020, it had been shown in 35 different galleries, just over half of these in North American locations and the rest in Europe, Brazil, Russia, Israel (twice), Turkey and Japan.[3]

    The Clock is simultaneously a celebration of film and TV history and an interpretation of our fascination with time and timepieces. These two aspects reinforce each other. For example, there is palpable tension in the clips building up to noon. Marclay intersperses this time in *The Clock* with extracts from the climax of the 1978 British film *The 39 Steps* starring Robert Powell, when the hero hangs onto the hands of Big Ben to stop a bomb exploding at midday. This image of someone being suspended from a municipal clock is a celebrated cinematic image that is used in various film scenes, from some involving Harold Lloyd in *Safety Last!* (1923) to some of Christopher Lloyd's scenes in *Back to the Future* (1985). For audiences familiar with the history of film, the anticipation of noon in *The Clock* is intensified through the association with one of the most celebrated cinematic representations of time, Fred Zinnemann's 1952 western *High Noon*. There is an editorial similarity between *High Noon* and *The Clock*, as Zinnemann also edited *High Noon* to run (almost) in real time and time is noted in the film with repeated images of clocks.

---

[1]Jones (2011).
[2]Zalewski (2012).
[3]These locations are taken from Wikipedia. (n.d.). The Clock (2010 film). Retrieved from https://en.wikipedia.org/wiki/The_Clock_(2010_film). Accessed on December 10, 2020.

The Social Life of Busyness, 29–64
Copyright © 2021 by Clare Holdsworth
Published under exclusive licence by Emerald Publishing Limited
doi:10.1108/978-1-78743-698-520211004

Marclay's choice of clips is constrained by the representation of time in film and TV culture. Although he was particularly attuned to the diversity of temporal tropes and sought to incorporate clips that concern when time is dragging or is a backdrop to the narrative of the film, cinematic time is biased towards more frenetic and anxious temporal experiences.[4] Throughout *The Clock*, people are late and/or in a hurry, appointments are missed and people are late for a train or for a scheduled lift in a car. Although the artwork is played 'on time', the action on the screen is often 'out of time'. While I was watching *The Clock* in the afternoon, I was struck by the number of clips in which people were going to sleep or waking up. This sense of being behind or out of time is interspersed with anticipation of what is to come. Awaited time may be dreaded with nervous glances at clocks and watches. Other times are welcomed if they indicate the opportunity for change or a break, such as the end of the school day or leaving work, or time for food and/or a drink. Although *The Clock* represents linear time, its pace varies between times of intense anticipation that involve multiple clips, such as of midday, regarding which Marclay had a greater choice of movie extracts, and more relaxed times when there are fewer cinematic references, such as 3.32 a.m.[5] This change of pace can be unexpected and sudden. For example, at 12.01 p.m., immediately following the frenetic cinematic anticipation of noon, *The Clock* switches to simultaneous clips of banks being shut for lunch. Images of blinds been shut abruptly in windows neatly dissipate the tension of what is going to happen at midday. People are simply going to stop working and have lunch.

The Clock is not just about time and/or an homage to cinema history. Marclay's skilful editing of the fragmented clips creates continuity between them. For example, a telephone ringing in one cinematic extract will be answered in the subsequent, but different, clip. The clips are edited to give the impression of spatial, embodied contiguity as well as temporal contiguity, underscoring the interconnectivity of time and space. Moreover, while the audience's focus is on *The Clock*'s visual imagery, Marclay pays equal attention to its soundscape. To ensure sonic continuity, he has created a new soundtrack by editing the audio of each visual clip.[6] Marclay disrupts the coupling of sound and vision by sometimes carrying forward the audio from one clip into the following scene. This sonic/visual disruption heightens the experience of anticipation when watching the installation.

Beyond its simple foundational premise and its initial delight in identifying cinematic clips, *The Clock* provides a subtle rebuttal of philosophical suspicions of clock time. By compelling the audience to be acutely aware of clock time, *The Clock* presents a philosophical paradox that inadvertently addresses Bastian's call for critical horology.[7] Time in *The Clock* is linear *and* it conforms to a phenomenological interpretation of time by continually segueing between past,

---

[4]Zalewski (2012).
[5]Design Boom (n.d.).
[6]Zalewski (2012).
[7]Bastian (2017).

present and future. Marclay's editing of cinematic images of clocks subverts the conventional phenomenological critique of problematic, objective clock time. *The Clock's* multiple succession of edited 'nows' continually synthesises past, present and future. Its past is collective and individual. The video is a collection of clips assembled from the archives of cinema history and includes clips from celebrated films that are instantly recognisable (such as *High Noon*) and more obscure contributions. One of the intriguing things about watching *The Clock* is trying to recognise as many films as possible; thus, this collective past is also intensely individual. *The Clock* is also an historical record of time because it represents different cultural aspects that are linked to time. Images of blinds being pulled down at service counters at noon capture mid-twentieth century temporal norms; in the twenty-first century, banks and shops no longer close for lunch. *The Clock's* present is unavoidable. The paradox of spending time watching it is that it is very easy to become immersed in its visual and sonic experience while knowing exactly what the present time is. This simultaneously intensifies and dismisses the present; you know the current time but what time it is does not matter – what is important is what might happen next. *The Clock's* future is, therefore, equally avoidable. Its narrative of suspense is continual even though there is no reprise, plot or denouement. Its continual, unfolding narrative is that something is always about to happen, though what that is will never be revealed. The paradoxical qualities of *The Clock* make it compelling to watch. Its frenetic pace and repetition of images involving hurrying, lateness and anxiety capture contemporary obsessions with busyness. *The Clock* accedes to the popular motif that there is not enough time to get things done while requiring its audience to be still and do nothing but watch the clock. The installation celebrates and taunts equally twenty-first century obsessions with time and its measurement, thus, neatly capturing vicarious fascinations with time and busyness. Its appeal is the invitation to spend time simply clock watching, that is, giving in to a collective captivation with the passing of time.

This first empirical chapter is inspired by *The Clock* to account for busyness in relation to clock time not simply as an objective measurement of how time is spent but also in terms of how fascination with clocks is a shared component of busyness. Clock time is intriguing because of what it reveals about how time is spent, but this intrigue is heightened by our disbelief about what records of clock time tell us about how time is spent. Dissonance between temporal measurement and expectations is an important theme in academic interpretations of time and it also imbues everyday accounts; making sense of time is not simply a challenging academic exercise. Rather than taking this dissonance between measurement and experience as evidence that the measurement of time is misdirected, I consider how accounting for clock time can unsettle temporal assumptions and reveal collective rhythms. That is, the measurement of time is more potent when carried out communally rather than individually, echoing how the magic of *The Clock* comes alive through collective viewing. Clock time does not simply locate individuals within time and space; it is also a necessary component of timing and the collaborative coordination of activities. My exploration of busyness through clock time consists of three components. I begin by exploring the legacy of time use data to account for the social inequalities of the distribution of clock time through a scoping study of time use analysis. In the second part of the chapter, I consider the shared rhythms of clock time and what these can reveal about the collective intensities of busyness. I use a data set of times extracted from the Mass Observation Archive diaries for this rhythm analysis. In the final section, I reflect on what we can learn about ourselves and interpersonal relationships through the self-study of clock time based on my own experiences of keeping a time use diary.

A Brief History of Time Use Data

Fascination with time has engendered the detailed collection of statistics about time. Echoing how Marclay was able to piece together a film that runs for 24 hours from cinematic clips, official statistics about time use record how individuals spend each 10/15/30 minutes over a 24-hour period. In their 2019 book, *What We Really Do All Day: Insights from the Centre for Time Use Research*, two leading authorities on time use data analysis, Jonathan Gershuny and Oriel Sullivan, summate collective survey data into a singular 'Great Day' to take account for how time use changes over time. Their approach neatly expresses the dual ambition of time use to account for collective experiences of time and to reveal inequalities in this collective expression.

Time use data are an intriguing category of official statistics. These data do not collate observations about the characteristics of a population (e.g. a census provides details about who is living in a particular place) or about their lifestyles, practices or beliefs (such as surveys on lifestyle, opinions and political intentions). Time use surveys collate what people are doing at specific times. The very fact that these data are routinely collected in many advanced economies underlines Thompson's observation that time is a site of exploitation and resistance.[8] The history of the development of time use data is not neutral; it reveals the political foundation of recording how time is spent. Using diaries to record time use is a technique that has been around for over one hundred years.[9] In the mid-nineteenth century, the French sociologist and engineer Frédéric le Play pioneered case-study methods to study the daily economic and social life of the family, which he argued was instrumental to social and economic moral order. Le Play's case-study method involved the use of time diaries. Employing integrated time use diaries to collate data on the totality of activities was first proposed in England and the USA to advance the philanthropic project of the moral reform of the poor.[10] National time use surveys were introduced in the USSR and the USA in the 1920s, although it wasn't until the 1960s that more systematic and cross-national surveys were instigated. The geographical coverage of time use data continues to be focussed on more advanced economies where it is more reasonable to make assumptions about the spatial and temporal demarcations of the day

---

[8]Thompson (1967).
[9]Frazis and Stewart (2007, pp. 73–97).
[10]Chenu, Lesnard, and Jacobs (2006, pp. 335–359).

(e.g. to distinguish between formal employment and domestic tasks).[11] The collation of time use data in the Global South is more uneven and is often initiated by NGOs or research organisations to detail the extent of unpaid activities and the temporal conditions of poverty.[12]

It is intriguing that time use data were first collated in countries developing very different economic systems. The inception of the collection of data from time diaries in the USSR was motivated by the Soviet political ambition to eradicate the inefficiencies of a single person doing housework and replace it with collectivised activities. These early Soviet surveys focussed on collecting data on time spent performing activities in the home. They began in 1922 and 1923, were interpreted during the 1930s and resumed in the 1950s. This legacy of time use data collection arguably makes the USSR one of the most prolific producers of time use studies in the world.[13] Time was integral to the emerging Soviet economic system, and the contributions of time use data to the Soviet economic system did not just revolve around the archaic problem of housework. The Soviet system celebrated the cult of productivity, and workers who exceeded their productivity targets became cult heroes. The most celebrated of these was the coal miner Alexey Stakhanov, after whom the Stakhanovite movement was named to inspire other workers to demonstrate their commitment to the socialist economic system. Stakhanov's celebrity was not just confined to the USSR, and he appeared on the cover of *Time* magazine in 1935.[14] The willingness of workers to follow the Stakhanovite movement and dedicate themselves to the cult of productivity served to demonstrate the economic superiority of the socialist economic system. The detailed collation of time use data underscored this political ambition to maximise individual productivity through the collective marshalling of individual effort rather than through management techniques.

While the USSR was developing time use data to promote collective productivity, sociologists in the United States were also exploring the use of time use surveys, though for very different purposes. The sociologist Robert Merton is said to have carried out the first collection of time use diaries in the USA, though his study was never published.[15] The early US studies were initiated to provide empirical evidence for theories of human behaviour. However, these were ineffectual as there was too much noise in the empirical data to confirm or disprove theoretical assumptions. Unlike the development of the first USSR studies, which were directed towards maximising collective productivity, the early American studies sought to advance understanding of human behaviour. Their initial preoccupation, similar to that of the USSR, was with women's domestic work. As Melissa Gregg explains, the foundational studies that aimed to understand

---

[11]Charmes (2015).

[12]Antonopolous and Hirway (2010).

[13]Chenu et al. (2006).

[14]*Time: The Weekly Magazine*, December 16, 1935. Retrieved from http://content.time.com/time/covers/0,16641,19351216,00.html

[15]Chenu et al. (2006).

and improve everyday behaviour focussed on documenting women's domestic routines and encouraging female readers to engage with the scientific practices of home management.[16]

If the political–economic backdrop to Soviet time use was the Stakhanovite movement, the equivalent in the USA was scientific management, which includes Frederick Taylor's development of time study and Frank and Lillian Gilbreth's advancement of motion study. The integration of 'time–motion' study into scientific management meant that the Stakhanovite principles stating that productivity could be maximised through hard work were rejected in favour of insistence on optimising efficiency. Taylor's method of time–motion study is interventionist rather than responsive. It involves breaking down a job into its component parts, timing each of these elements and rearranging these tasks into the most efficient method.[17] The Gilbreths' pioneering of motion study combined filming with the study of time to generate standardised best practice.[18] They famously broke away from Taylor in 1914 over their claim that scientific management should be used to improve workers' welfare rather than to blindly pursue profit, which they associated with Taylor's work, as well as because of their desire for self-publicity.[19] These disagreements about how the study of time should be utilised and for whose benefit underscore the necessity to consider the socio-political context of how time is counted. The origins of the 'scientific' study of time were stimulated by moral and economic ideas about essential and correct ways of doing things in time, at work and at home.

Moving forward to the present day, the collation of time use data is now an activity carried out by national research institutes. The American Time Use Survey (ATUS) diary day starts at 4.00 a.m. on one day and ends 24 hours later at 4.00 a.m. on the day of the interview.[20] The detail of the ATUS is collated using a computer-assisted interview rather than a self-completed paper diary. Respondents are asked to describe all activities they did during the previous day, starting at 4 a.m. The interviewer uses established codes for some standard activities such as sleeping; all other activities are recorded verbatim. In contrast, the European Commission's time use harmonisation project recommends the use of a 'leave-behind diary' to be filled in on two days, one weekday and one weekend day.[21] These self-completion diaries also start at 4 a.m. and require respondents to document the primary and secondary activities that they do for each 10-minute interval, where these activities take place and with whom (if anyone) they are done.

The simplicity of these time use questionnaires contrasts with the complexity of time use data. The trade-off, as with all systematic forms of data collection,

---

[16]Gregg (2018).

[17]Taylor (1919).

[18]Gregg (2018).

[19]Price (1989, pp. 88–98).

[20]*American Time Use Survey Users' Guide*. Retrieved from https://www.bls.gov/tus/atususersguide.pdf

[21]Harmonised European Time Use Surveys - 2018 guidelines. Retrieved from https://ec.europa.eu/eurostat/web/products-manuals-and-guidelines/-/KS-GQ-19-003

is between obtaining the level of detail required and ease of completion for respondents. Ask for too much detail to be recorded and respondents will not complete the task; if not enough detail is asked for, the data collected are of limited value. As the study of time use has expanded beyond its original purpose (i.e. to perfect particular elements of society and/or the economy), the challenge of measuring time use is to develop meaningful tools for data collection that are suitable for the divergent interests of time use scholars.

Time Use Over Time

The value of time use data is that it records collective accounts of time rather than explains what is happening to individual temporal experiences. Because this method of data collection must make assumptions about how time is spent, this will result in biases in the data. Interpretation of the data relies on being able to code time use into predetermined categories and analyse variation in these categories over time and between social groups. I have carried out a scoping study of this analysis to assess what time use data can reveal about changes in time use during the first years of the twentieth century and what these changes might imply about busyness. This approach adopts a rule-based method to identifying research publications rather than simply collating references from search engines, which are biased towards publications with the most citations and/or those that confirm researchers' assumptions. Using a systematic approach to selecting the literature widens the geographical coverage and should ensure that well-known researchers in the field and more obscure or summary articles are included.

Scoping Study: Method

In April 2019, using the Web of Science database, I searched for published papers using three terms: time use data, time use diaries and busyness.[22] I included busyness as it is the focus of my research, though busyness is not a particularly effective search term as it is too vague and, for these purposes, too subjective. Time use is a more appropriate search category but it generates a large number of results; using the terms time use data and time use diaries reduces this to a manageable number. Searches using all three search terms found 4,649 publications, and the earliest outputs date back to the 1960s, though the majority were published in the twenty-first century. In 2015, the number of studies increased to 332 from 280 in the previous year, so 2015 can be described as a watershed year. Searches using the three search terms found over 300 outputs per year for each year after 2015; before this, the number of studies per year is lower. These searches illustrate the intensification of time use analysis as more data become available and techniques for their analysis are more widely shared.

For my purposes, I am interested in analyses that consider change over time. In the second stage of the review, I selected outputs that compared time use data for at least two different time points. These were selected through the examination

---

[22]Hyphenated and non-hyphenated search terms were used.

of the title (for the first run-through) and then the abstract of each publication. From the initial search results of 4,659 publications, I identified 41 publications that specifically compared two time periods and that permitted access to the publication.[23] Nineteen of the publications identified examined trends in European countries, 11 in North America and eight in Asia/Australasia, and three compared trends in multiple countries in different continents. Half of the papers were published since 2016, with only two published in the twentieth century. The full details of the 41 publications are provided in the appendix. In Table 3.1, I have extracted the study aims and the main findings for each paper. The main findings summarise the trends in time use identified in each study: what use of time has increased, decreased or stayed the same?

Scoping Study: Findings

The review demonstrates continuity and change in time use. What it does not do is demonstrate an unequivocal change in one direction towards either a speeded-up or a more leisured society. If anything, the evidence points to the latter, though certainly not sufficiently to fulfil early twentieth century aspirations for a leisure society and a reduced working week.[24] The overall balance of time spent on paid work, unpaid work and leisure has not fundamentally changed since the 1960s, although who does these activities has changed. Analyses of trends in leisure suggest that the amount of time devoted to 'free time' has increased,[25] though Gimenez-Natal and Sevilla's[26] multi-country analysis suggests that this is country specific and more pronounced for men than women, and also more pronounced for people with fewer educational qualifications. North American couples report spending more leisure time together over a 40-year period.[27] People are also sleeping more in the twenty-first century.[28] More detailed analysis of how leisure is spent suggests that the quality of leisure time has deteriorated. The proportion of leisure time spent doing sedentary activities has not changed, though more time is taken up with screen-based activities in the twenty-first century.[29] The increase in time spent on screen-based activities is accommodated by a decline in other sedentary activities. For children, the increase in screen time is caused by combining screen-leisure with other activities.[30]

---

[23]I could not access a few publications, for example, conference proceedings, and these were excluded from the scoping study.

[24]See, for example, Keynes (1932, pp. 17–26).

[25]Bittman (1998, pp. 353–78), Lenhart (2018, pp. 306–328), Vilhelmson, Elldér, and Thulin (2018, pp. 2898–2916) and Genadek, Flood, and Garcia Roman (2016, pp. 1801–1820).

[26]Gimenez-Nadal and Sevilla (2012, pp. 1338–1359).

[27]Voorpostel, Van Der Lippe, and Gershuny (2010, pp. 243–265).

[28]Lamote de Grignon Pérez, Gershuny, Foster, and De Vos (2019) and Leech (2017, pp. 202–209).

[29]Van Der Ploeg et al. (2013, pp. 382–387) and Vilhelmson et al. (2018).

[30]Mullan (2019, pp. 997–1024).

Table 3.1. Summary of Scoping Study of Longitudinal Time Use Analysis Research Publications.

No.	Authors	Study Aims	Geography	Time Period	Identified Trends in Time Use
1	Mullan, K. and Wajcman, J.	To compare work extension practices (work both beyond the workplace and outside standard business hours), total work hours and subjective time pressure in 2000 and 2015	UK	2000 and 2015	Small *increase* in work extension (working beyond formal hours and workplace) associated with time pressure (2015 only). *Increase* in work hours due to work extension facilitated by working with a device
2	Lamote de Grignon Pérez et al.	To investigate changes in sleep time in the UK between 1974 and 2015 using the two British time use studies that allow measuring 'time in bed not asleep' separately from 'actual sleep time'	UK	1974 and 2015	*Increase* in sleep time
3	Etile, F. and Plessez, M.	To investigate the extent to which labour-market changes explain the decline in the time spent home cooking by married women in France between 1985 and 2010	France	1985–1986 and 2009–2010	*Increase* in women's employment and wages accounts for 60% of *decrease* in time women spend cooking
4	Fernandez-Lozano, I.	To explore how work schedules allow Spanish fathers to take care of their children when they are not at school or childcare centres, comparing 2003 and 2010	Spain	2003 and 2010	*No change* in available time (time not working excluding 9–5 on weekdays) at weekends. *Decrease* (36 minutes) in available time during weekdays. Women have more available time

Table 3.1.   (*Continued*)

No.	Authors	Study Aims	Geography	Time Period	Identified Trends in Time Use
5	Lenhart, O.	To examine changes in East German time use following the German Reunification of 1990 and to consider the evidence for a convergence of East German time use with West German practices	(East and West) Germany	1990 and 2000	East German time use is becoming more similar to West German time: *decrease* in working time and *increase* in leisure time in East
6	Mullan, K.	To analyse changes in children's (8–18 years) daily time use of screen-based activities (TV, video games and computers) and the time children spend using computers and mobile devices throughout the day (2014–2015 only)	UK	2000–2001 and 2014–2015	Children's (aged 8–18) screen-based activity *increased* ½ hour a day due to boys playing video games *Increase* in screen time activities done concurrently with other activities
7	Mullan, K.	To examine changes in school-age children's (8–16 years) time use in the UK between 1975 and 2015	UK	1974–1975, 2000–2001 and 2014–2015	*Increase* in time children (8–16) spend at home doing screen-based activities and homework. *Decrease* in unstructured play and small *increase* in sport. Gender influences activities
8	Neilson, J. and Stanfors, M.	To investigate how coupled individuals allocated time together, alone, with children and as a family, exploring changes between 1990 and 2010 in Sweden using three waves of the Swedish Time Use Survey	Sweden	1990 and 2010	*Increase* in time couples spend together

9	Sullivan, O. and Gershuny, J.	To address evidence for 'speeded-up' society using time use diary evidence from the UK on change in the frequency and distribution of activities over 15 years	UK	2000 and 2015	Small *increase* in multitasking for men, *no change* for women, *no change* in number of activities during the day, *decrease* in feeling rushed, *increase* in ICT use though not associated with feeling rushed
10	Taillie, L. S.	To examine who cooks and time spent home cooking between 2003 and 2016 by gender, educational attainment and race/ethnicity	USA	2003 and 2016	*Increase* in time spent on home food preparation, especially for men, though women still cook more
11	Vihelmson, B., Elder, E. and Thulin, E.	To analyse changes in free time activity patterns during a period when private Information and Communications Technology (ICT) use was introduced, expanded and went online	Sweden	1990–1991, 2000–2001 and 2010–2011	*Increase* in 20–29 year-olds' overall free time and online screen time. *Decrease* in offline time
12	Kim, J. W. and Jin, K.	To analyse changes in the unpaid work time of married men (domestic chores and childcare time) using a time use survey	Korea	2004, 2009 and 2014	*Increase* in men's unpaid work time
13	Kim, O.-S.	To explore changes in adolescents' time use (sleep, school and leisure time) and time famine (lack of time for these activities) between 2004 and 2014	Korea	2004 and 2014	*Increase* in sleep time, *decrease* in schooltime (weekdays and Saturdays), *decrease* in schooltime (Sundays), *increase* in leisure on Saturdays, *decrease* in leisure on Sundays

Table 3.1.   (Continued)

No.	Authors	Study Aims	Geography	Time Period	Identified Trends in Time Use
14	Klunder, N. and Meirer-Grawe, U.	To examine the division of labour for everyday food routines for German couples, comparing dual-earner couples, couples with additional female income and male breadwinner couples	Germany	2001–2002 and 2012–2013	*Decrease* in daily time for food routine; working mothers spend less time preparing food.
15	Leech, J. A.	To assess change in sleep duration among Canadians from 1998 to 2010 and to examine any associations with non-work-related screen time	Canada	1998 and 2010	*Increase* in average sleep duration and *increase* in recreational screen time
16	Schulz, F. and Engelhardt-Wolfer, H.	To analyse time budgets for total childcare and six specific childcare activities on weekdays and weekends for German mothers and fathers	Germany	2001 and 2013	*Increase* in total childcare time for mothers and fathers. Highly educated parents read more
17	Zuzanek, J.	To analyse changes in the allocation of time to paid work, domestic work, personal needs and free time, as well as accompanying changes in perceived time pressure and subjective well-being	Canada	1981, 1986, 1992, 1998, 2005, 2010	*No change* in overall paid and domestic work; *increase* in paid and domestic work for parents aged 20–64 with at least one child <12. *Increase* in part-time and long hours worked
18	Genadek, K. R., Flood, S. M. and Roman, J. G.	To examine trends in couples' shared time in the United States: comparing time spent alone or with spouse/child	USA	1965 and 2012	*Increase* in couples' shared time, concentrated in leisure

19	Gershuny, J. and Harms, T. A.	To refute Vanek's (1974) observation that housework time has not declined over the previous half century using US Department of Agriculture and ATUS data	USA	1925–2011	*Decrease* in women's housework time and *increase* in time women spent doing childcare and shopping
20	Dotti Sani, G. M. and Treas, J.	To test the hypothesis that more educated parents devote more time to childcare than other parents and how this changes over time	Canada, USA and nine European countries	Various years between 1965 and 2012	*Increase* in parents' childcare time
21	Glorieux, I. et al.	To analyse gender trends in paid work, childcare and unpaid work	Belgium	1999, 2004 and 2013	*Increase* in time men spent on childcare and *increase* in women's paid work
22	Hofferth, S. and Lee, Y.	To analyse trends in time fathers spend doing childcare since 2003 and whether fathers' time use was linked to family structure and partners' employment	USA	2003 and 2013	*Increase* in time spent by fathers doing childcare
23	Han, J. and Koo, J.	To investigate whether Korean work schedules have moved away from a 9 to 6 standard schedule towards more flexible schedules	Korea	1990, 1995, 2005, and 2010	*No change* in work schedules
24	Procher, V. and Vance, C.	To analyse gender differences in time spent shopping	Germany	1996–2009	*Decrease* in time couples spend shopping. Convergence of gender differences

Table 3.1.   *(Continued)*

No.	Authors	Study Aims	Geography	Time Period	Identified Trends in Time Use
25	Smith, L. P., Ng, S. W. and Popkin, B. M.	To examine how patterns of home cooking and home food consumption have changed from 1965 to 2008 by socio-demographic groups	USA	Various surveys between 1965 and 1966 and between 2007 and 2008	*Decrease* in time spent on home cooking
26	Van der Ploeg, H. P. et al.	To determine changes in non-occupational sedentary behaviours in the Dutch adult population between 1975 and 2005	The Netherlands	1975, 1980, 1985, 1990, 1995, 2005	*Decrease* in number of minutes of non-occupational sedentary time, though *no change* for proportion of non-occupational time spent sedentary. *Increase* in screen time
27	Chau, J. Y. et al.	To examine population trends in sedentary behaviours in non-occupational activities and more specifically during leisure time	Australia	1992, 1997 and 2006	Small *increase* in total non-occupational sedentary time. *Increase* in sedentary transport and education. *Increase* in leisure screen time, small *decrease* in other non-sedentary leisure activities
28	Gimenez-Natal, J. I. and Sevilla, A.	To document general decreases in men's market work (paid work) and any linked increases in men's unpaid work and childcare; and to document increases in women's paid work and childcare and any linked decreases in unpaid work	Australia, Canada, Finland, France, The Netherlands, Norway and the UK	Various years between 1971 and 2000	Men: Leisure *increased* in AU, FO and UK; *decreased* in FR, NL and NO; *no change* in CA. Paid work: *decrease* except FR and NL; childcare *increase*; unpaid work *increase* Women: leisure *decrease* except *increase* in FI and *no change* in CA; childcare *increase*; unpaid work *increase* except FR

	Authors	Aim	Country	Years	Findings
29	Sevilla, A., Gimenez-Nadal, J. I. and Gershuny, J.	To compare trends in the quality of leisure (pure leisure, co-present leisure and leisure fragmentation) and relative growth in leisure time, by level of education	USA	1965–2003	*Increase* in time spent doing leisure for men and women, especially for less educated. *Decrease* in quality of leisure
30	Craig, L., Mullan, K. and Blaxland, M.	To explore how having children impacted (a) paid work, domestic work and childcare (total workload) and (b) the gender division of labour in Australia over a 15-year period	Australia	1992, 1997 and 2006	*Increase* in total workloads for mothers and fathers, especially 1997–2006. Divergence in parents' and non-parents' workload.
31	Hook, J. L.	To examine household task segregation using 36 time use surveys from 19 countries (spanning 1965–2003) combined with original national-level data in multilevel models	19 Countries	1965–2003	*Increase* in cooking and housework and *decrease* in gender segregation. Gender segregation more pronounced in time-inflexible households in countries where work hours and parental leave are long
32	Kuroda, S.	To measure trends in average hours worked (market work) and leisure for Japanese over the past three decades	Japan	1976–2006	*Increase* in market work from 1970 to mid-1980 then *no change*. *Increase* in market work on weekdays
33	Voorpostel, M., van der Lippe, T. and Gershuny, J	To investigate to what extent couples' joint leisure time has changed in the past four decades and to what extent joint leisure time varies between men and women and between single and dual-earner couples	USA	1965, 1975 and 2003	*Increase* in leisure time and leisure time spent with spouse

Table 3.1. (Continued)

No.	Authors	Study Aims	Geography	Time Period	Identified Trends in Time Use
34	Zick, C. D. and Stevens, R. B.	To describe how the time spent in food-related activities by Americans has changed over the past 30 years	USA	1975, 1985, 1998 and 2006	*Increase in* total time spent eating; *decrease in* food preparation and cleaning up
35	Mestdag, I. and Glorieux, I.	To assesses how commensality (eating together) patterns have evolved in Belgium over the last four decades and which factors have an impact on commensality	Belgium	1966, 1999 and 2004	*Decrease* in time spent eating together
36	Gershuny, J.	To explore the contradiction between empirical increase in leisure time in advanced economies and concomitant increase in feeling busy	UK	1961, 1983 and 2001	*Decrease* in paid work for men; *increase* in paid work for women, *increase* in unpaid work for men, *decrease* in unpaid work for women leading to *increase* in non-work for men and *no change* for non-work for women. Men with higher human capital have and *increase* in paid work. Paid work more concentrated in weekdays and *increase* in number of activities, especially on weekdays
37	Sayer, L. C.	To analyse trends and gender differences in time use, comparing paid work, unpaid work and free time	USA	1965, 1975 and 1998	Women: *increase* in paid work and *decrease* in unpaid work. Men: *decrease* in paid work and *increase* in unpaid work. Overall men have more free time

38	Zander, U., Meirer-Graewe, U. and Moeser, A.	To investigate changes in time use patterns of the German population for eating and drinking as well as for household work, including changes in time use for meals eaten at home and away from home as well as the division of labour for nutrition provision activities between men and women	Germany	1991–1902 and 2001–2002	*Increase* in time spent eating and drinking, *decrease* in gender segregation
39	Sullivan, O.	To explore changes in patterns of men's and women's time spent in domestic labour over the past twenty years, considering structural factors such as employment patterns and social class. To identify which groups of the population of couples have experienced change	UK	1975, 1987 and 1997	*Increase* in men's domestic work and *decrease* in gender segregation
40	Bittman, M.	To analyse trends in free time for working-age Australians	Australia	1974 and 1992	*Increase* in free time
41	Bittman, M.	To analyse evidence for a reduction in (paid) work time; the leisure revolution; the self-provisioning of services; and the growth of the 'symmetrical family'	Australia	1974 and 1987	*Increase* in wage-earning women's work and free time and wage-earning men's unpaid work. *Decrease* in wage-earning women's unpaid work and wage-earning men's paid work. *No change* in wage-earning men's free time

There is no evidence of an overall increase in paid work. The most discernible trend is how the distribution of paid work has changed between men and women, with men taking on more unpaid responsibilities and women increasing the amount of time in paid work. Greater gender equality in the distribution of paid and unpaid work is a defining characteristic of longitudinal time use data, though this process of gender equalisation is context specific and is happening in varying intensities in different countries.[31] More detailed analysis explores how time in paid and unpaid work is spent. Analysis of the temporality of paid work assesses the evidence for social acceleration. Mullan and Wajcman's analysis of technology and work extension[32] employing time use diary data collected in the UK finds evidence of a discernible increase in work extension in the twenty-first century, and this is concentrated among managers and professionals.[33] This increase in work extension is associated with time pressure and is facilitated by working with a device. Sullivan and Gershuny use the same data sources to find a small increase in the level of multitasking done by men, an increase in ICT use and an overall decline in the levels to which people always feel rushed.[34] Gershuny's earlier analysis of working time over a longer time period (from the 1960s to the early 2000s) finds that work has become more concentrated in the working week and that there is an increase in the number of activities during weekdays.[35]

Trying to decipher trends in unpaid work produces equally murky results. As noted above, the clearest trend relates to the distribution of who is doing unpaid work, but changes in how much time is spent on unpaid activities and what this involves are less clear. There is evidence that time spent on childcare has increased[36] and less time is spent on domestic duties.[37] Evidence about time spent cooking is inconclusive; Smith Taillie's analysis find that Americans spend more time cooking,[38] while analysis of France, Germany and an earlier analysis of the USA reveals the opposite trend.[39]

The overall conclusion of these analyses is that the empirical data do not confirm popular and theoretical interpretations of how time use is changing. The conviction that universal busyness has been brought about by the intensification of demands at work cannot be confirmed through analyses of time use data, as these do not reveal an increase in the amount of time dedicated to paid work.

---

[31]Hook (2010, pp. 1480–1523).
[32]Work extension refers to working beyond regular hours and/or working outside of a defined workspace.
[33]Mullan and Wajcman (2019, pp. 3–20).
[34]Sullivan and Gershuny (2018, pp. 20–38).
[35]Gershuny (2005).
[36]Craig, Mullan, and Blaxland (2010, pp. 27–45), Gimenez-Nadal and Sevilla (2012), Hofferth and Lee (2015, pp. 318–329), Schulz and Engelhardt-Wölfler (2017, pp. 277–297) and Zuzanek (2017, pp. 27–38).
[37]Gershuny and Harms (2016, pp. 1–22).
[38]Taillie (2018, p. 41).
[39]Etilé and Plessz (2018, pp. 939–970), Klünder and Meier-Gräwe (2017, pp. 179–201), Smith, Ng, and Popkin (2013, p. 45).

The most notable trend regarding paid work is that women are doing more in the early years of the twenty-first century than during the latter decades of the twentieth century. There is evidence of paid work simultaneously becoming more concentrated (an increase in the number of people working a five-day week and a general decline in Saturday working) and more extended (managers and professionals are more likely to work outside normal hours). Trends relating to unpaid work are varied. Although time spent on some activities that can be replaced by technology has declined, some labour-intensive activities, particularly childcare, continue to take up a similar amount of time, if not more. There is no evidence of people have less 'free time', assuming that activities coded as leisure correspond to temporal freedom. Leisure time is more fragmented and, for women in particular, more likely to be spent with other people, particularly children.[40]

The Usefulness of Time Use Data

Amassing data on time use have not provided a cohesive picture of how time is spent nor even the direction of any change in the use of time. In their conclusion to *What We Really Do All Day*, Gershuny and Sullivan conclude that on balance, analyses of 'general time use trends in some respects run contrary to expectations'.[41] In particular, the overall amount of time dedicated to work, sleep and leisure has changed less over the preceding 50 years than is popularly assumed. The disappointment that time use data does not confirm popular convictions about the intensity of temporal experiences is not surprising. Fascination with time does not oscillate around the order of time but, as *The Clock* reveals, around its disorder. If the montage of *The Clock* followed a predictable sequence of time, with people doing what is expected where and when, it would have less appeal. *The Clock* captivates its audience by keeping it constantly guessing what happens next. The original intention of collating time use data was to advise governments and organisations about how time is allocated, not about how time is spent *per se*. As the use of these data has expanded beyond the realm of official data, the potential of time use data to inform individual experiences and hence social, economic and cultural explanations of time has developed, though its purpose is not necessarily to confirm popular expectations.

The question to ask about time use data is whether it is even relevant to the study of busyness. The answer is not straightforward. In many respects, the answer is no, because the collation of time use data needs to make too many assumptions about the classification of time and must assume it is linear and external. The measurement of time is not the same as the perception of time and we should not expect this to the case.[42] Thus, the main consistent finding of time use analysis, which is that working time has not increased in advanced

---

[40]For a discussion of the gendering of leisure time, see Bittman and Wajcman (2000, pp. 165–189).
[41]Gershuny and Sullivan (2019, p. 326).
[42]Robinson and Godbey (1997).

economies in recent years and leisure time has not contracted, can be rejected as a red herring. Time use data cannot account for the intensity of activity at work and home, and recording how much time is spent doing discrete tasks misses the point of the significance of an increase in the pace of life, which cannot be easily measured.[43] This distrust of time use data is captured by the journalist Brigid Schulte in her book, *Overwhelmed*.[44] She begins her book with a description of a meeting with the American time use analysis expert John Robinson to discuss the findings of his research and his analysis of her own time use diary. Schulte is suspicious of Robinson's calculation that in the week she recorded she had 27 hours of leisure time and worked for 50 hours. Robinson categorised particular activities as leisure, such as a yoga class, but these were not experienced as such by Schulte. She contrasts Robinson's careful and leisurely approach to counting temporal frequencies with the frantic experiences of the predominately female researchers she encountered at the 2010 International Association for Time Use Research conference in Paris two months after her meeting with Robinson. At the conference, in contrast with her characterisation of Robinson's obsession with the methodical, dispassionate counting of time use, she found a frenzied focus on overwork, which many of the conference participants were experiencing in their own lives. These researchers were identifying with the hot topics of time overload and stress rather than with the objective analysis of time allocation. According to Schulte, time use analysis was shifting from the objective to the subjective as a new generation of predominately female time scholars were entering the discipline and seeking to find synergies between their own temporal experiences and their subject matter. Time use data that rely on the assumption that activities are allocated in discrete times and space are irrelevant for the study of contemporary time squeeze, as this phenomenon ultimately comes about through the dispersal of activities in time and space.[45] Data that rely on bounded assumptions about when and where things happen are not suited to unravelling busyness.

Schulte's emotional rejection of time use concurs with more scholarly contributions such as Rosa's detailed rebuttal of time use data. However, the evidence from the analysis of time use that trends in how time is spent are relatively stable over time cannot be so easily dismissed. Statistics rarely provide thrilling accounts of social change as there is an inherent conservatism to data that can never match the theoretical claims made about social change. The question to ask when using time use data is not whether people in modern advanced economies have more or less free time but which groups have 'gained or lost free time'.[46] Time use analysis confirms the durability of temporal structures of everyday life and how these are unevenly distributed. The persistence of how time is spent and the lack of clear absolute trends in time use in contrast to the significance of relative differences, cannot be so easily dismissed. Perhaps the obduracy of the temporal distribution

---

[43]Rosa (2013).
[44]Schulte (2014).
[45]Southerton (2020).
[46]Zuzanek (2017, p. 28).

of the 'Great Day', rather than anticipating busyness and linking the associated quickening pace of life with changes in the timing of tasks during the day, contributes to the overwhelming frustrations of busyness. For many people struggling with the inequalities of time distribution (and time use analysis consistently shows that this is mainly women), being busy is associated with the intensity of responding to divergent responsibilities within bounded time constraints that are not evenly distributed and have little flexibility. Frustrations with busyness are exacerbated by awareness of the unfairness of temporal distribution, and time use analysis efficiently demonstrates the validity of these claims.

Synchronising Time

Analysis of time use data underlines enduring inequalities in the distribution of tasks in time. These data, therefore, confirm the relational significance of temporality; what matters is how much time is spent doing particular tasks, the relative contribution of different groups and the persistence of gender inequalities. In time use data, the relational qualities of temporality are expressed through differential responsibilities undertaken by distinct social groups. However, busyness is not just experienced through the dissonance of time; it is also manifest in the intense synchronisation of activities. Busy times can be characterised by lots of people trying to do (almost) the same thing at the same time. So if busyness is an outcome of uneven temporal intensity, this means not only that we have lots of things to do but also that we are trying to do things at the same time and coordinate activities with other people.[47] Families getting up and getting ready for the day, travelling to work, timing mealtimes and breaks, attending meetings and leaving work are obvious, if somewhat mundane, components of time squeeze.[48]

Empirically capturing the coordination of activities in time–space is not straightforward. One of the pioneers of this empirical challenge is Torsten Hägerstrand, who started to develop the discipline of time geography in the 1950s. Time geography defines places through coordinates and prioritises the analytical significance of paths of individual movements in time–space.[49] The problem with time geography is that while it is intuitive – it is based on self-evident phenomena – its application is abstract and mundane to equal extents. The conundrum of time geographies is that to analyse everyday paths, they have to be converted into abstract representations and the detail concerning time and place removed. The potential of time geographies has been revitalised through the application of geographic information systems that facilitate analytical ways of visualising time geographies. These methods do, however, necessarily prioritise the spatial components of time geographies rather than the temporal dimensions.

An alternative approach to studying everyday time and space is to follow the philosopher Henri Lefebvre's conceptualisation of rhythm analysis.[50]

---

[47]Schwanen (2006, pp. 882–894).
[48]Southerton and Tomlinson (2005).
[49]Hägerstrand (1970, pp. 7–21).
[50]Lefebvre (2004).

This approach starts from Lefebvre's observation that everyday life is experienced through multiple rhythms and as such the study of the everyday requires attention being paid to how rhythms are reproduced, experienced and understood.[51] These rhythms are not simply the 'norms, habits and conventions'[52] of temporality but express the interplay between time's biological, psychological and social dimensions.[53] Of particular resonance to my more specific interest in the shared experiences of timing is Lefebvre's distinction between circular and linear rhythms. Circular rhythms capture repetitive activities that continuously begin again and include natural as well as social rhythms. In contrast, linear rhythms are those that occur as 'consecutive reproductions or pulses of activity'.[54] In other words, we need to be attuned to the different ways in which everyday routines can collide, and following a linear path is only one way of revealing the time and space of everyday life.

While watching *The Clock*, I had noted how certain times – the hour and half hour – received more recognition than others and were more likely to be spoken in the cinematic clips than other times, which were captured by a timepiece. Marclay deftly plays with the significance of 'o'clock time', building up to the anticipation of noon and midnight and reverting to mundane temporal references immediately after these temporal climaxes. I was aware of the same arrhythmical temporal referencing in the Mass Observation Archive one-day diaries. Through repeated readings, I observed that some clock times during the day were referenced more than others and that the one-day diaries could be used to analyse the rhythms of temporal intensity and synchronisation. I have, therefore, used the MOA diaries to quantify the rhythms of clock time by extracting time references from all of them.

One-day Diary Format

Before I discuss analysis of temporal rhythms, it is necessary to describe the format of the diaries. There is no proscriptive format for the MOA one-day diary, and one of the most intriguing details of the diary is the variation in how correspondents write them. The 2017 Autumn Directive[55] requested correspondents to write about a day when either they or their partner were at work. If no one in the household was in employment, they were asked to choose any day.[56] The directive

---

[51]Lefebvre's theorisation is developed in studies of the complexities of individual and collective mobilities; see, for example, Stratford (2015).

[52]Adam (1995, p. 66).

[53]Stratford (2015).

[54]Southerton (2020, p. 153).

[55]The diaries were written between 9 September 2017 and 11 April 2018.

[56]Mass Observation volunteers are not representative of the UK population. Among correspondents to the Autumn 2017 directive: 61% are female; 54% are retired and 82% have or had occupations classified in Groups 1-4 of the UK Office of National Statistics occupational classification (Managerial, Professional, Assistant Professional and Administrative occupations: in the 2011 UK census these four groups accounted for 65% of working population).

asked correspondents to write about everything that happened from when they got up to when they went to bed, including what time, where and with whom (if anyone) events occurred. The significance of food and eating was also highlighted in the directive. Correspondents were encouraged to reflect in the diary on why they had carried out an activity at a particular time. They were also asked to reflect on how their day had been organised: how the schedules of others influenced what they did or when they did it, how much flexibility they had, how much planning they did and whether different parts of the day had gone as planned. Correspondents were encouraged to reflect on their thoughts and feelings as well as on the events and to comment on time pressures, specifically when they felt most and least pressed for time. They were asked to relate this to what they were doing, who they were doing it with, whether they felt activities were under or out of control, and whether the time pressure (or lack of it) was anticipated or unexpected and whether it was enjoyable. Finally, correspondents were asked to provide photographs or sketches of their day. The detailed instructions were clear about the data that the directive was seeking to collate but not about how the data should be recorded. Correspondents' responses to the directive are, not surprisingly very varied. Some kept to the brief and answered as many questions as possible, while others simple wrote about their day. The messiness of MOA data is what makes them both fascinating and frustrating. The variability in the format of the diaries makes visible the different ways in which time can be experienced and unsettles the assumption that time is a divisible and discrete resource.[57]

One quarter of the diaries are handwritten, and one diary was submitted as a cartoon. The diaries vary in length from half a page to 15 pages, and the modal length is three pages. Thirty-one correspondents include images, which are all photographs except for the cartoon diary and one correspondent who provides two sketches. Several correspondents write that photographs are not appropriate, because their day was too boring or was spent at work. Diarists' responses to the specific questions about time pressure are varied and just under a half (44%) of correspondents write about their emotional experiences of time pressure. The choice of day is evenly distributed throughout the working week (10 correspondents write about a weekend, mostly Sunday), though there is a slight bias towards the start of the week, with Monday the most popular day (28 responses) and Friday the least common (20 diaries).

With the exception of the cartoon diary, correspondents adopt one of two approaches to organising the diary around when (and where) events occur. The first approach is to write a time-structured diary which divides the day into specific time points and the diarist details the activities that they were doing at each time. Some of these time-structured diaries use a table format and all conform to a stylistic device of noting the time on the left-hand side of the page. The second approach is to write a time-narrated diary in which the diarist describes the activities of the day and (sometimes) the times that activities happened. In time-narrated diaries, the narrative is driven by activities rather than temporal

---

[57]Nowotny (1994).

structure. These diaries usually take the form of a long essay, though some might identify key time points in the margin. References to clock time segue between being deterministic (activities happen because of the time, such as leaving the house to go to work) and incidental (activities happen at certain times, such as a meeting starting or finishing). Both types of reference to time are used in time-structured and time-narrated diaries. To illustrate the differences between these two approaches, I provide fictional examples of a time-structured and time-narrated diary in Table 3.2. Although I have categorised diaries into these two styles, this does not imply that there is a clear-cut distinction between structured and narrated approaches. The categorisation simply indicates the dominant style in each diary. Categorising a diary is easiest for diaries that are written using a table format, for which structured clock time is the only temporal narrative. Other diaries have a more varied style. For example, diarists might begin their day with

Table 3.2.   Illustrations[a] of a Time-structured Diary and a Time-narrated Diary.

Time-structured Diary	Time-narrated Diary
7 a.m.: Woke up when the alarm went off. Grey December day, no motivation to get up *7.35 a.m.*: Reluctantly get up and head for bathroom. Clean teeth, take tablets, shower and moisturise with my own handmade creams. Tell daughter to get up *8.05 a.m.*: Finish ablutions, get dressed *8.10 a.m.*: Downstairs. Cat is cross at our tardiness and demands food. Daughter sees to cat (including his Christmas advent treat) while I finish cleaning up from last night's meal, which we had somehow overlooked *8.15 a.m.*: Routine of breakfast. For me: leaf tea, blended fruit, more tablets (vitamins and cod liver oil) and toast. Daughter has cereal and a piece of my toast *8.35 a.m.*: Daughter leaves for work	The alarm goes off at 7. It's a miserable grey December day and I can't be bothered to get out of bed. It's a working at home day today so less need to be on time. I lie in bed thinking about work that I need to do, glancing at the clock. After half an hour I realise I'm getting late. Usual morning routine: cleaning teeth, taking tablets, showering, moisturising with my own handmade creams. I always take too long in the shower. Once finished I observe that my daughter is not up, so I remind her and go to get dressed Coming downstairs and into the kitchen, the cat is cross as always and demands his breakfast. I realise I forgot to finish the washing up after last night's meal so I see to this while my daughter sees to the cat. She gives him his Christmas advent treat before his breakfast Time for breakfast. For me it's toast, leaf tea and a blended fruit drink. My daughter has cereal and steals a piece of my toast before leaving for work

[a]These illustrations are fictional and are provided to illustrate the two main approaches to writing about time in the one-day diaries.

a structured account of clock time, but as the day develops, clock time becomes more incidental. In diaries that combine time structure and time narration, I have made a judgement about the dominant stylistic reference to time.

Of the 134 diaries written in response to the 2017 Autumn Directive that were collated, I classify 36% as time-structured and 64% as time-narrated. The frequency of time points noted in the diaries varies considerably. The time-structured diaries are more consistent in recording times throughout the day, but they do not necessarily record more time points than time-narrated ones. Some of the time-narrated diaries are very detailed in recording time, but others make no reference to clock time at all. In diaries that mention no (or very few) clock times, the temporal narrative is indicated through the sequencing of events: before, after, then, etc. It is noteworthy that while it is possible to describe a day with no reference to clock time, all diarists write about where events happen. All diarists require some spatial clarity to describe everyday events (where events happen), but temporal precision is not necessary (when events happen).

Analysis of the characteristics of correspondents by diary type is presented in Table 3.3 and reveals no patterning of how the diaries are written by gender, though age and employment status are associated with diary format. Correspondents in paid employment are more likely to write a time-narrated diary than those

Table 3.3.   MOA One-day Diary Format by Gender, Age and Employment Status of Diarist.

Characteristics	Number of Diaries (%) by Format	
	Structured (%)	Narrative (%)
Gender[a]		
Female	28 (34)	54 (66)
Male	20 (39)	32 (61)
Age group[b]		
<30	3 (43)	4 (57)
30–49	6 (17)	30 (83)
50–69	21 (45)	26 (55)
70+	18 (41)	26 (59)
Employment status[c]		
In paid work	11 (22)	33 (78)
Not in paid work	37 (44)	48 (56)

Source: Author's analysis of diary format: Mass Observation Archive (University of Sussex): Replies to autumn 2017 Directive Part I: One-Day Diary: Organising and Experiencing Time.
[a]P-value for Pearson's chi-squares test is 0.61, that is, not significant.
[b]P-value for Pearson's chi-squared test is 0.05, that is, significant at 95% confidence level.
[c]P-value for Pearson's chi-squared test is 0.01, that is, significant at 95% confidence level.

who are not. Similarly, time-structured diaries were not very frequently written by those in the age group 30–49 compared with those in older age groups. It is worth noting that many retired correspondents write that time does not really matter to them as much now they are no longer working, though they are more likely to frame their day through the structure of time compared with those in paid employment. It is tempting to interpret these data as evidence that the perception of time changes over the life-course,[58] but this interpretation should be treated with caution because of the biases in the data. An alternative interpretation is that the days of diarists in paid work are structured by external timetables and these are taken for granted, while retired diarists have to structure their own day.[59]

Telling the Time

After classifying the diaries, the next stage of the quantitative analysis was to extract all clock time references from the diaries and put them into a database. In total, 2,052 time points were extracted. Most clock time references refer to specific times (e.g. 8 a.m.) even if the activities written about did not necessarily happen at that precise time. Some are vague (e.g. 'at about 9 o'clock'). These approximate times have been recorded as an exact time in the database. Temporal references can also be for a time period (e.g. 8.00–9.00 a.m.), and both clock times (i.e. 8.00 and 9.00) are recorded. Times noted more than once in the diaries were only logged once in the database. The clock times in the database were classified according to the diarists' gender and employment status and the diary format (time-structured or time-narrated).

The first observation is that, as Marclay found when making *The Clock*, clock time references are dominated by the 12 points of clock time, particularly the hour and half hour, and thus the cyclical rhythm of the clock dominates how time is referenced in the diaries. Of the 2,052 time references in the diaries, 96% (1970) refer to one of the 12 clock points and the distribution of these 1970 time references is shown in Fig. 3.1. Of these, over half, 36% and 25%, refer to the hour and half hour respectively. This is not surprising, because many technologies used for time management are based on 30-minute intervals; electronic diaries, for example, use 30-minute slots for meetings which start on the hour or half hour (other times usually have to be entered manually). The duration of 30 minutes is also used for promoting health and well-being, as this period of vigorous exercise, walking or reading has been proven to enhance well-being. Thus, half hours are a frequent demarcation of time, and this is evident in how diarists record time.

The dominance of 12 and 6 for clock time is not the only pattern that emerges from these data, and the symmetry of clock time references is also striking. After 12 and 6, the next most popular clock points are 3 and 9, and these have

---

[58]Wittmann (2016).

[59]For further discussion of the differences in the MOA one-day diaries over the life-course see: Holdsworth (2019, pp. 155–176).

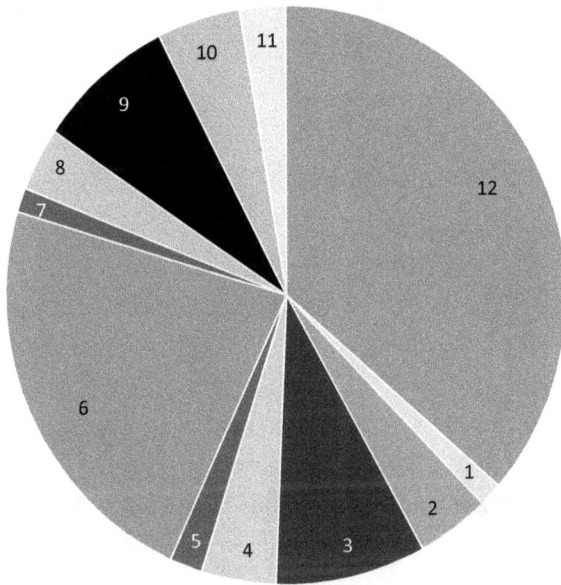

Fig. 3.1.   Distribution of Clock Points in MOA Time Database. *Source*: Author's extraction of times from Mass Observation Archive (University of Sussex): Replies to Autumn 2017 Directive Part 1: One-day Diary: organising and experiencing time.

almost identical frequencies in the database. These are followed in frequency by the remaining even clock points, 2, 4, 8 and 10, which all have similar frequencies, though there is a slight bias towards 10. Finally, the least popular clock points are 5, 11, 7 and 1, in declining frequency. This analysis suggests that the recording of clock time is not simply a neutral expression of spatialised time but reveals cultural preferences for rounded, rather than precise, clock time and those at the beginning and halfway through the hour. Despite the heterogeneous quality of the data set and the different approaches that correspondents take to writing a one-day diary, it is possible to see a symmetry in the references to clock times.

Diurnal Rhythms

The symmetrical recording of clock time is not the only pattern that can be identified in the data set. It is also possible to discern a linear rhythm in the distribution of recorded time over the course of the day. To analyse this, I have counted the number of discrete clock time references in the database for each hour. The distribution of these is illustrated in Fig. 3.2.

This analysis reveals, not surprisingly, that the most intensely referenced hours are 7, 8 and 9 in the morning. There is a slight lull in noting time in mid-morning (11), an increase around lunchtime and a second lull in the afternoon.

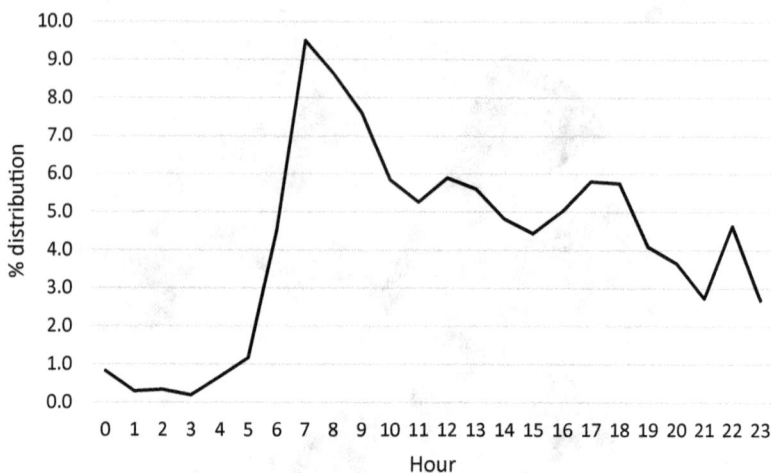

Fig. 3.2.   Percentage Distribution of Time References by Each Hour Period in MOA Time Database. *Source*: Authors' extraction of times from Mass Observation Archive (University of Sussex): Replies to Autumn 2017 Directive Part 1: One-Day Diary: Organising and Experiencing Time.

More references to time points are made in the late afternoon and early evening, though this does not match the intensity of the morning rush. Evenings (7 p.m. onwards) are distinguished by a gradual decline in time references, though there are slightly more temporal references between 10 p.m. and 10.59 p.m. compared with 9 p.m. and 9.59 p.m. because the former is the modal hour for going to bed.[60]

This linear rhythm in the intensity of recording time over the day does not correspond to the distribution of time in *The Clock*. In his research for *The Clock*, Marclay found that noon and midnight were particularly dominant in cinematic representations of clock time. In the MOA diary database, morning times are more prevalent. Marclay reports that morning time is his favourite period in *The Clock* as it is dominated by people getting up and starting the day and mirrors what happens in everyday life.[61] However, while cinematic time suggests that the intensity of time builds up during the day, the MOA data suggest that clock time becomes less intensive after the morning rush.

---

[60]This pattern of time counts over the day is statistically significant. I calculate confidence intervals for the percentage distribution of time points in each hour, restricting the analysis to time points between 7 a.m. and 10.59 p.m. (1,438 time points in total). If time points were evenly distributed, each hour would account for 6.25% of time points (I exclude the time points between 11 p.m. and 6.59 a.m. as it is not reasonable to assume that time points are evenly distributed at night). Divergence from an even distribution of time points is significant if the confidence intervals (calculated for 90% and 95% significance) exclude 6.25% of time points.
[61]Zalewski (2012).

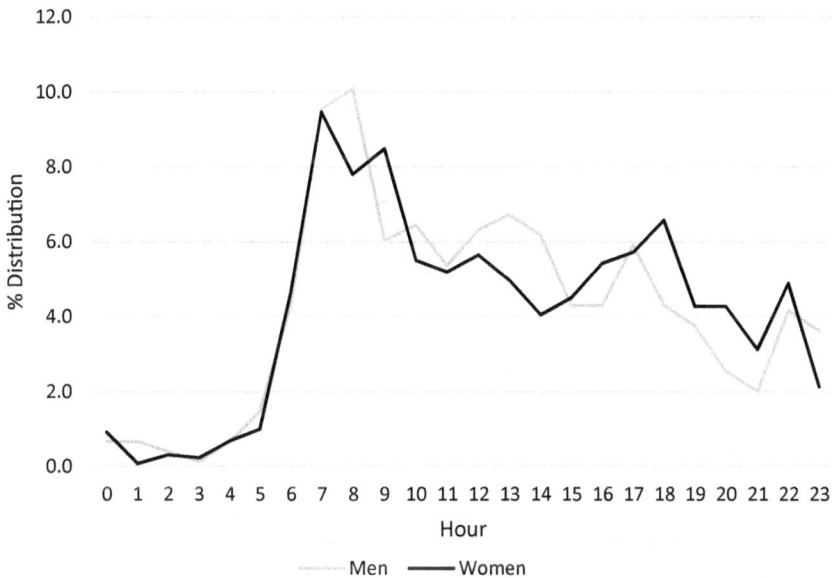

Fig. 3.3. Percentage Distribution of Time References by Each Hour Period by Gender in MOA Time Database. *Source*: Authors' extraction of times from Mass Observation Archive (University of Sussex): Replies to Autumn 2017 Directive Part 1: One-Day Diary: Organising And Experiencing Time.

The database allows for a comparison of the distribution of clock time by gender (Fig. 3.3) and employment status (Fig. 3.4). As with diary type, there is no clear difference between men's and women's recording of time. Women appear to get up slightly earlier than men and are more aware of time in the evening than at lunchtime, the latter being more discernible in men's diaries. This may be because many women have the responsibility for preparing family meals in the evening and/or putting children to bed. The difference by employment status is more striking. The dominance of morning times is associated with diarists in paid work. Once at work (and most diarists work a conventional 9–5 working day), their adherence to time slackens and the mid-morning lull is a feature of their diaries. There is an increase in temporal references at lunchtime and again when it is time to go home. Clock times for those in work do not detail the timing of the working day but when works starts, pauses (e.g. lunch) and ends. For those not in paid work, the distribution of clock times is flatter, although there is a slight decline in the frequency of clock times mentioned during the day (and this might be explained by fatigue in writing the diary over the course of the day) and a slight increase in intensity in the evening, though interestingly not at lunch time. The difference between the intensity of time references for those in and out of work suggests that for the latter, who often write in their diaries that time is less important than it used to be, time is noted more uniformly over the day.

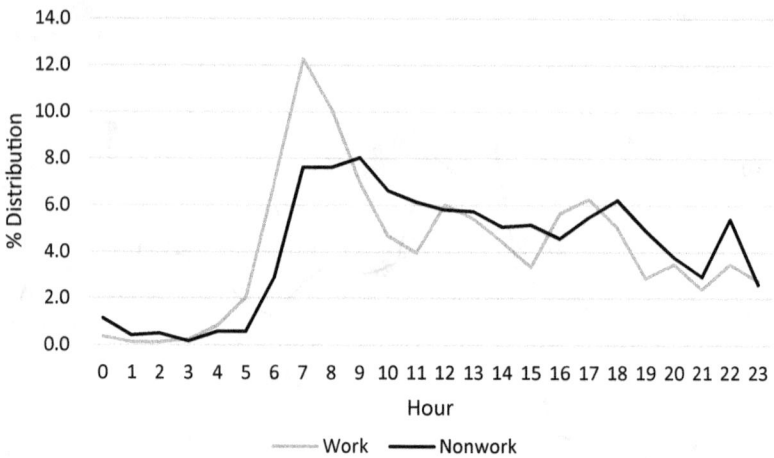

Fig. 3.4.   Percentage Distribution of Time References by Each Hour Period by Employment Status in MOA Time Database. *Source*: Authors' extraction of times from Mass Observation Archive (University of Sussex): Replies to Autumn 2017 Directive Part 1: One-Day Diary: Organising and Experiencing Time.

MOA diaries are used by other time scholars. In particular, Southerton has analysed diaries collated in 1937, when the archive was first established.[62] He is struck by how these diaries are organised around institutional time points, particularly meal times. He suggests that this adherence to collective time has dissipated over the twentieth century and contrasts the 1937 MOA diaries with interviews carried out in 2000. My analysis suggests that collective time points are very much discernible in the 2017/2018 data set. I concur with Southerton that how these collective temporal moments are experienced has changed – for example the image of shutting for lunch in *The Clock* is of a particular time and place. However, the coordination of these activities remains an important feature of everyday life. The method used for researching time and timing is clearly important here. If diaries are used to explore temporal experiences, then they are more likely to record collective events such as eating meals, as this is one of the main uses of a diary. My analysis suggests that the diaries are not particularly suited to documenting change over time. Instead, along with official time use data, diaries are more sensitive to the persistence of temporal rhythms.

The diurnal rhythms repeated in these diaries provide a quantification of Lefebvre's observation that there will be rhythm in all places where there are interactions among place, time and energy.[63] The concentration of time references between 7 a.m. and 9.59 a.m. is a function of the intertwining of individual biological rhythms

---

[62]Southerton (2020).
[63]Lefebvre (2004, p. 15).

of getting ready for the day, social rhythms orchestrated through education and work routines, and psychological immersion into the day. It is not surprising that diarists provide lots of detail when documenting mornings; morning routines have more resonance than at other times of the day. A shared fascination with how people organise mornings is a staple feature of self-help books on time, which I consider in chapter four. Morning routines provide a grounding for individual immersion into consciousness. These routines also awaken awareness of the self and others. Time references demarcate individual routines and how these synchronise or collide with the timings of others: family members, pets, fellow commuters and travellers, colleagues, etc. Times are given for getting up and getting ready (and coordinating bathroom routines with family members or housemates); having breakfast; getting children ready for the day; feeding/looking after pets; going out to work or to do non-work tasks; and taking children to school. The morning hours are more intensively accounted for by time because of the temporal ordering of activities that are required to start the day and because these activities have to, to some extent, be coordinated with those of others. In contrast, the mid-morning period, which might be presumed to be a time when work activities are more intensive, is not as heavily referenced by time. The distribution of time points in the afternoon mirrors the distribution in the morning, though overall there are fewer references to time. The decline in intensification of temporal references to the end of the day compared with the morning does reflect temporal fatigue in writing the diary. Most diarists wrote their diary in the evening or the following day, and while many diaries start with a detailed description of the morning, this can fade away during the day. Moreover, morning routines are easier to recall because, as many diarists write, these are predictable. People get up, get washed, get dressed, have breakfast, walk the dog, get the children ready for school and leave home and/or start work at the same time each day. Diarists were specifically asked to write about meals, and I find that diarists are more precise about what they eat for breakfast than for other meals, because they eat the same breakfast every day. Evening routines are more varied and are harder to recall with precision.

There are two concluding observations to make from this analysis. The first is that adherence to clock time varies. Even when specifically requested to record when activities happen, most diarists do not provide this temporal detail. While some diarists are punctilious in how they record clock time, this is the exception rather than the rule. Most of them refer to clock times to identify changing schedules in the day. The second is that the intensity of clock time, when it is important, is unavoidable. Busyness that focusses around clock time is required for scheduling and coordinating activities with others. Mornings are busy because people have to do the same activities at the same time and in the same place. The time squeeze of busyness revealed in the diaries is relational, not individual. As the day unfolds and people adopt more positional rather than personal roles, the detail of clock time is less important. As the intensity of coordination diminishes, the necessity of keeping to time becomes less important. Employed diarists write about temporal discipline in relation to the practices of work, and this is particularly acute in the times and spaces adjacent to work itself and in time that is not structured by specific employment responsibilities.

Tracking Time

Most MOA diarists did not keep a detailed time use diary. It is more intuitive to write about the sequencing and coordination of activities rather than the precision concerning when things are done, and how much time is spent doing particular activities. This lack of interest in detailing the time of an individual day contrasts with a shared fascination with the quantification of time. There is a popular appeal in calculations of how long we spend doing mundane everyday activities, such as answering emails (the 'average' American worker spends 2.6 hours each day doing this),[64] browsing social media (globally, the average is 144 minutes each day)[65] or waiting for a kettle to boil (12 minutes each week for UK workers[66]). The badge of honour of busyness is earned, and sometimes crushed, through declarations about how much time is spent being productive. The contradiction here is that while we might want to know how much time other people (or the 'average' person) spends doing activities, we rarely ask these questions of ourselves: none of the MOA diarists used the discipline of keeping a one-day diary to track their time. In this final section of this chapter, I consider this reluctance to reveal the individual detail of time, and what can be learnt from the practice of tracking time.

Tracking Time: Method

I kept a detailed time use diary for one year, starting on 4th February 2018. My time use diary is an adaptation of Laura Vanderkam's method for getting 'off the clock'.[67] Vanderkam is a US-based time management specialist and I include her book *Off the Clock* in my analysis of self-books in chapter four. For now, I focus on the first stage of Vanderkam's method for managing time, which requires readers to track time over at least a week. To facilitate this activity, Vanderkam provides readers with a simple Excel spreadsheet divided into either 30-minute or 15-minute segments to record time use, starting at 5 a.m. (one hour later than the American Time Use Survey). She has kept her own time use diary continuously since April 2015 and analyses her diary every Monday morning. I kept my diary for 49 of the possible 52 weeks. Unlike Vanderkam, I did not record my time when away on holiday and three weeks are excluded from the diary, two weeks of annual leave when I was away from home and one week over Christmas. I found that I needed to switch off and have some time when I was not required to make a note of time.

Keeping any diary over a period of time requires a routine that works. My solution was to colour in time rather than write it down. I chose to document time for every 30 minutes rather than 15 as I found during the first few weeks that this level of temporal detail was sufficient. I also coded activity at the same time as

---

[64]Plummer (2019).
[65]Clement (2020).
[66]Choiceadmin (n.d.).
[67]Vanderkam (2018).

recording it. Using differently coloured highlighter pens, I coded each 30-minute interval according to the main activity that I did during that time. These activities are as follows:

1. *Sleep.* The most straightforward to record, though it is difficult to accurately record a broken night's sleep.
2. *Travel.* Travel by car, bus, train, plane or boat (excludes cycling and walking). Also includes times waiting for transport (though some time spent at airports/stations is classified as food, craft or work if I spent a period of time doing that activity).
3. *Work.* Time spent on activities connected with paid employment. I attempted to keep an accurate account. Coffee with colleagues, chats in the morning on the way to the office and lunch at my desk are not recorded as work (these are coded as socialising or food). It is inevitable that some non-productive work time is recorded as work. If work is carried out simultaneously with another activity, the other activity has priority. For example, thinking about work at breakfast is recorded as food. Activities that are only orientated towards work are not recorded as work, for example travelling to work is recorded as travelling.
4. *Food.* Time spent preparing, eating and cleaning up. A food-related activity is often carried out with other activities, for example lunch with a friend. For these activities, I divide the time between the two, so an hour's social lunch is recorded as 30 minutes for food and 30 minutes for socialising.
5. *Self-care.* This includes a variety of activities: everyday habits such as having a shower, getting dressed and getting ready for bed. It also includes going to the hairdressers, having a manicure or a massage, meditation and relaxation classes, medical appointments (for myself) and packing in preparation for travel.
6. *Shopping.* Time spent purchasing goods but does not include online browsing (this is recorded as doing nothing; see 11 below). Also includes waiting for car/cycle repairs.
7. *Housework.* Time spent cleaning (except for daily washing up, which is recorded as food) and gardening.
8. *Exercise.* Walking and cycling (including walking/cycling to the train station, gym or shops), swimming and yoga, and Pilates classes.
9. *Socialising.* Time spent with other people. Includes talking on the phone or online, volunteering, lunch with friends and visiting family. It also includes time spent taking relatives to hospital appointments.
10. *Craft.* Mostly sewing and crochet but also some painting (decorating is recorded as housework). These are often carried out in conjunction with other types of activity, such as crocheting on a train or waiting for a medical appointment. I divide this time between activities (e.g. half an hour for craft and the same for travel).
11. *Doing nothing.* In theory, anything not listed above. It is not time spent literally doing nothing, but time for which there is little intention other than the activity itself. It captures activities that are not orientated towards

carrying out responsibilities for other people. Includes lying in bed, browsing the internet, watching TV (though time spent watching TV while crocheting is craft time), reading for pleasure (not time spent reading academic books, though the distinction is blurred) and going to the theatre, cinema or an art gallery.

My interpretation of how I spend time and how this is recorded on my spreadsheet is only applicable for me. Anyone else tracking time in this way would make different decisions about the classification of time. For example, I am not particularly fond of gardening and I classify it as housework rather than a separate activity. I enjoy sewing, though other people might classify this as housework. There are, therefore, two stages to the project of tracking time. The first is deciding which activity dominates, the second is coding it so that it is categorised as a type of activity that summarises its purpose or intention. My classification distinguishes between activities that are carried out by myself or with other people, between paid and unpaid work, sedentary and mobile activities and between activities involving consumption and those involving production.

Tracking Time: Results

The results of my time use diary over the 49 weeks are shown in Table 3.4. The aim of keeping the diary was not to collate these data or to calculate how I spend time (and whether I achieved a badge of busyness or not) but to reflect on how

Table 3.4.   Number of Hours and Percentage of Time Spent Per Activity.

Activity	Total Number of Hours Per Activity	% of Time Devoted to Each Activity
Sleep	2,476.0	30.1
Travel	577.0	7.0
Work	1,668.5	20.3
Food	557.0	6.8
Self-care	451.5	5.5
Shopping	117.0	1.4
Housework	178.0	2.2
Exercise	368.0	4.5
Socialising	304.0	3.7
Craft	910.5	11.1
Nothing	624.5	7.6
Total	*8,232.0*	

Source: Authors' personal time-diary.

difficult it is to account for time. Tracking time was both a chore and a satisfying achievement. Like Vanderkam, I transferred my colour diary into a spreadsheet first thing each Monday morning, and this ritual became an affirmative way of starting the working week. I quickly became more observant of clock time and how long it took to complete discrete tasks. While researching and writing this book, I did not have a set working week with times when I needed to be in an office but I became disciplined in starting/pausing/ending work at the hour or half hour as this facilitated filling in the diary. However, it is difficult to keep to the discipline of continually accounting for time. I periodically got fed up with the exercise and fell behind in tracking days. I started recording a routine of mornings and evenings rather than being alert to the detail of each day.

The diary did, though, provide an extremely useful external check on how much time I was devoting to different tasks over the year and the amount of time I dedicated to myself and others. The year during which I kept the diary was particularly challenging. A few weeks after I started it, both my sister and my partner were diagnosed with cancer. During many of the 49 weeks of tracked time, how I spent my time was determined by the needs of others: making hospital visits, attending appointments and simply being there through the treatments that left both my sister and my partner extremely ill. Tracking time enabled me to be kinder to myself, to acknowledge that the regimes of the rhythms of every day continued and that it did not matter if these were disrupted at times or if I was too emotionally tried to work. The time use diary revealed that even though I sometimes felt as if everything was disrupted and it was impossible to get anything done, my use of time did not alter radically. I carried on working and crafting, the latter often to take my mind off other responsibilities.

While tracking time was affirmative in revealing the rhythm of every day, it also made me nervous that I would be caught out by this activity. Although studying time might ultimately reveal more about ourselves than anything else, this knowledge may not be something that we want to or can share with others. Revealing the truth about time use to be shared with others opens up a personal vulnerability. For me this vulnerability was the thought that I might fail to earn a badge of honour for working long hours in a working environment where almost everyone conforms to an expectation that overworking is the norm. I became obsessed with ensuring that at the very least I fulfilled the notional contract of working 1,650[68] hours during the year and did not have to request additional time off work. I regularly checked how many hours I was working to ensure that I did not miss this goal. Tracking time become a goal-orientated task, not just to reassure myself that life was not on hold, but also to ensure that I kept my responsibilities to myself, my family and my employer. In the end, I learnt that tracking time became a practice that constituted how I spent time and was not simply a neutral activity of recording time use. My diary segues between the objective recording

---

[68]1,650 hours is calculated by assuming a working week of 37.5 hours over a 44-week period.

of time and the subjective interpretation of how this time was spent and how I would like others to see how I spend my time.

Summary

Clocks, according to Michelle Bastian, might not have the imaginative appeal of maps but this does not imply that clock time is of little popular interest. The fascination with time makes Marclay's *The Clock* possible (along with the collective allure of cinematic culture) and facilitates the longitudinal collation of time use diaries and the individual practice of diary writing. These shared practices do not rely on a universal interpretation of clock time. Time can be told in different ways, from detailing the intensity of activities (as in the collection of time use data) to the segueing of activities (this is how the majority of MOA diarists write about time). Underpinning these different ways of telling the time are strongly bound linear and cyclical rhythms that facilitate the coordination of activities in time and space.

To return to the possible theoretical explanations of busyness, the analyses of different aspects of clock time cannot support a linear explanation of social change, especially through the lens of individualisation. This is because studying clock time is essentially a collective endeavour, from the analysis of gender differences in how time is spent in time use analysis to identifying the shared pinch points of time squeeze during the morning rush. Moreover, turning attention to individual use of clock time can reinforce the timing of collective activities but it also exposes vulnerabilities about the self. Detailing the precision of individual time use, rather than relying on subjective declarations of busyness, reminds us that our time is not our own but highly normative and shared with others.

In this chapter, I have explored how busyness cannot be separated from clock time, as the latter is more than a simple expression of external, linear time. Clock time is relevant because it reveals the inequalities in how time is used and the social norms that reproduce this diversity. The measurement of clock time does not provide a consistent account of temporal change, but it does confirm that social and economic changes have differential impacts on people's lives. Thus, one of the social lives of busyness is dealing with temporal inequality. Clock time is ultimately a collective measure of time, and its second contribution to busyness is the simple observation that coordination of everyday lives necessarily involves synchronising with others. Individual linear rhythms necessarily collide in time and space, and this mundane component of busyness should not be overlooked.

Chapter 4

Organised Time

A Brief History of the Filofax

Philofaxy is a website dedicated to the use of time planners and organisers.[1] Written by enthusiasts, it collates advice on how to use planners, reviews of different makes, models and printable inserts, and a brief cultural history of the planner. Its name references the most widely known brand of organiser, the Filofax. Filofaxes are cultural artefacts associated with a specific social group in a particular place at a specific point in time: the yuppie[2] working in a global city in the 1980s. In an iconic episode of the classic British sitcom *Only Fools and Horses* entitled 'Yuppie Love', originally aired on 8 January 1989, its central character, Del Boy, a happy-go-lucky chancer from London's East End played by David Jason, endorses his ambition to be upwardly mobile by brandishing the required artefacts: a black Filofax and an outsized mobile phone. Though Filofaxes were cult items in the 1980s, the practice of time organisation is not simply a fad of that time.

The first personal organisers were produced by an American company, Lefax, which was founded in 1910 in Philadelphia. In a 1928 edition of Lefax's Radio Log and Catalogue, the company promoted the value of its planners to workers who were finding that their day was too short and would like to have more time for both work and play.[3] Lefax's advice is that the only way to get more time is to use it more efficiently, ideally through purchasing and using one of their planners. The Filofax was born in 1921 when a London stationer, Norman and Hill, started importing them. The name Filofax was invented by a secretary at Norman and Hill, Grace Scurr, as 'a contraction of the product being a "File of Facts" '.[4] These original planners were mainly sold to professionals; Lefaxes were popular with engineers and Filofaxes with the military and clergy.[5] The boom years for Filofax were, not surprisingly, in the mid-1980s, though this popularity was followed by a sudden slump. In 1990, shares in the company were trading at less than

---

[1]Philofaxy (n.d.).
[2]Yuppie stands for young upwardly mobile urban professional.
[3]Lefax (1928)
[4]Hall (2010).
[5]Hall (2010).

The Social Life of Busyness, 65–87
Copyright © 2021 by Clare Holdsworth
Published under exclusive licence by Emerald Publishing Limited
doi:10.1108/978-1-78743-698-520211005

20 pence from a 1987 peak of 200 pence.[6] Though they enjoyed an iconic status, Filofaxes were not the only planners available, and the expansion of unbranded generic organisers eroded the company's dominance of the planner market.

While planners no longer have the iconic status of the Filofax in the 1980s, they are not an anachronistic tool. Planners have developed during the first decades of the twenty-first century, partly in response to the competition from digital technologies that might be assumed to render a paper-based format obsolete. Instead of being associated with a particular person, location and time, planners take varied forms. Planners are no longer only used by professional workers and can be a good tool for anyone wanting to record their efforts to embrace a lifestyle approach. It is possible to buy planners to enable dream futures and healthy lifestyles, reform habits and nurture relationships. Buying a planner is not a straightforward purchase; diverse choices need to be thought through. Planners can be in different sizes (mini, pocket, personal, A6, A5 or A4), can contain different inserts (the Philofaxy website provides 41 different inserts for A4 or A5 planners, 18 for A6, 20 for personal and 9 for pocket-sized planners) and can be personalised (there are numerous YouTube videos on how to pimp a planner). Other choices include colour (there is a discernible trend towards more pastel colours and away from the uniform black), the type of cover (hard or soft back) as well as the size of internal pockets and storage options. A considerable amount of time can be spent choosing and organising a time planner.

Just like the aesthetics of planners in the twenty-first century has moved away from a uniform monochrome form, the target audiences of these planners have also changed. The 1928 Lefax catalogue assumes that customers are male. For example, the inserts include specific forms for a 'salesman' and Lefax's radio handbook was written by 'men who know the radio'.[7] The owner of the 1980s bulky black Filofax was assumed to be yuppie man, which is what Del Boy aspired to be. The twenty-first century 'personalised' pastel planner that enables the user to achieve her dreams and ambitions is sold as the solution to women's busy multitasking lives.[8] Leslie Knope, the mid-level bureaucrat played by Amy Poehler in the US comedy *Parks and Recreation*, which ran from 2009 to 2015, kept a red planner with her at all times.

Planners are a divisive material artefact that can engender a range of responses from devotion to ridicule. The users of planners, however, find them indispensable, though this reliance also makes them subject to mockery. For example, although Leslie Knope does not do much with her planner, the very fact that she carries one around can be easily interpreted by a television audience. In this chapter, I examine this paradoxical status of time organisation: that we are equally enthralled by and suspicious of strategies and tools whose aim is to organise busy lives. As with other technologies, how planners are used depends on social

---

[6]Hall (2010, p. 3).
[7]Lefax (1928).
[8]See, for example, the catalogue and blog of Kikki Retrieved from https://blog.kikki-k.com/?hl=en

norms and practices.[9] In this chapter on organised time, I consider the norms and practices of time management through analysis of self-help literature. While it is easy to dismiss self-help books as a vulgar publishing format, I am interested in their status as important cultural texts and what they can reveal about the practices of busyness. This analysis is carried out in two parts. In the first section, I review a selection of self-help texts and analyse how they represent sociocultural norms and practices surrounding the use of time, especially a gendered interpretation of temporality. In the second part of the chapter, this analysis takes a different direction to explore the relevance of philosophical interpretations of temporality for time management techniques. To do this, I examine David Allen's text *Getting Things Done*. My reading of Allen's book considers how a philosophical engagement with temporality can contribute to strategies of time management.

Self-help and the Self

The publication of self-help books on time management is big business.[10] The North American self-improvement industry is calculated to be worth around $10 billion.[11] In July 2019, the online shopping service Amazon.com listed over 200,000 self-help books and the monthly median sales[12] for bestselling self-help titles was $750k. Self-improvement incorporates diverse topics. Amazon.com provides authors with 28 different book subcategories to classify self-help texts, which range from texts offering advice on motivation (the sub-category that generates the highest monthly median sales for bestsellers, at $300k) to books on hand-writing analysis (the lowest sales, $200). Books categorised as time management are mid-way down the list of categories arranged by sales, generating $20k a month for a bestseller. The use of categories on Amazon.com is only indicative of differential popularity by topic, as some books are classified under multiple headings and time management books can also be categorised as motivational texts. Likewise, the category for time management includes a variety of self-help topics. For example, in July 2019, the bestselling book listed under this subcategory was *The Unexpected Joy of Being Sober: Discovering a Happy, Healthy, Wealthy Alcohol-Free Life* by Catherine Grey.

Self-help books are undeniably popular but equally the genre can be treated with suspicion and even ridicule.[13] This distrust can be dated back to public reaction to the first self-help book, published by Dr Samuel Smiles in 1859 and titled

---

[9]Wajcman (2015).

[10]For a review of this literature in the twentieth century, see Starkar (1989).

[11]La Rosa (2018).

[12]Median sales are calculated as the monthly volume of sales generated by a book listed in the top 30 best sellers for 30 days.

[13]There is a growing online community commentating on self-help literature, some of which deliberately takes a more critical and humorous approach. For example, Lisa Linke's and Misty Stinnett's podcast 'A comedy self-help podcast to make life suck less'. Linke and Stinnett draw attention to the assumptions about white, male, heterosexual privilege that permeate twenty-first century self-help literature. Retrieved from https://gohelpyourselfpodcast.com/category/about.

Self-Help: With Illustrations of Character and Conduct. Smiles' intention was to show how working class men could improve their social position through hard work and education. *Self-Help* promoted the idea that individual endeavour, rather than birthright, should matter in terms of achieving a respected social position.[14] While *Self-Help* was a bestseller among its intended audiences, it was also a divisive book and was ridiculed by the secure and educated middle classes.[15] The idea that individuals can seek advice on how to improve themselves, rather than one's social position being an intrinsic quality, has polarised responses to self-help literature from this first publication. The Victorian disparagement of self-help has not dissipated completely with its popularity in the twentieth and twenty-first centuries. Contradictory attitudes towards the literature cannot just be explained with reference to class distinction, which influenced Victorian reactions. An important shift in this literature is that modern texts are directed towards the anxieties of the professional middle classes rather than towards readers seeking to join their ranks.[16]

While Smiles' original text was concerned with self-improvement and conduct calibrated by an existing class position, during the twentieth century the genre is more directed towards techniques of self-management. The changing focus of self-help texts encapsulates the diverse unravelling of the genealogy of the self. By this I mean the different ways in which individuals come to know themselves and their world and learn how to act upon themselves and other people. Since the 1960s, self-help literature has endorsed the preoccupation with the self in late modernity as both a problem that needs to be fixed and a goal to be realised.[17] Yet the idea that self-help encapsulates – that we should seek advice on how to live our lives, from how to interpret dreams to being more productive at work – is paradoxical. On the one hand, the rationale for self-help promotes an expectation that care of the self is an individual's responsibility, but on the other it endorses the assessment that people need guidance on how to enact these self-responsibilities. Therefore, the genre simultaneously promotes individual responsibility for self-regulation and self-determination that includes repertoires of how to nurture oneself.[18] Self-help is subtler than a simple manifestation that self-care can be enacted through individual autonomy.[19] Rather, self-help captures how responsibility for the self is not just about promoting well-being through an ethic of discipline and reflexivity but also about the expectation that this ethic will be nurtured by making use of appropriate resources and technologies.[20]

A further problem with the ethos of self-help literature as manuals for self-care is that the premise that there can be a definitive method for developing an open and inquiring mind is an oxymoron. Curating an inventive and open self may

---

[14]Clausen (1993, pp. 403–418).
[15]Clausen (1993).
[16]McGee (2005).
[17]Rimke (2000, pp. 61–78).
[18]Hazleden (2003, pp. 413–428).
[19]Atkinson (2011, pp. 623–637).
[20]Rose (2007).

stimulate people to question the very norms and constraints that constitute the self in the first place.[21] In other words, the expectation that individuals develop strategies to maximise self-potential through being open to the possibility of self-inquiry will also instil resistance to external technologies and methods of self-invention. The paradox of self-help literature is that while these books invite the reader to be the best they can be, the methods used to achieve this and the criteria by which it is judged are not internal but external. For example, Micki McGee's examination of self-help culture in the USA describes how workers are increasingly turning to self-help to help them navigate unstable and competitive modern workplaces.[22] But rather than being able to mollify readers' anxieties, self-help literature is more effective in reproducing readers' worries about how to lead a productive and meaningful life.

Self-help texts on time management target anxieties about productivity and the expectation that efficiency is the responsibility of the individual worker. In her detailed genealogy of the development of productivity, Gregg identifies how the principles of self-help texts concerning time turn individuals away from each other; the timing of activities becomes an individual matter rather than a collective concern.[23] The industry that has developed around self-help books for time management replaces bureaucratic and vertical management systems with individualised, diverse and horizontal systems and the corporate fetishising of speed.[24] The expectation that time management is an individual responsibility is emblematic of the rise of networked, fluid styles of working predicted by Luc Boltanski and Eve Chiapello in their study, *The New Spirit of Capitalism*.[25] I will return to the relationship between organisational structure and temporality in the following chapter on working time. For the purposes of this chapter, it is sufficient to acknowledge the tandem development of organisational structures that emphasise responsibility and speed and self-help literature on how to negotiate fluid distributions of power and authority.

Self-help Books on Time Management and Busyness

Given these paradoxical qualities of self-help, my initial analysis of these texts does not focus on authors' discussions about the external criteria for curation of the self that offer advice on how time *should* be organised. I was drawn to how the texts mirror readers' busy, chaotic lives, and I treat these books as exemplars of the stories that are told about busyness. During repeated readings of a sample of titles, I was struck by the similarities in the writing styles, language, presentation and content across the different texts. Authors simultaneously incorporate normative understandings of time while addressing the unique capacity

---

[21]Atkinson (2011).
[22]McGee (2005).
[23]Gregg (2018).
[24]Du Gay (2017).
[25]Boltanski and Chiapello (2005).

of readers to make the most of their own time. I became intrigued by self-help texts as cultural artefacts that condense the complexity of time into simple, but often abstract, homilies and rules. My analysis also systematically incorporates a gendered approach.[26] Gendered assumptions have permeated self-help from its inception; Gregg's historical analysis of time management details how gender discourses were integrated into the development of productivity techniques in the nineteenth century.[27] My analysis identifies how gendered assumptions continue to be interwoven into the twenty-first century self-help texts about time.

Sampling *Self-help*

There are a large number of published titles on time management and the first task is to collate a sample of these texts. While it would have been preferable to select titles by book category, for example, using the Amazon category 'time management', the primary use of these categories is to maximise sales rather than classify titles, and books can be listed under multiple categories. For this reason, books listed as time management cover a diverse range of topics and the category does not function as a sampling tool.[28] I have, therefore, used a snowball sampling approach, and the sample should not be taken as a representative selection of self-help books on the busyness of time management. To select books, I started with Tony Crabbe's book *Busy: How to Thrive in a World of Too Much* on Amazon.co.uk and followed both customers' linked purchases and views to identify a sample of similar titles. I purchased books over a two-year period starting in the summer of 2017. I identified 35 self-help books that focus on time-, family- and organisation-related issues. From this initial sample, I selected 15 books published since 2000 that specifically provide commentary and advice on dealing time management in different contexts. The selected books include some that are focus on productivity at work and others that are concerned with temporal tensions between home and family life. Only four of the books are written by women. While women write many self-help texts and a genre of self-help written by and for women has emerged in the twentieth century,[29] I found fewer female-authored self-help books on time management. The books are produced by different publishers and include bestselling texts as well as less popular titles. The books are, starting with the most popular and ending with the least popular according to Amazon.co.uk rankings in December 2020:

---

[26]By drawing attention to these representations of gender, I do not intend to suggest that gender is the only social identity that is implicitly produced in self-help narratives of time: ethnicity, sexuality, disability and class should not be ignored. However, the limitation of these texts is that these identities are not visible, while gendered assumptions are more transparent.

[27]Gregg (2018).

[28]Titles are continually produced, reprinted or discontinued, so the population from which a sample could be taken is not constant.

[29]Simonds (1992).

Hal Elrod. (2017). *The Miracle Morning: The 6 Habits that Will Transform Your Life Before 8am.* London: Hodder & Stoughton.

Brian Tracy. (2004/2012). *Eat that Frog: Get More of the Important Things Done Today.* London: Hodder & Stoughton.

Greg McKeown. (2014). *Essentialism: The Disciplined Pursuit of Less.* London: Virgin Books.

Gary Keller with Jay Papasan. (2013). *The One Thing: The Surprisingly Simple Truth Behind Extraordinary Results.* London: John Murray.

David Allen. (2015). *Getting Things Done: The Art of Stress-Free Productivity.* Revised Edition. London: Piatkus.

Jake Knapp and John Zeratsky. (2018). *Make Time: How to Focus on What Matters Every Day.* London: Bantam Press.

Alex Soojung-Kim Pang. (2016). *Rest: Why You Get More Done When You Work Less.* London: Penguin Life.

Graham Allcott. (2014/2016). *Productivity Ninja: Worry Less, Achieve More, Love What You Do.* London: Icon Books Ltd.

James Wallman. (2019). *Time and How to Spend It: The 7 Rules for Richer, Happier Days.* London: WH Allen.

Tony Crabbe. (2014/2015). *Busy: How to Thrive in a World of Too Much.* London: Piatkus.

Brigid Schulte. (2014/2015). *Overwhelmed: How to Work, Love, and Play When No One Has the Time.* London: Bloomsbury.

Leo Babauta. (2009). *The Power of Less: The 6 Essential Productivity Principles that Will Change Your life.* London: Hay House.

Laura Vanderkam. (2018). *Off the Clock: Feel Less Busy While Getting More Done.* London: Piatkus.

Grace Marshall. (2012). *21 Ways to Manage the Stuff that Sucks Up Your Time.* High Point, NC: Discover Books.

Catherine Blyth. (2017). *On Time: Finding Your Pace in a World Addicted to Fast.* London: William Collins.

The most popular, Hal Elrod's *Miracle Morning*, was ranked 984 out of all books on Amazon.co.uk, and the least popular, Catherine Blyth's *On Time*, was ranked 987,091. Rankings on Amazon.co.uk are also given for subcategories, and four of the texts I selected for my research are in the top ten books listed in the 'Self-Help Time Management' category: *Eat that Frog* (no. 3); *Essentialism* (no. 4); *The One Thing* (no. 6); and *Getting Things Done* (no. 8). *Getting Things Done* is the bestselling book in the 'Time Management' subcategory. It is noteworthy that the four books authored by women are in the lowest five sales rankings of the

15 books selected. Although I do not claim that these books form a representative sample, when it comes to time management, it would appear that male authors have an advantage.

Analysing Self-help

The analysis was carried out using summative content techniques.[30] This approach starts with identifying and coding the content of a text with the intention of contextualising this content. I began the analysis by reading each text in turn; from this initial analysis I identified nine substantive and stylistic themes that were repeated in more than one text. In the second stage of the analysis, I returned to each text and coded and manually counted each code under the nine themes.

The content analysis pays close attention to representations of gender. This has been carried out in a number of ways. First, as part of this quantitative stage of analysis, I counted references to gender, including the presumed gender identity of people mentioned in the text. Second, following this initial quantitative analysis, I explored how authors' accounts of time pressure and their solutions are gendered and how gendered language is used in the books. Finally, I considered how authors' own biographical experiences made references to gender roles.[31]

The first part of this analysis explores how these books are manifestations of being busy rather than cures. It does not make financial sense to sell a definitive solution for time-related problems; it is more lucrative to get readers hooked on the obsession of trying to manage time and endlessly looking for remedies.[32] If these books provided definitive solutions to the problem of time deficit, they would quickly become obsolete. To keep the brand going, authors need readers to sign up for more: subscribe to listings, listen to podcasts and attend seminars and book personal/organisational coaching sessions with the author and/ or associates. Self-help books are not, for the most part, standalone texts but are supported by a diversity of virtual material. I have focussed primarily on the published texts as the supporting material is more transient (websites, e.g., are changed, updated and continually added to). This analysis interrogates how these texts and their supporting materials are more aligned with a non-teleological ethos which suggests that time has to be continually managed through ongoing calibrations rather than offering definitive solutions for achieving the definitive goal of a managed life, even though these texts ostensibly promote the latter.

I describe the busyness of these texts through nine stylistic and substantive themes that are repeated across the texts though are not manifest in all of them. There is no text that reproduces all nine themes. Moreover, as I have stressed previously, the selection of books cannot be taken as a representative sample,

---

[30]Hsieh and Shannon (2005, pp. 1277–1288).

[31]I have written about the gendering of self-help books on time management in Holdsworth (2020b, pp. 677–694).

[32]For a discussion of this paradoxical quality of self-help literature, see Cherry (2008, pp. 337–348).

and if the analysis was repeated with other texts, different themes would probably emerge. These nine themes are identified to illustrate how these texts reproduce busyness; they are not intended as a definitive guide to writing a self-help book on time management.

I have grouped the nine themes according to how they correspond to three salient features of self-help: aesthetics, authenticity and gender norms. Aesthetics refers to the 'busy' stylistic devices and how the distinctive style of self-help reproduces paradoxical expressions of busyness. Authenticity captures how authors make claims about time and temporality. Gender norm themes acknowledge how the texts incorporate gendered assumptions. The nine themes are as follows:

> More is more; Three is a magic number; Distract the reader (aesthetics)
>
> Do your research; Keep it vague; recycle (authenticity)
>
> Get married, have children; Name drop; Go to war (gender norms)

Aesthetics

One of the most striking features of self-help texts on time management is that they are very busy books. These texts keep readers to the important job of performing busyness through strategies that 'manage' time. I had the opportunity to encounter this paradoxical manifestation of busyness as time management at a workshop on time maximisation led by a motivational speaker. The speaker's watch was broken, but rather than sourcing a replacement, they had brought along an alarm clock and had perched it on top of the lectern. They repeatedly picked up and looked at the alarm clock during the workshop while repeating the phrase 'I'm hopeless with time'. The impression this gave was more evocative of Walt Disney's busy White Rabbit obsessed with his oversized watch than a considered exploration of how to make the most of time. Thus, an aspect of these texts that has fascinated me the most is how, curiously, authors reproduce the habits that they are seeking to overcome.

More is More.   While these texts might ostensibly promote a philosophy of less is more, this is achieved by dedicating lots of space to long lists of activities to perform and rules to guide these actions. Some texts are simply a list of activities; Grace Marshall's 21 ways of managing things (her book about this regarding time is admittedly part of a book series on '21 ways' to do various things) are presented in 21 chapters; over two-thirds of the pages in Leo Babauta's book extolling *The Power of Less* are given over to listing activities to do; and a third of Graham Allcott's book about worrying less and achieving more deals with suggested tasks and advice on how to become a *Productivity Ninja*. Jake Knapp and John Zeratsky list 87 numbered tactics on how to *Make Time*. Other texts list activities at the end of each chapter: Crabbe offers 24 go-to activities and 22 experiments to beat busyness; Gary Keller's *The One Thing* incorporates 49 big ideas; and the simplicity of Brian Tracy's time management strategy in *Eat that Frog* can be achieved in 42 different ways.

The incessant productivity of self-help is particularly evident in virtual publications. Laura Vanderkam's website includes a blog which she launched on 27 March 2009 and contributes to every other day. She also publishes two podcasts, one of which, 'The best of both worlds', has over 100 episodes.[33] Her continual production of outputs on the theme of being 'off the clock' is exhausting but this paradox forms the essence of self-help. The readership has to be continually cultivated and maintained. The curation of time is a busy habit.

Three Is a Magic Number.   The multiple methods for time management are often streamlined into numbered lists. A discernible feature of lists of things to do is that they are usually restricted to products of the number three. There are a few exceptions to this convention, for example, Allen's two-minute rule for doing something immediately, which is repeated in many texts, and James Wallman's seven rules for richer and happier days. However, most lists of things to do are grouped in products of three. The magic quality of the number three itself is required for core activities: Tracy sticks to three goals; Babauta recommends that the most important tasks should also be limited to three, and Blyth encourages readers to complete a 'life edit' in three steps. Lists that include more than three things are limited to products of three. For example, both Hal Elrod and Babauta propose six principles of self-improvement; Babauta also advises changing 12 habits; Crabbe recommends focussing on 15 people who matter most; habits can be changed in 30 (Babauta), 60 (Blyth) or 66 (Keller) days. The magical quality of listing activities using products of three underscores the non-randomness of advice. A defined list of things to do is restricted to a numerical quantity which has a cultural significance distracts the reader from the busyness of this advice. Numbers make the busy habits of time management more defined and reassure readers about the objectivity of the advice provided.

Distract the Reader.   The visual style of many texts is busy and distracting. Tables, bullet points and numbered lists are all used to organise manifold advice. Multiple fonts denote different types of text, usually distinguishing the main text from exercises, examples and summaries. **Important recommendations can be in bold**, or for even more impact, CAPITALS IN LARGE FONT CAN BE USED to 'shout' at the reader. Diagrams and comic doodling are used to reinforce the transformation from busyness to serenity. Random quotes from the (predominantly male) great and the good are scattered throughout some books. These confirmatory homilies come from philosophers and scientists (e.g. Aristotle and Einstein), politicians (Winston Churchill dominates), writers (more Mark Twain than Shakespeare) and anonymous proverbs. The overall effect of these stylistic devices is that they make some texts very difficult to read, and rather than promoting a calm and methodical approach to time use, they mirror the frenzied hustle of readers' lives. I read these texts linearly, which became increasingly harder to keep to the more that I read. However, this is not how these books are designed to be read. Although an author might use a linear style, for example, by working through a numbered list, the chaotic aesthetic surrounding the list encourages

---

[33]Vanderkam's blog and podcast are available at: https://lauravanderkam.com/about/.

readers to browse rather than read. Numerous distractions on the page make it difficult to focus on each point in turn.

The aesthetics of time management books is overwhelmingly distracting. However, authors may use their online resources to present a calmer aesthetic. How images are used in online material is particularly striking: the monochrome and/or messy aesthetic of busyness is contrasted with calming and colourful natural images. The end goal of self-help is often visualised with the image of a person standing on top of a mountain/towards an ocean who is looking ahead (their back to the camera), usually with their arms outstretched. Large landscapes with natural colour, such as pictures of autumn trees or blossoms, are also popular. The contrasting aesthetics of self-help – monochrome confusion versus colourful natural tranquillity – reinforce the duality of these books: they diagnose the problems concerning time and offer tantalising cures for their resolution. It also subtly inverts the aesthetics of earlier cultural manifestations of time, such as the popularity of black for Filofaxes in the 1980s. Representing the goal of time management through colourful images inverts time to a pre-modern sentiment. As the artist and writer David Batchelor argues, the fear of colour and the dominance of 'whitescapes' defines modernity and progress.[34] The use of monochrome images to denote busyness and spatialised clock time appeals to the sentiment that modernity takes us away from time.

Authenticity

Writing about self-help might be compared to the 'psy' professions; however, there are no academic or practice-based training requirements so anyone can call themselves a motivational speaker, author or life coach. In the absence of formal qualifications and accreditation, authors must authenticate their authority to advise readers about how to manage their lives by establishing their reputation as self-made gurus.[35] Some authors, such as Babauta and Elrod, completely rely on their own experiences, and their writings share how they have transformed their lives. Others, such as Allen, promote their experience in advising organisations. Other writers blend the personal and professional – Knapp and Zeratsky had careers in high tech, where they developed a fascination with time before becoming successful time consultants. Two of the female contributors are journalists, Catherine Blyth and Brigid Schulte, and their books are written to appeal to women's emotional experiences of time. The accreditation of self-help authors is also confirmed by the success of geography. Authors predominantly live in global cities – London, San Francisco or New York, for example – or holiday locations such as Spain.[36] However, authenticity is not just confirmed by the status of the

---

[34]Batchelor (2000).

[35]Gregg (2018).

[36]The geography of authors' biographies neatly encapsulates Richard Florida's interpretation of the relationship between the creative class and urban success. See Florida (2005).

author but is also addressed in the presentation of the advice. The following themes capture the different ways in which authors seek to reassure their readers.

Do Your Research.   One rationale for writing self-help texts is to summarise scientific research that readers will either not have the time to read or not be able to understand; self-help texts are, therefore, promoted as conduits for public engagement with scientific studies. For example, Wallman makes numerous references to the large amount of research that he has read. Crabbe and Pang meticulously detail the research that they use to inform their analysis and prescriptions about time. Other authors are vaguer, or, as Schulte does, revert to journalistic techniques and interview researchers. References to academic research almost exclusively incorporates psychological experimental research; social science or philosophical writings on time are rarely considered.

There are though no stated methodologies for this research. The authors do not adhere to the principles of scoping, systematic or narrative reviews.[37] For example, no inclusion criteria, which are required for systematic or scoping reviews, are given for identifying the studies referred to. Writers choose studies that support their recommendations and observations. Research reviews also fall short of the requirements of narrative reviews because they do not provide any interpretation or critique. The authors present research instead as objective evidence to support their understandings of time, although how this research is acquired is subjective. There is little or no discussion of alternative findings, so scientific research is valued for its assumed objective qualities; despite this, the authors do not apply any principles of objectivity to their own knowledge discovery. This lack of methodology also applies to research that authors have carried out themselves. For example, Vanderkam develops her time management advice from her own analysis of readers' time diaries but she does not provide a methodology or sampling framework for this analysis.

Keep it Vague.   The trick to writing quantitative, repetitive and normative rules about how to use time is not to be too specific. The advice offered is often vague, abstract or metaphorical. For example, Crabbe recommends that readers draw a pie chart of how they use their time and consider whether this meets with core values, though how readers can do the first task is not discussed. Blyth suggests nine ways to 'cuff time thieves', including noticing 'where time leaks', erecting 'ladders to distraction' and smoothing 'the flow'.[38] After an exhaustive account of being overwhelmed, Schulte concludes that women need to 'shorten their time horizons' and aim to be authentic.[39] Keller and Papasan recommend that to achieve the *One Thing*, practitioners 'block time' in order 'to find your answer' and to implement it.[40]

Using particular language to describe these tasks rather than the detail of what they entail is part of the branding of self-help. Readers must learn the language

---

[37]Greenhalgh, Thorne, and Malterud (2018).
[38]Blyth (2017, pp. 211–212).
[39]Schulte (2014, p. 286).
[40]Keller and Papasan (2013, p. 220).

of time management before they can embark on its practice. The authors use jargon or acronyms to distinguish their advice. These often evoke popular culture. For example, tactic number 24 of Knapp and Zeratsky's strategy to make time is 'Laser: Block Distraction Kryptonite',[41] which challenges the reader to give up a dominant distraction habit, such as an over-reliance on social media. The authors' oblique reference to the comic hero Superman reinforces the idea that an individual's exertion is required to make the most of time.

Particular language is used to disguise the possibility that advice might just be common sense and to simultaneously convince readers that they are members of a distinctive club. This tactic of othering is used explicitly in Elrod's miracle morning method, which entices readers with the opportunity to lead extraordinary lives, in contrast to the 95% of society that are destined to lead mediocre lives. The language of self-help diverts attention from the detail of how to manage time and implicitly presents these vague tactics as exclusive measures of esteem or superiority. Self-help literature promises collective solutions (i.e. they are available to everyone) to individual aspirations to be distinctive.

Recycle.   Self-help books on time, for the most part, reinvent the wheel. There are more books written on how to manage time than there are ideas and techniques on how this can be achieved. Not surprisingly, there is a considerable amount of repetition, sometimes without citation. For example, I found a redrawn interpretation of Allen's flow chart from *Getting Things Done* in a later text. Other advice is more generic: suggestions about decluttering space, getting up early, doing exercise, curating to-do lists, not starting the day with emails, spending time offline, delegating tasks or outsourcing and focussing on relationships are all reproduced in different ways. The craft of the self-help author involves promoting their unique interpretation of this generic advice. The familiarity of the advice is also reassuring. The task of the twenty-first century guru is not just to facilitate self-knowledge but also to reinforce what we already know. This recycling of intuitive, if obvious, advice neatly captures the duality of responsibility for the self that is achieved through internal disciple and adherence to cultural resources and technologies.

Gender Norms

Most self-help books on time management are authored by men, but this simple observation hides more significant gender distinctions. Women have contributed to the development of time management since its inception in the nineteenth century through the publication of domestic manuals that dictate methods for women's organisation of time at home. In the UK, the popularity of Smiles' original text for men can be compared with Mrs Beeton's *Book of Household Management*, first published in 1861.[42] While men could aspire to join the middle classes by adhering to Smiles' principle of self-help, women were instructed on how to keep a middle class household (and in particular how to manage domestic staff)

---

[41]Knapp and Zeratsky (2018, p. 105).
[42]Clausen (1993).

though dedication to Mrs Beeton's advice. In the USA, women's domestic management developed from the mid-1800s into a cult of domesticity that positioned the responsibilities that women were deemed to have to their families through practising self-denial and self-sacrifice.[43] The aesthetics of the nineteenth century US domestic management was spiritual as well as practical; women had a duty to manage homes efficiently to support their families and country. The twenty-first century self-help texts are clearly very different in tone from these domestic manuals. However, representation of gender norms remains a persistent feature through the authors' biographies, their use of anecdotes and the language they use.

Get Married, Have Children.   It is courteous of authors to acknowledge friends and family in their books (I have done the same), but many self-help authors go further than this and incorporate their personal lives into their text. Fifteen of the 16 authors state their marital status and all but two that they are married with children. When family is incorporated into these texts it is in a static way: family is a place to go to, to relax, not a space of activity and anxiety. Family is also a symbol of success. Living by his principles of *The Power of Less* has enabled Babauta to raise six children, and McKeown states that one of his main achievements as an essentialist is to have more time to spend trampolining with his children; Knapp identifies his 'backstory' with an epiphany which suggested that he was not spending enough with his children. In contrast, two of the texts written by women, Schulte and Blyth, do engage with the busyness of segueing between our intimate life and our professional life. Schulte documents the challenges that women face while multitasking in relation to discrete responsibilities. Vanderkam has also made this a feature of her blog and writes extensively about managing time with her six children. She acknowledges that juggling the demands of a large family does not always mean that everyone gets to do what they want. She also makes frequent use of outsourcing, and (baby)sitters feature regularly in her accounts of how she juggles her busy family life.

While managing issues such as children being ill are acknowledged in some texts (especially those authored by women), accounts of spending time with children are mostly representative of the Apollonian child: they are innocent and pure and, thus, are capable of asking perceptive questions about parental time use.[44] The authors are concerned about ensuring the success and well-being of their children, not about picking up the pieces if their children go off the rails. And while care is directed towards the innocent rather than the unruly child, caring for adults (such as partners or parents) does not feature. Parents are acknowledged as inspiring but caring for elderly parents is not a task that authors consider. Care is a bounded and time-limited activity and, thus, very different from Baraitser's depiction of the enduring temporal qualities of care.[45] Assumptions about family structure and the domains and practices of care, in particular that care is a choice

---

[43]Gregg (2018).
[44]The distinction between Apollonian and Dionysian representations of childhood is a classic dichotomy discussed in sociological studies of childhood. See Jenks (1996).
[45]Baraitser (2017).

and an activity to be enjoyed rather than endured, endorse a normative view of care that does not engage with the complex emotions and temporalities that looking after others necessarily involves.

Name Drop. Smiles' original self-help reproduced anecdotes about successful men to reinforce the message that self-improvement could be achieved by any reader. The use of anecdotes continues in the twenty-first century self-help texts but they are about celebrities (in business, sport, politics, media and the arts), intellectuals, academic researchers, personal acquaintances and clients. Anecdotes are used to personalise the text and enhance authenticity. Some mentions, mainly of clients, are anonymous and occasionally pseudonyms are used, but for the most part, the value of the anecdote is in the name and how readers can identify with this person. There is a striking gender bias in these anecdotes.[46] For example, Allen disperses quotes throughout the text of *Getting Things Done* and quotes from 80 different sources, but 68 of them are male and only 6 are female, with another 6 anonymous or not identified with a male or female gender. To explore this dimension further, I categorised anecdotes identified with male or female gender in the nine texts that use this stylistic device. The distribution of these anecdotes by gender identity is presented in Table 4.1

Across all of the texts, just over two-thirds of anecdotes are identified with the male gender. Female writers reference a larger proportion of anecdotes associated with female identity. Vanderkam includes an even number of references to male and female gender identities, while Schulte's text is dominated by anecdotes involving women. In Schulte's book, though, these include brief portraits of how women are managing or not managing time.[47] In all of the texts, there is an overwhelming use of positive male anecdotes and only selective references to struggling women. This brings a stark observation into view: gender norms are not subtlety interwoven in these texts but are repeated through the identification of male success and female absence and/or failure. The dominance of 'successful' men reinforces gender divisions in the use of time and the perpetuation of patriarchal authority.[48]

Go to War. The masculinist tone of self-help is not just restricted to normative, static representations of family and the gender identities of anecdotes; it is also striking in the language that is used. Tackling the problem of time use can be presented as a challenge and one that requires physical and mental determination.[49] For some writers, this is achieved through the metaphor of war. Crabbe's

---

[46]For this analysis, I distinguish between names that are identified with either the female or the male gender This necessarily requires a binary distinction and I acknowledge the limitations of this approach. For the most part, transgender identities are not discussed in these books, with the exception of the celebrity Bruce/Caitlyn Jenner.
[47]Another distinctive feature of Schulte's discussion of the people she meets to talk about busyness with is that she fleshes out these accounts with brief physical descriptions of body shape and hair colour and style.
[48]Holdsworth (2020b).
[49]See Gregg (2018).

Table 4.1.   Number of Anecdotes and Percentage of References to Female Gender Identity in Self-help Books.

Author	Title	Number of Anecdotes (References to Business People, Writers, Researchers, etc.; Fictional References are Excluded)	% Female Gender Identity
Catherine Blyth	*On Time: Finding Your Pace in World Addicted to Fast*	70	29
Tony Crabbe	*How to Thrive in a World of Too Much*	29	21
Hal Elrod	*The Miracle Morning*	56	18
Jake Knapp and John Zeratsky	*Make Time: How to Focus On What Matters Every Day*	38	32
Greg McKeown	*Essentialism: The Disciplined Pursuit of Less*	57	19
Alex Soojung-Kim Pang	*Rest: When You Get More Done When You Work Less*	177	10
Brigid Schulte	*How to Work, Love and Plan When No One Has the Time*	82	72
Laura Vanderkam	*Off The Clock: Feel Less Busy While Getting More Done*	51	50
James Wallman	*Time and How to Spend It: The 7 Rules for Richer, Happier Days*	191	29
Total		751	29

Source: Author's own analysis.

buzz words around busyness refer to machine guns, missiles and attacks. Allcott's productivity ninja has to be ruthless and agile and know how to use weapons, stealth and camouflage, though is not super-human. Knapp and Zeratsky's list of tactics for making time include encouragements to 'bulldoze your calendar', 'pound the pavement' and 'stay hungry'.

This militaristic language encapsulates expectations of self-sacrifice and acceptance of a duty to manage time. Metaphors involving heroes and saviours reinforce the cult of exceptionalism of time management: that only the entrepreneurial are capable of the self-discipline required.[50] An exclusionary language of war, endeavour and sacrifice is a sleight of hand that suggests that not everyone can be a saviour of time, though the requirement to be productive is universal. This call to duty also recalls the ethos of service in the nineteenth century domestic management texts. However, its alignment with military endeavour rather than obligations to care for others is implicitly masculinist and defines the success of time management as an individualistic trait rather than a collective practice.

Social and Cultural Norms of Self-help

Self-help books on time management are paradoxical. On the one hand, they claim to provide a definitive method for maximising productivity and free time but equally require that readers, in Deleuzian fashion, are never finished with anything.[51] The busyness of self-help books is part of their appeal; self-made gurus of time need to keep their followers busy and engaged and cultivate new followers. Enticing and keeping an audience requires not so much novel strategies but the reassertion of social norms and the repetition of techniques that prioritise individual distinction and distance rather than collective endeavour. Recycling advice about time use and the mitigation of busyness consolidates social norms about the use of technologies, relationships (which are universally assumed to be nurturing and never disruptive) and the necessity of coordinating body and thought through the physical tactics of time management and the vitality of time rather than through the non-event. These norms of busyness also capture inequalities in time use and implicitly reproduce social differentials regarding who can manage time and who cannot. Gendered and heteronormative assumptions permeate these texts and writers reconfirm these stereotypes in their own biographical accounts of becoming a self-made time guru. This reproduction of temporal inequalities in self-help book echoes one of the findings from the analysis of time use, which is that social differences in temporal experience are more significant than overarching temporal trends.

Examining these texts as cultural artefacts also reveals the ephemeral quality of self-help books. These texts have all been published since 2004, yet I was struck by how quickly they have become out of date. In particular, many authors viewed taking advantage of more opportunities for global travel as the main benefit of successfully managing time. Even before Covid-19 lockdowns, this endorsement would have felt out of tune with popular recognition of the need for greater individual and collective environmental responsibility. I anticipate that the next wave of self-help books could integrate concerns about environmental justice with strategies for individual use of time, and the frenetic publishing cycle of self-help books will continue.

---

[50]The metaphor of the saviour is a recurrent them in entrepreneurial narratives; see, for example, Sørensen (2008, pp. 85–93).

[51]Deleuze (1992, p. 5).

David Allen's *Getting Things Done*

The thematic analysis of the aesthetics and social norms of self-help texts does not consider what these authors have to say about time and temporality. I have not deliberately ignored this temporal advice. I have adapted my working habits in response to reading these books and now track my time (as described in Chapter 3), ensure that morning routines start with major writing tasks and not the trivia of email, have a daily goal for writing and stop when this is met, take regular breaks (including daily walks) and regularly declutter my desk. But no author has attempted to analyse the how conceptual interpretations of habits and time have shaped this advice. In this section, I consider how philosophical interpretations of time are relevant to tactics for managing time. This analysis involves interrogation of the temporal methods in one text: Allen's *Getting Things Done*.

Getting Things Done was first published in 2001 and continues to be a bestselling self-help text on time management. The first edition sold an estimated 2 million copies, and a second edition was published in 2015.[52] Allen has also published a spin off: *Getting Things Done for Teens*. The resources he uses for his method are listed on his website.[53] Allen's organisation, Next Action Associates, delivers one-to-one coaching and public and bespoke seminars. *Getting Things Done* is not just a book; it is a trademarked method for improving productivity. For this method to work effectively, users need to be committed to the endpoint of being productive and willing to continually apply themselves to its practices. In the second edition, Allen acknowledges that the principles of his method were initially developed for corporate executives and high-achieving professionals, though he claims that it can equally apply to carers, students, artisans and retirees. He encourages his readers not to view his method as a one-off solution to time management but as a lifestyle practice. The second edition of *Getting Things Done* follows the trend in self-help time books that has departed from detailing the techniques of productivity to selling a lifestyle. The lifestyle component of *Getting Things Done* is more of an add-on, though, than an integrated aspect of the ethos of the book.

The Method

Allen's book is primarily a manual for productivity. He does not write about how readers can benefit from the promise of being 'off the clock' or making/spending time. He describes a methodology for getting things done rather than extolling its benefits, which has led to the book being criticised for not being particularly engaging; at the seminar on time management that I attended, it was dismissed by other participants as 'hard work'. In addition, the text is not immune from the stylistic traits and reliance on cultural norms that are the trademarks of self-help. I have already described how Allen's use of random quotations is highly

---

[52]Sherr (2015).
[53]Allen's website is titled 'Join the Global Productivity Movement'. Retrieved from https://gettingthingsdone.com/.

gendered. However, more than other books examined for this analysis Allen's text promotes a method for a systematic process of actions that is based on a flow diagram[54] for which the input is 'stuff'. This method can be summarised as follows:

- To apply Allen's method, users must interrogate stuff in two ways: what is it and is it actionable?
- For non-actionable stuff there are three outcomes, this stuff needs to be trashed, incubated for future action (preferably in a tickler file) or kept for reference. So, a non-actionable email should be deleted, stored in a future actions folder, or archived.
- The means for dealing with actionable stuff are more complicated. The first question to consider is what should be done next; that is what is the next action that the initial thing coming into the in-tray requires?
- For most actionable stuff Allen's method applies the two-minute rule. If an action will take less than two minutes, then it should be done now.
- For longer actions, there are two choices: delegate or defer. If a longer action is passed onto someone else, the delegator should wait for this to be completed. For deferred actions, there are two choices: allocate a specific time to complete it (i.e. put in the calendar) or do it as soon as the required time is available.
- There are sidesteps for actions associated with complex projects, which have to be reviewed with reference to project plans.

What I found distinctive about Allen's contribution is that it comes closest to being consistent in interpreting time. Allen's temporal interpretation is not based on his own detailed reading and referencing of philosophical literature; it emerges through his development of a systematic methodology of practice. His method for productivity endorses the ideal that individuals should do tasks according to their own temporal pace and requirements and should not organise activities around the priorities of other people. I suggest that his method can be summarised in three ways: commitment to a pragmatic theory of habit; adherence to a phenomenological interpretation of temporality to synthesise past, present and future; and, as a consequence of the first two, an understanding that it is not possible to manage time – it is space and other people that have to be managed.

Pragmatism

My first observation is that Allen's method for productivity implicitly concurs with John Dewey's neo-pragmatic philosophy about action. Dewey contends that ends and means are the same thing; ends are 'a series of acts viewed at a remote stage'.[55] Means are closer to us than ends, so it makes sense to focus on means rather than ends. The simplicity of Dewey's argument is that ends are simply the last acts that are thought of and means are 'the acts to be performed prior

---

[54]Allen (2015, p. 40).
[55]Dewey (1922, p. 34).

to it in time'.[56] His interpretation leads to a non-teleological conclusion that '[t]o *reach* an end we must take our mind off it and attend to the act which is next to be performed. We must make that the end'.[57] Allen's method requires the user to consider what actions need to be done in relation to a new thing in an in-tray. The question to ask is not how important a task is for someone else, nor how it relates to longer-term goals and aspirations. Instead, productivity is about asking whether I can do something and if so, how long will this take? This method requires adherents to think about means rather than ends and, thus, adhere to a pragmatic interpretation of habit. The means are very immediate – to get things done – and adherents should not be preoccupied with the ends, that is, with the assumed benefits of leading a more ordered and productive life.

Synthesising Time

The second conceptual principle of Allen's method is that it implicitly adheres to a phenomenological synthesis of time into past, present and future. Allen restricts the present to two minutes. The only actions that can take place in the present are those that can be completed in this time. All other tasks, if they cannot be delegated to someone else, must be synthesised into the future to be moved into the past. Allen's method of synthesising present, future and past is demonstrated in his recommendation of tickler files. A tickler file can be thought off as a 3-D diary, and perhaps the easiest way to describe it is in terms of its material form. Creating a tickler file requires a file box divided into 43 compartments: the first sections are numbered 1–31 and the remaining 12 are labelled January–December. If today's date is the 4th March, the sections in the tickler file would be ordered from 4 to 31, then 1 to 3. All sections would be in the March file. Today I would open the section in the tickler file for today's date (number 4) and complete the actions noted there and then place this section at the back of the March file, and so forth each day. At the end of the day, the numbered sections start with 5, ready for review on the 5th March. At the end of March, I would take all actions noted in the April compartment and distribute these in sections 1–31. Allen's synthesis of the present into the future (deferring) or the past (doing), and of the future into the past (doing a deferred activity) is ongoing. There is no point in not doing actions in the present and then simply pretending they have gone away (unless they have simply been filed for information).

Managing Space and Other People

In committing to a pragmatic conceptualisation of action that enables the synthesis of the present into the past and future, time is not treated as an external, linear entity that can be managed. If the now is reduced to two minutes, then there is not much time to organise. Adhering to Allen's method requires knowing when to

---

[56]Dewey (1922, p. 34).
[57]Dewey (1922, p. 34).

do deferred activities and pay close attention to what can be done in the present. However, users need to be more concerned with the organisation of space than worrying about time.[58] The first stage of using Allen's technique (before applying the workflow method) is to set up an efficient workstation. Allen is adamant that for his method to be effective, all users should have at least one exclusive work-space where most syntheses of actions take place. He is not a fan of hot-desking or hotel offices if the majority of work is done at these stations. Allen recognises that many users will have workstations at 'work' and home and advises against sharing home offices with any co-resident. He requires that all new practitioners set aside a least one day to sort out an office and to arrange the space for the coordination of workflow activities. When working with clients one-to-one, he describes this initial stage of clearing out and re-assembling the technologies of workspaces as one of the most satisfying elements of coaching. In the 2015 edi-tion, he acknowledges the usefulness of digital organisational systems, though he retains his commitment to an assemblage of physical and digital infrastructure. Allen endorses the use of in-trays, filing systems, paper clips and staplers – as well as digital technologies such as smartphones and cloud storage.

In my initial reading of *Getting Things Done*, I interpreted his method of the continual categorisation of stuff as re-territorialising space. This interpretation is reinforced by the language that Allen uses. He writes about the importance of 'place-makers' and 'airtight' management to create fences around work processes. The importance of being in control of space seems to flow against a Deleuzian tide of de-territorialisation.[59] A more careful examination of Allen's text finds that he is responding to de-territorialised workspaces and the subtle shift from hierarchical to horizontal forms of management that characterise many corpo-rate organisations in the twenty-first century.[60] By providing a way of re-fenc-ing space within organisations, Allen's method draws attention to the duality of Deleuze and Guattari's molecular interpretation of power, which is reinserted through individual action rather than structures.[61] Therefore, Allen is not out of step with the subtle shift from the distributions of power ordered through

---

[58]There are clear synergies between Allen's method and Marie Kondo's bestselling text *The Life-Changing Magic of Tidying*. This book was first published in 2011, and has outsold *Getting Things Done* with an estimated 6 million sales. The 'Konmari' method of tidying is a lifestyle practice, not a one-off activity, and is supported with the requi-site websites and a more recent television programme. Kondo's method of tidying pro-motes focussing on what items users should keep, which is stuff that is identified with bringing joy, rather than focussing on what should be thrown away. Kondo's method of identifying what to keep rather than discard synthesises the past and present into the future through the active production of space. In both methodologies, space is not a static entity where stuff happens but is continually reproduced through processing things. Kondo (2011).

[59]Elden (2005, pp. 8–19).

[60]Du Gay (2017).

[61]Deleuze and Guattari (2004).

the authority of discipline to more dispersed forms of control. But his method exposes how boundaries must be continually reworked and redrawn as airtight.

Getting Things Done provides a method of simultaneously reinforcing and distributing power. A key component of the method is delegation. The method assumes that there is a hierarchy of power through which tasks can be distributed, though Allen notes that delegation can be upstream and downstream. His method for delegation recommends a particular order of actions: first, send an e-mail; second, a written note; third, a text message or voice mail; fourth, add the matter to the agenda of the next face-to-face meeting; and fifth, talk directly to the person. He dislikes the fifth option as this requires upsetting both workers' time schedules. His preference for e-mail runs counter to most self-help texts, which advocate getting offline. Delegation is not a one-off activity but should be monitored through tracking and 'waiting for' lists. This method of delegation adheres to the idea that power is manifested through controlling and monitoring of others in the workplace.

Ultimately, as with the previous analysis of the aesthetics and norms of self-help books, this analysis of the temporality of self-help underscores how these texts assume the uneven politics of time. While the endorsed tactics might promote the mantra of self-sustainability, they depend on a reader's ability to manipulate others through strategies of delegation. This ability is not simply a matter of self-efficacy; it is determined by individuals' positions within hierarchies or controlling systems of power and by their justification of requesting others to do tasks.

Summary

If busyness is a fault, then the temptation is to fix it. The proliferation of texts on time management and making the most of time are testimony to the collective experience that busyness has taken over life and it is the responsibility of individuals to overcome this. The popularity of self-help speaks to a collective expectation that busyness is a fault to be fixed by individuals, albeit individuals surrounded by a supporting cast of one-dimensional family and friends. These texts emphasise self-responsibility without reference to dependency and assume that the 'problem' of time needs to be fixed by isolating individuals from each other. However, for these texts to be persuasive and ultimately to sell, authors' ambitions involve (re)producing social temporal norms rather than proposing methods to radically transform everyday life. These are busy books that are supported by a range of activities and online resources to captivate an audience. The multiplicity of advice on how individuals can take control of time cannot assume that self-responsibility is enacted in socially neutral space, and these texts are infused with implicit gendered assumptions about who can take control of time.

An intriguing distinguishing feature of these books is how self-help authors avoid writing about time and temporality. One reason for this is that ultimately time management is a red herring. Thus, in Allen's productivity method, the 'now' is demarcated as two minutes, and what needs to be managed is making decisions about whether to act now or delegate/defer tasks and knowing when deferred activities will be done. His method for time management involves ensuring the ongoing synthesis of past, present and future. These methods of time management reveal that the resources that can be manipulated are the organisation of space and other people. That is, it is the management of assemblages of space, technologies and people that make the synthesis of time possible.

On first reading self-help books, it is easy to dismiss or embrace these texts as intense representations of the individualised self. This conclusion is valid as the advice offered in these texts depends on the technique of self-isolation. However, a more careful analysis of both the social and the cultural norms of self-help and the phenomenological principles of time management resonates with Deleuze's conviction that people are in continuous orbits of (in)activity and that it is the assemblages of (non-)human things that keep this motion going. Indeed, the paradox of self-help texts offering advice on how to curate the self is partly resolved through their promotion of ongoing resources and techniques. What matters more is the conviction that changing habits, becoming more productive and having more time for oneself is the most important thing, rather than perfecting these techniques.

Chapter 5

Work Time

Sorry We Missed You

Ken Loach's 2019 film *Sorry We Missed You* portrays an ominous ordeal involving twenty-first century working temporalities.[1] Set in Newcastle-upon-Tyne in the north of England, the film follows the experiences of the Turner family – Ricky and Abby and their children Seb (aged 15) and Liza Jane (aged 10/11) – and their struggles with debt. Ricky has been in and out of building work since the 2008 financial crash, though has proudly never depended on state support. He is persuaded to take up a franchise opportunity driving for a parcel delivery company out of their Newcastle depot.[2] The depot's foreman, Maloney, entices Ricky with the promise that Ricky will be working for himself and not for the company.[3] Ricky initially warms to this reworking of responsibilities and what he perceives to be the freedom to be his own boss. The reality of working 'with' the delivery company is very different. Ricky is responsible for his own van, ensuring that his route is covered and that he delivers the parcels on time. The timing of Ricky's working day is tracked with a scanner – known as the 'gun' – for which he is also responsible. He quickly adopts accelerated practices to comply with the tracker and maximise his income – running between deliveries and urinating into a bottle in his van. His new job initially starts well; he proves to be a reliable driver and is quickly offered a more profitable route. He is even allowed a few pauses – the viewer sees him sitting with Liza Jane by the open doors of the back of his van as they share a sandwich overlooking a sunny, hilly landscape.

However, Ricky's conflicting responsibilities soon begin to unravel. His work responsibilities exacerbate the family debt problems. He buys rather than rents a van and sells Abby's car to pay the deposit for the van loan. Abby works as a home carer, and after selling her car she has to make her round of visits by bus. The film contrasts Ricky's accelerated working day with Abby's dedicated care for

---

[1]Laverty (2019).

[2]Ricky's franchise can be defined as dependent self-employment: he works for one client, cannot employ other workers and cannot contribute to the strategic development of his company.

[3]Laverty (2019, p. 17).

The Social Life of Busyness, 89–112
Copyright © 2021 by Clare Holdsworth
Published under exclusive licence by Emerald Publishing Limited
doi:10.1108/978-1-78743-698-520211006

her clients and her time waiting at bus stops. As the responsibilities of Ricky's job intensify, they increasingly clash with those he has towards his family. Liza Jane resents the amount of time he spends at work. Their older child, Seb, is a moody teenager and talented artist who is having a difficult time at school. Seb reacts negatively to Ricky's temper, which is exacerbated by his exhaustion. Abby finds herself in a peacemaker role and as increasingly in opposition to her husband. Ricky is broken by two events: a violent robbery of his van, which he is financially responsible for because the company's insurance does not cover all of the losses, and his scanner breaks, so he will have to pay for that too. Seb is cautioned by the police for shoplifting and Ricky has to abandon work to be Seb's responsible adult at a police station. The film ends with Ricky driving in desperation to his delivery route, battered by the men who stole from his van and the grinding responsibility of work that provides no flexibility for him to fulfil his family responsibilities.

Ricky is more than busy. The temporalities of adhering to the responsibilities of being a delivery driver are quantitatively different from the cult of busyness. While it might be tempting to view Ricky's ordeal as a manifestation of acceleration that constitutes all working life, his problems do not just come about due to the challenges of speed. The distinctive features of this new kind of work are its reworking of time, space and responsibility. Ricky is caught in a trap. He has the 'freedom' to own his van and work for himself, but his performance is tightly controlled by the company he works 'with'. When things go wrong, Ricky is on his own. The responsibility to deliver dominates. The company offers no support; it simply provides the parcels that need delivering and the route that must be followed – any diversions, problems or errors are Ricky's responsibility. He is required to conform to the company's control of time–space. Its model of responsibility assumes that time-space is uniform and regulated, that is, it is always possible to be in a particular place at an exact time to deliver a parcel. The uneven temporalities of the 'real' world, such as traffic jams, uncooperative customers and physical exhaustion do not feature in the precise timings of deliveries. Similar assumptions about spatial and temporal confluence surround Abby's job as a carer, although she is able to find some flexibility by working at night or through her breaks to meet her clients' needs. There is no flexibility in Ricky's work 'contract' and the unrealistic exceptions of one-sided responsibility within tightly bounded time-space eventually break Ricky and his family.

If *Sorry We Missed You* sets an apocalyptic tone about new forms of work in the twenty-first century, this is not just because it exaggerates the acceleration of work. Ricky's experiences represent new forms of dispersed responsibilities that jar with assumptions about time–space. Ricky cannot rely on assumptions about traditional forms of contracted labour, because responsibility is not shared but delegated. Both Ricky and Abby are required to commit to devolved responsibilities and respond to multiple people – family, bosses, clients, teachers, the police, etc. The trap they fall into is that they cannot respond to these multiple demands because there is no flexibility concerning where and when these responsibilities are enacted.

Sorry We Missed You expressively captures the challenges of working temporalities in the twenty-first century. However, the film's emphasis is not so much on the acceleration of working life (though Ricky has to work quickly) but on the impossibility of the different directions that Ricky and Abby are pulled in. In this chapter, I explore the centrality of busyness at work as a constellation of responsibilities in diverse spatial–temporal settings. This approach, therefore, develops my previous analysis of organisational time, though in this chapter I investigate more diverse forms of work than those assumed by self-help writers, whose are interested almost exclusively in workers in corporate organisations. My intention is not to understand busyness at work as a singular outcome of temporal change. Instead, I interpret work-related busyness as a conduit of the messy integration of acceleration, competing work ethics, diverse organisational structures and thinking habits that consolidate people's justification of work performance. To work through these competing explanatory forces, the empirical material in this chapter is divided into two: an exploration of busyness among employees working in different types of organisations using case studies from the Mass Observation one-day diary data set and analysis of *The Guardian*'s series 'My writing day' to explore the spatial and temporal dynamics of working alone. Before I present these empirical data, it is necessary to flesh out the key features of the moral economy of work and how these relate to the frustrations of work-related busyness.

The Moral Economy of Busyness

The narrative of *Sorry We Missed You* is anchored in a particular time and place – the North of England, where the population is enduring austerity following the 2008 global financial crash. The Turner family's experiences encapsulate how the austerity policies were not simply economic measures; as Sarah Marie Hall writes, they define personal and relational everyday life.[4] Yet within this specific context, the film's broader narrative captures temporal features of the changing landscapes of work. It is tempting to develop this narrative to explore how twenty-first century obsessions with busyness are an outcome of changing organisational structures of work that in turn are a product of social, economic and political relations. This requires writing about work as a unified practice. In the social and political sciences, the cultural history of work as an incubator and bellwether of social change is a recurrent and dominant theme, and writers who develop these accounts are less interested in the detail of work.[5] Theoretical accounts of work and social change necessarily distil the moral qualities of work. That is, writing about work in a meaningful way while avoiding the details of specific work practices (i.e. what work actually entails doing) necessarily draws attention to the consequences of work and how work itself is the outcome of moral positions. The most celebrated account of this is Max Weber's *Protestant Ethic and the Spirit of Capitalism*, which identifies the importance of the diligence of the Protestant work ethic for the development of capitalism.[6] Weber describes the value of work for Calvinists as an expression of virtue and closeness to God

---

[4]Hall (2019).
[5]See, for example, Frayne (2015).
[6]Weber (1905/1930).

rather than a punishment for sin. In Weber's account, the moral fervour of Calvinist doctrine conveniently assimilates the everyday activities of work into its outcomes. *The Protestant Ethic* is so canonical and overfamiliar in social science that it is easy to overlook the historical detail of Weber's treatise.[7] The book is both an historical analysis and a foundational work of social theory, though it is more celebrated as the latter. The reception of *The Protestant Ethic* neatly illustrates the tension between writing accounts of both sociocultural change and historical detail, and few writers have Weber's audacity to try and do both.

Fragmenting Work Ethics

My examination of busyness is directed towards the detail of everyday experiences rather than attempting to distil a generalised work ethic of the first decades of the twenty-first century. Such an approach would be inappropriate and impossible because busyness is not about adherence to a particular ethic but, as Ricky and Abby experienced – about being pulled in different directions. Busyness captures the fragmentation of work ethics in the twenty-first century, the vestiges of a Protestant work ethic that endorses hardworking respectability; distaste of futile effort and the expectation that we should not strive to work hard but to work well; and the enduring appeal of anti-work sentiment. These diverse positions predate twenty-first century concerns about burnout and busyness. As noted previously, E.P. Thompson observed that values can be lost and gained in the struggle for the imposition of work discipline, and the merits of hard work versus spending time well were debated in Victorian accounts of the morality of work. Writing in 1899, Thorstein Veblen sought to identify the *Theory of the Leisure Class* in contradictory attitudes towards work, specifically the distinction between the repetition of industry and the guile of exploit.[8] According to Veblen, humans are drawn to deep-rooted judgements to seek abstention from industry and futile effort to work effectively and maximise opportunities for exploit. However, work ethics cannot be easily reduced to a binary distinction between hard work and agility. Tom Lutz's detailed account of endorsements of anti-work sentiments in diverse cultural forms reveals the vibrant history of scepticism and disrespect for hardworking respectability that does not simply scorn a hard work ethic but unsettles normative assumptions about what it is like to succeed or fail by these rules.[9] Thus, the cultural history of work is enlivened by diverse and contradictory work ethics, and I suggest that the twenty-first century busyness captures this ambiguity about how we should work and the uneven distribution of work and responsibilities. What sinks Ricky and Abby is not the challenges of how they are expected to work – Ricky is proud that he has never relied on benefits and is willing to work long hours and to work quickly – but the unreasonable and unsustainable responsibilities that are placed upon them.

---

[7]Weber's work is dismissed by some historians as inaccurate. For an assessment of this judgement, see Ghosh (2019, pp. 121–155).
[8]Veblen (1899/2007).
[9]Lutz (2006).

Unfairness and Inequality

The moral economy of busyness revolves around the uneven distribution of the responsibilities and rewards of busyness rather than simply around what is achieved through work. Accounts of overwork are, therefore, personal and collective to the same extent.[10] We recognise the universal requirement to be productive while simultaneously assimilating this as an individual problem because we are asked to do more than others. Colleagues who complain about being busy implicitly understand this sense of injustice as meaning that the responsibilities they are expected to perform are unreasonable.

The unfairness of busyness is not just a personal response; I suggest it can be interpreted as an expression of more deep-rooted inequalities in the twenty-first century capitalism. The argument that we are living in a time of intense and widening inequality has received considerable academic and popular support.[11] More pertinently, both Thomas Piketty[12] and Andrew Sayer[13] have separately argued that wealth is increasingly accumulated through returns on capital, not productivity. In other words, in the twenty-first century wealth is acquired not through hard work but through what can be extracted from other people; it is the rentier rather than the industrialist who can acquire vast wealth. Sayer repeats the early twentieth century economic interpretation of 'improperty' – the ability to extract unearned income from unequal ownership – to explain the rapid growth in the wealth of the richest members of society.

Extraction of wealth can be achieved not just through ownership of capital but also through the exploitation of time. For example, Timothy Ferriss's best-selling justification of a four-hour week is a clear manifestation of the economic benefits of temporal exploitation.[14] Ferriss advises his readers that to become members of the 'new rich' they need to develop their outsourcing to make other people or technology do the work for them. Outsourcing enables the new rich to lead a lifestyle of mini-retirements. He contrasts this attitude to the accumulation of wealth with that of the old rich, who invested capital to sustain a lifestyle of lavish consumption. The new rich do not chase money for money's sake; instead they seek to maximise opportunities to make money from other people to free up their own time. Being a member of the new rich relies on the temporal exploitation of the busyness of others. To repeat Veblen's interpretation of the leisure class,[15] the new rich value guile over industry.

Ferriss's endorsement of outsourcing inverts the assumption that busyness is a universal condition; no one has enough time, from the corporate executive to the delivery driver. His solution does not propose a universal relaxation of working time. He advocates a more pernicious redistribution. His vision of temporal exploitation

---

[10]See, for example, Berg and Seeber (2016) and Schor (1992).
[11]See, for example, Dorling (2014/2019) and Pickett and Wilkinson (2010).
[12]Piketty (2014).
[13]Sayer (2016).
[14]Ferriss (2007/2011).
[15]Veblen (1899/2007).

is confirmed by Sharma's ethnographic study of workers employed in different vertices of global capitalism.[16] Her account fleshes out in detail the diversity and inequality of temporal experiences which are unevenly distributed by networks that extend beyond organisational structures. Her analysis of power-chronography makes visible the uneven exploitation of time, which is relevant to the experience of the new rich but is also more intermeshed into the fabric of everyday life.

In writing about work-related busyness, I attempt to capture how experiences of occupational time squeeze are not simply a matter of individual commitment to maximising exploits but are embedded in the complexity of organisational structures and relationships. Moreover, I try to avoid writing about the moral outcomes of work, as this would entail writing about work as a unified activity. My approach follows the work of writers such as Johanna Briggs in detailing the diversity of what workers do all day and indeed whether work is busy or not.[17] Therefore, unlike other empirical investigations, in particular Gregg's detailed analysis of professional employees in the knowledge economy,[18] this analysis does not delve into the intricacies of particular types of work. As an alternative, I consider how different organisational structures integrate varied amalgamations of time–space. Some workers, such as Ricky, have to work within a very tightly bounded expectation of being in a particular place at a certain time, but most professional workers have more flexibility. Both arrangements are problematic: Ricky is unable to work within such tightly bounded constraints, while Gregg details how work can take over intimate life, and vice versa, if boundaries between the domestic and work are too fluid. Yet these dissimilarities in organisational configurations of times and spaces are rarely considered in moral evaluations of work, even though they are fundamental to the temporality, and, thus, the busyness, of work. The first half of this chapter, therefore, details case studies of different experiences of the temporalities of work. In the second part, I consider a more unique experience, working on one's own. If busyness is all about managing colleagues' expectations and spatial–temporal organisational structures, then working in isolation could be the solution. The second half of the chapter challenges this assumption, as even working for oneself can never be independent of the requirement to assimilate broader responsibilities.

Case Studies of Working Time

I use the Mass Observation Archive diaries to explore the relationships between distinctive organisational structures, the specific spatial and temporal arrangements of work and experiences of time squeeze. The advantage of using this data source is that it provides varied accounts of different working days, though for the most part the diaries are quite mundane. Contributors to the MOA are not employed in particularly time-pressured occupations at the more extreme

---

[16]Sharma (2014).
[17]Briggs (2015).
[18]Gregg (2011).

temporal limits of global capitalism. Thus, rather than capturing the intense acceleration of work, these diaries detail the interdependencies of working time and ongoing personal justifications during the working day. The mental chatter about being busy does not just revolve around what people have to get done but also around the justification of what they are asked to do.

I have chosen five case studies of everyday working life from the 134 MOA diaries. These examples are restricted to employees in organisations and also exclude students and retired correspondents. The case studies were selected after careful reading of all of the diaries and were chosen to illustrate the temporalities of different types of work in discrete organisational structures and diverse spatial arrangements. The choice is biased towards diarists who provide a more detailed account, as this detail is necessary for the narrative analysis technique that I have used.[19] This analysis identifies how the diary is structured (how the diarist reports the time and whether the diary is time-narrated or time-structured, as detailed in chapter three); how it is performed (the emotional tone of the diary); the substance of the diary (how each diarist narrates time pressure over the day); and what functions the diary serves in revealing how correspondents react to temporal pressures experienced over the day.

The five case studies and their pseudonyms[20] are as follows:

John: Engineering works manager (manufacturing work).

Cathy: Library assistant (service work).

Linda: Speech therapist (care work).

Alex: IT project manager (project work).

Julie: Business analyst (home work).

The five case studies are not intended to be representative of the diversity of organisational configurations, though they do illustrate how it is impossible to write about work practices as cohesive activities even for workers engaged in similar occupational types (all five diarists are engaged in professional or semi-professional occupations and four of the five in health care and service industries).

John

MOA Number: S5915. Pseudonym: John. Male engineering works manager, 50–59, married, no children. Diary for Friday 23 February 2018.

I classify John's diary as time-narrated, even though it is a hybrid of time-structured and time-narrated approaches. His morning routine is time-structured and his attention to temporal detail has been refined over the last few years, although he hates not being able to spend more time with his wife. After his precise

---

[19]Riessman (1993).
[20]The pseudonyms are names that I have given to the diarists.

morning routine, his diary takes a more narrative form and he shifts to writing about what happens between different time periods. In total there are 28 references to specific times. In his diary, he is critical of other people encountered during the day and he complains about the situation at work.

Most of his day is spent supervising work colleagues. He reflects that he is the only person at work who is committed to the job and everyone else just turns up for the salary. After his regular morning tour of the works, John identifies a major technical problem at work. Tests on a new piece of equipment are not going well and he decides that it requires dismantling and review. He meets with the managing director to discuss the equipment and the MD informs him that the failure of the equipment is John's responsibility and that John should spend the weekend at work to fix it. John rejects this suggestion. He writes in his diary that he is becoming increasingly frustrated that he is expected to do more at work with no extra pay, and to do work that he is not qualified to do. He writes that he is looking for a new job.

No progress is made regarding the faulty equipment. By lunchtime he is fed up and focusses on clearing his desk. Every Friday work finishes at 1.30 p.m., and John is in no mood to work beyond this time. He leaves work at 1.33 p.m., the earliest he has done so a while. John spends the afternoon writing an objection to a neighbour's planning application. He then works in his engineering garden-workshop listening to classic rock music, aiming to cheer himself up. He has set himself a deadline to finish the model he is working on and is pleased with his progress. On going to bed, John reflects that the frustration of his working day is that more and more is expected of him with less support.

Cathy

MOA Number: C5706. Pseudonym: Cathy. Female library assistant, 30–39, no children. Diary for Tuesday 23 January 2018.

I have classified Cathy's diary as time-narrated though it segues between the two different styles. There are 25 references to time, some of which are precise, for example, 8.03, 10.54 and 12.06, and she records that her husband's (whom she refers to as 'hubby') alarm goes off seven times between 6.30 and 7.18. Cathy gets up at 6.55. Her diary is very detailed and revolves around the people with whom she engages during the day, including physical encounters – family, friends, colleagues and customers – and virtual ones, such as with Chris Evans[21] on the radio. In contrast, Cathy writes little about herself, other than about her ablutions and her failed attempt to commit to Veganuary.[22] She pays careful attention to small details and distinguishing features of her clients and colleagues.

Cathy does hint that she has suffered from mental health problems in the past. She works in another small town approximately 10 miles away; although

---

[21]Chris Evans hosted the BBC Radio 2 breakfast show between January 2010 and December 2018.
[22]Being vegan for the month of January, Cathy is already a vegetarian.

she could make the journey on her own by changing buses, she chooses to travel with her husband to his work in a different town and to catch a bus from there. This change of routine came about after she had a panic attack when she had to change buses. Cathy now appreciates the short time that she spends driving to her husband's work. On a Tuesday, she does not have to catch a bus from her husband's work as she gets a lift from a work colleague. They go shopping before starting work, as her colleague loves to shop and Cathy is happy to go along. Cathy purchases toothpaste, lip salve and some sweets, and also buys glass pebbles for a craft project at work. Cathy works in a team of six in the library with a team leader. Work starts at 10 a.m. and is organised into three 2-hour and one 1-hour period, with half an hour for lunch (which I assume is taken during these shifts, as she leaves work at five). Most of her day is spent on the enquiries desk, where she attends to the various requests from customers as well as carrying out library administration and preparation. She also spends a shift re-shelving.

In her diary, Cathy details her encounters with customers, both new and regular, and describes how she was particularly thrilled that one new customer turned out to be her former deputy head teacher from primary school. She speculates about the ethnic origin of non-white customers, more out of curiosity rather than prejudice. Reading her diary, I was struck by her patience with others, even those clients who were rude or annoying. She is concerned about a colleague who is unhappy in his work and writes that she 'does not want him to get angry with a customer'. Cathy readily agrees to change her shifts so that he can work where he is happiest. In the afternoon she assists a home library service volunteer, whom she describes as someone who 'likes a bit of attention', and Cathy does her best to oblige, though the volunteer 'rubs her up the wrong way'. Cathy jokes that she is a 'grumpy old sod' in not tolerating the volunteer, but she appears to be anything but grumpy with other people. She responds to all requests for help during the day and goes along with the wishes of others, from shopping with her colleague in the morning to swapping shifts with another colleague and, in the evening, when she and her husband go to her mother-in-law's for tea, to watching the TV programmes chosen by her husband and mother-in-law.

Cathy's day, from getting up to travelling to work, carrying out duties at work and spending time with her in-laws is lived through other people. Except for washing and eating lunch, she does not carry out any other activity on her own. She does not acknowledge the relational necessity of her home and work life, nor does she write that she needs more time for herself. While working at the enquiry desk, she is able to complete her own administration tasks and can segue between doing tasks she has been assigned and doing things for other people. My interpretation of her diary is that her day is deeply embedded and relational it is not something that she remarks on, either as an endorsement of her day or as a source of frustration. Cathy anticipates and accepts being busy doing things for other people.

Linda

MOA Number: T4715. Pseudonym: Linda. Female speech therapist, 40–49, married with two school-age children. Diary for Tuesday 21 November 2017.

Linda's diary is a time-structured account of her day. Visually, her diary segues between morning domestic activities, daytime work and evening domestic activities punctuated by time. Her first time reference is 6.13 a.m., which is when she checks her phone to ensure that she gets up by 6.25 a.m., and her last time point is 11.40 p.m., which is when she goes to bed. She records 44 time points in total over the day (her diary is 11 pages long); the smallest time gap between discrete points is five minutes and the longest is one hour and five minutes. Her diary is observant of her own behaviour and her interactions with other people and non-human entities. It is also humorous and written in a self-deprecating tone, and her reflections on her day are subtlety directed towards herself. Linda's temporal awareness is not just related to recording clock time. She has a clear perception of when things should happen and how long activities should take. She needs to be up by 6.25 a.m. at the latest, she knows when her children need to be up, what time she needs to leave the house and when to bring appointments with patients to an end.

Linda's close attention to time is matched by the equal detail she provides of the materiality of space. She details her routes to work, her visits to patients and her return home, difficulties in parking, the layout of the office (and the challenges of finding a hot-desk) and how patient visits are punctuated by intercoms, bells and access codes. Her diary presents an integrated account of the assemblage of roads, pavements, technologies, infrastructures, family members, pets, colleagues and patients that she encounters over the day.

Linda's work is bounded in caring spaces and there is little flexibility within these. Consultations with patients are time limited as they cannot be ended by the resolution of patients' conditions. It is up to Linda to manage the temporal boundaries of each appointment, and if she fails to do this it will segue into later appointments. Because she deals with patients with limited cognition, visits are coordinated with other colleagues and family members. Her frustration is that despite her attempts at punctuality she finds this precision impossible to maintain. In particular, while moving between the bounded spaces of home, office and consultations she enters 'Bermuda triangles of time'. These are spaces such as hallways, corridors and pavements where time accelerates though nothing seems to happen. One tactic for staying on time is to set her car clock 15 minutes fast to trick herself into thinking time is more advanced than it is and to avoid being late for appointments. Having the clock run fast means that she has to mentally calculate the actual time. What she does not have time for during the day is time for herself, and she is constantly behind with administrative tasks, such as submitting her travel expenses. Linda has a managerial role; she is responsible for the shift rota and has accidentally put herself down for a rota on a day she had previously booked off. Her struggles to fulfil her responsibilities to herself are her main source of temporal frustration. Linda compares her adherence to time and her responsibilities towards others with colleagues whom, she observes, do not share her commitment. She is the last to leave work on the diary day and contrasts her work ethic to that of colleagues, who have their coats on ready to leave on time.

Linda's drive home is frustrating. She takes a detour to avoid a rush-hour traffic jam but queries why she has done this because the extra mileage does not save time compared with waiting in the queue. Her caring responsibilities segue into domestic space as she cooks tea for her family and supervises her children's homework. She resists her family's request to prepare the evening meal early (her husband and son want to watch a football match) and is not happy with the 'horrid' meal that she serves up. She finally winds down in the evening, absorbed in knitting baby socks for a colleague.

Alex

MOA Number: P6034. Pseudonym: Alex. Male IT manager, 30–39, cohabiting, no children. Diary for Wednesday 6 December 2017.

Alex's diary is time-narrated. There are only six time-anchoring points (times for when the alarm goes off, he leaves for work, meetings at work, leaving work to return home and when he gets home). The time in between these anchoring points is narrated through his negotiation of relationships at work. Alex writes about his anxiety in relation to work and about his relationships with different colleagues, vendors, subcontractors, clients and software testers with whom he interacts during the day and how their interests in projects may come into conflict. His diary is personal, and he does not explain his working context for another reader, which makes it hard to follow.

Alex's contract is home based, and he spends a lot of time travelling to support specific projects. But on this day, he is going into his employer's office as he has been asked to answer some questions about some software relating to a large project that has recently completed and to identify some improvements in the software that the operators have requested. There is no requirement for Alex to be punctual, and he leaves home slightly later than planned. Most of his day is spent in meetings and his work time his dedicated to negotiating complaints, criticisms and requests from different members of the project team. In contrast, it does not take Alex long to fix the problem with the software. He is anxious about his working day because of the working relationships that he has to manoeuvre around more than the challenges of the actual productive work that he has to do. He is conscious that he finds it difficult to be assertive.

Alex's day is technologically tethered, though his use of technology is not associated with dystopic acceleration. He uses technology as a mind cleanser rather than as a stimulant. In the morning, as part of his routine to get him ready to face the relational challenges of work, he plays a simple computer game (*The Simpsons: Tapped Out*) and updates social media before heading for work. In the evening, he watches a film on triple speed with his partner and enjoys being able to watch more television because of this facility.

Julie

MOA Number: P7940. Pseudonym: Julie. Female business analyst, 40–49, married, two school-age children. Diary for Thursday 21 December 2017.

Julie's diary is time-narrated in a precise and detailed style. She includes 16 references to clock time that are evenly distributed throughout the day but are mostly bunched up around mealtimes. The precision of her diary is rather matter-of-fact; she writes about the unfolding of events over the day – from getting up and sorting out her children's breakfast to getting them to school, her working day, having lunch and engaging in after-school and evening activities. Julie works exclusively at home, and in the absence of a spatial segregation between work and home her coordination of morning activities is almost exclusively through getting other members of her family ready for the day. She does not comment on time pressures, only hinting at the pinch points of getting her children up and getting them to school. For example, her older teenage son is not good at getting up and he is now allowed to sleep in later as long as he gets ready quickly and does not make anyone else late. On this day, her younger son goes to an after-school club, and Julie's choice to drive rather than cycle to school means there is less time pressure at the end of her working day, as she can pick him up sooner if she drives rather than cycles.

Compared to other diaries in the MOA data set, Julie's diary is particularly bland.[23] She does not write about negotiating competing responsibilities; everything happens in an ordered fashion. Other than mentioning an after-school Christmas concert, Julie does not write about activities that happen during the day. She does not describe the detail of her job and there is no detail about what her work as a business analyst involves. Although she is a home-based worker, she works closely with various people in the UK and overseas, particularly India. Work revolves around networking with this globally dispersed team. Her work consists of dealing with e-mails and a continual series of conference calls. Julie begins by precisely recording the timing of these – she has calls at 9.30 a.m., 10 a.m., 11.30 a.m. and 1.30 p.m. This temporal detail is lost in the afternoon, maybe because of the fatigue of writing her diary or the repetition of her day. She writes that in the afternoon, she simply has more calls and that between these she replies to e-mails and updates documentation. Unlike other diarists, Julie does not discuss the personalities and characteristics of co-workers, the organisational structure of work (though she does mention calling her boss for a quick chat), tensions in working relationships or anxieties about segueing between tasks. Instead she pays more attention to the activities that break up working in this virtual space: the timing of coffee breaks and details about her lunch and lighting a burner to make her workspace smell fragrant. The detail is about the material space that she is sitting in rather than the virtual space in which she works.

Work-related Busyness

These five case studies are not intended to be representative of work-related busyness. Engineering works manager, librarian, speech therapist, IT manager and business analyst are not necessarily the kind of jobs popularity associated with excessive time pressures, and not all of the case studies detail the performance of 'busyness'. If the point of this analysis were to identify extreme experiences of time pressure at work, attention would need to be paid to workers at the forefront of temporal intensity,

---

[23]In my first read-through of the diaries, I did not identify Julie's diary as one to be included in the analysis of busyness at work. Her account has become more relevant as home working has been strongly advised for many professional workers during the Covid-19 pandemic.

such as workers like Ricky and the subjects of Sharma's ethnographic study. My interest is subtlety different because busyness is not simply contained within particular job types. Although the specific details of temporal and spatial organisation at work generate diverse temporal pinch points, individual assimilation of responsibilities and positions within networks are also relevant. Putting it bluntly, some people are more amenable and/or better able to respond to the temporal demands of others. We saw in the previous chapter that effective time management is achieved through the management of space and other people. These case studies illustrate different responses to the configuration of work with time, space and organisational hierarchies. What emerges from the diarists' reflections on the demands placed on them at work is how they manage these and their judgement of the reasonableness of requested responsibility. Busyness as described in the diaries has little to do with productivity; it is not related to the volume of work but the justification of work and the diarists' ability to accommodate or refuse expectations at work.

Relational Hierarchies

Cathy's work in a small library team could be interpreted as the least time-pressurised job described in the diaries. This is not because she is not busy; her diary is full of the detail of what she does, much of which might be regarded as small stuff: buying toothpaste, shelving books, meeting an old teacher. Cathy's description of her day is without conflict. Her account probably corresponds with outsiders' opinion of working in a library as an unhurried and leisurely job that is not subject to time pressure. Other library workers would disagree. There are six other one-day diaries submitted by working librarians in the MOA data set. Their working days are very different. Three contributors complain about the time pressures and management structures of their jobs; two are matter-of-fact, with little commentary other than what they do at work and when; and the sixth is similar to Cathy's in detailing personal interactions during the day. Cathy acknowledges that one of her colleagues is not happy in his work and she is worried that he will take his anger out on customers. My interpretation of Cathy's day is not that working in a library is a routine, predictable job; it is that she prioritises the responsibilities that she has for others. She agrees to fit in with colleagues' work preferences and travel routines and lets her family choose which television programmes to watch. She does not write about her own discretionary time either at work or at home. She hints about previous episodes of anxiety, suggesting that her assimilation of responsibility is not necessarily benign. Cathy's diary epitomises a feminist ethic of care that foregrounds how dependency, rather than difference, defines us.[24] However, she is able to put other people's requests and needs before her own because her life is tightly contained within domestic spaces (her own home and her in-laws') and the library.

---

[24]Morwenna Griffiths writes, 'My freedom to do some things is increased if I do not have to consider others. But my freedom to be myself is bound by those others and our ways of leading a life together', which is very appropriate for Cathy's assimilation of responsibilities. Griffiths (1995, p. 30).

John's day is quite different. He describes a more hierarchical organisational structure in the engineering works that has a clear chain of command; he has a boss and workers for whom he is responsible. Unlike Cathy, he is less willing to respond to the requests of others and is unwilling to recalibrate his time to assimilate new responsibilities.[25] He complains that he asked to do more than others at work and his musings about work-related busyness focus on what he perceives to be an unfair distribution of tasks. John's recurrent internal complaining about the inequalities of time pressure is closer to theories of reflective modernity[26] than the feminist ethic of care that Cathy's diary describes. In these accounts, formal structures and repertoires that have collapsed have been replaced with expectations of individual responsibility which is navigated through the processes of reflective thought and choice-making.[27] Hence, while John's work remains structured around a formal hierarchy, he is conscious that he expected to be responsible for more tasks and be prepared to choose to dedicate time to these. Moreover, he believes his colleagues shirk their responsibilities and this observation intensifies his grievance about temporal inequalities. However, unlike Cathy, he is also prepared to put his own interests first. On the day, he writes about he declines the instruction to spend more time at work and keeps to the formal hours at work, leaving at lunchtime on Friday. He keeps himself busy with his own projects at home instead. He puts his own interests before the responsibilities of work and feels justified in doing so. John's complaint about productivity is relative: it is not simply that he is asked to do too much at work; what frustrates him is that colleagues are not expected to be equally hard working. John's account neatly illustrates how the moral economy of work is expressed through justifications of right and wrong and that these can be personal as well as structural.

Project Work

Alex's day is representative of Boltanski and Chiapello's description of project work.[28] They attribute this cultural change in the organisation of work to artistic critiques of both bureaucracy and Fordist models of production. According to Boltanski and Chiapello, this critique emerged in affluent societies in the 1960s and targeted large corporations for failing to improve the quality of life for their workers or to meet an expectation that work should facilitate development of the self.[29] This expectation is realised through project work, which is facilitated through relational networks rather than hierarchical bureaucratic structures. Good individual performance in one project ensures recruitment to future projects. Performance is measured by how an individual manages relationships as well as by objective criteria concerning productivity. Alex's anxiety is all about how he manages (or does not,

---

[25]Sharma (2017).
[26]Giddens (1991).
[27]Beck and Beck-Gernsheim (2002).
[28]Boltanski and Chiapello (2005).
[29]Du Gay and Morgan (2013, pp. 1–42).

as he perceives it) the competing demands of different players in the projects that he works on. The busyness of his day is not prescribed by the productive tasks that he has to do and that can be achieved within a fixed time frame. Alex's experiences of time pressure are related to ongoing expectations that he can simultaneously respond to competing demands and requests from within the project team. His account of a working day foregrounds the difficulties of managing relationships in project working rather than challenge of getting things done. His experiences invert the assumptions about speed and agility that infiltrate the contemporary management ethos. Alex can complete his productive tasks quickly, what takes the time is managing relationships in non-hierarchical organisational structures.[30]

Alex's anxiety about work illustrate that working quickly to complete tasks is not the same as being agile in managing relationships. His experiences of time pressure are defined by ongoing negotiation of de-territorialised relationships and working practices. These include relationships with colleagues with different interests in the company he works for as well as subcontractors, clients and vendors. What Alex finds time-consuming is responding to these competing demands and synchronising his time with other members of the project team. This synchronisation does not necessarily require spatial coordination, because meetings can take place in virtual space or can be repeated at different times (Alex notes that he will have to repeat one meeting as not everyone could be present).[31] Alex's account of project work underlines my previous observation of Allen's *Getting Things Done* method, that time management is effectively done through the management of other people. The challenge in project work is that managing other people in non-hierarchical structures takes time as delegation of tasks can be done in multiple directions.

Being on Time and in Place

While some types of work come and go as a result of technological and organisational change, other forms of work are more persistent. Speech therapy (Linda's occupation) emerged as a medical profession in the early twentieth century, and, as with other health and social care work, is not an occupation that will become obsolete, though it is reshaped through ongoing organisational reforms in health care. Accelerating health care into the twenty-first century is particularly problematic and has been shown to result in deteriorating employee well-being and patient care.[32] Linda's diary exemplifies the challenges of delivering care that, unlike virtual project work, cannot be performed without paying close attention to time–space.[33] Not only is it difficult to accelerate care that has to be given within defined times and spaces, but also these temporal boundaries are not necessarily transparent, because care work is not easily demarcated by the

---

[30]Du Gay (2017).
[31]Wajcman (2019, pp. 315–337).
[32]Kubicek, Korunka, and Ulferts (2013, pp. 1525–1538).
[33]Bowlby (2012, pp. 2101–2118).

conventions of arrival, progress and departure.[34] The busyness of Linda's work is generated through the requirement to synchronise where and when she works with a revolving assemblage of clients, colleagues and relatives in different locations. Her working day is, therefore, simultaneously territorial and dispersed, which requires careful adherence to clock time.

Linda's working day exemplifies the challenges of delivering care within the constraints of a system that relies on temporal and spatial precision. Linda also has to coordinate her visits with other care professionals and with relatives and patients. Her adherence to clock time is necessary for her own punctuality and the synchronisation with others. Her tactics for keeping time and her naming of 'Bermuda triangles' capture Bissell's description of the mental chatter of thinking habits that orientate Linda through the day.[35] What does get lost in the unfolding of Linda's day is her own sovereign control over time. She does not have time to complete her own tasks, such as submitting her expenses, because her priority is the spatial and temporal coordination of others.

Remote Working

Julie's day is defined by the absence of a physical co-presence with colleagues. Her working day revolves around timings of meetings with no requirement for physical punctuality. Unlike the others in the case studies, who describe their relationships with colleagues, her diary is distinguished by the absence of such detail. Other than a brief mention of a boss, there is no discussion of hierarchy or of tensions within the project teams. Nor is there any description of what she actually does, so her job appears to correspond with David Graeber's description of a bullshit job.[36] Julie herself is not dismissive of her work; she simply does not write about it and details her diary with description of the activities that happen around work. Her working day spent segueing between virtual meetings may well predict the form of work in the aftermath of the Covid-19 pandemic. In this virtual, socially distanced space, time pressures associated with the coordination of time and space and the ongoing negotiation of relationships are absent. Her schedule of online meetings is punctuated by lunch and lighting a burner. Equally, the absence of the tensions and pleasures caused by colleagues detailed in the other diarists' accounts are missing. The trade-off to giving up the intensity of busyness generated through the intermeshing of colleagues in time and space is the lack of varied detail of everyday encounters.

These five case studies illustrate how busyness at work cannot be defined as a specific thing brought about by a particular constellation of space, time and

---

[34]Baraitser (2017).

[35]Bissell (2011), I discuss the implications of Bissell's theorisation of thinking habits for these case studies of work-related busyness in Holdsworth (2020a).

[36]Graeber (2019). Other diarists in the data set do write about how their working day is pointless and the frustration of their work, which concurs with Graeber's depiction of meaningless work.

organisational structures. Busyness can be accepted as the requirement to be responsive to others, resisted as a form of injustice, experienced as the anxiety of managing diverse relationships, exacerbated by the restrictions of needing to be in particular places at specific times or supressed through the blandness of exclusive virtual working.

Working for Oneself

Organisational structures generate very different experiences of time pressure. However, not everyone works in an organisation. Self-employment is equally varied and includes entrepreneurs, freelancers, contractors and gig economy workers – such as Ricky – and it is not restricted to particular sectors. The number of people engaged in self-employment increased globally during the first two decades of the twentieth century. While this trend is greater in emerging economies, particularly South America, it is also a feature of more advanced economies. According to the Office of National Statistics, in 2019 there were an estimated 5 million self-employed workers in the UK, accounting for 15% of the workforce.[37] The USA has a much lower self-employment rate, 6.1%,[38] though other estimates put the proportion of self-employed workers closer to 30%.[39]

It is not possible to write about self-employment as a singular experience, and it is beyond the scope of this chapter to compare different practices of working for oneself. I have chosen to focus on a more celebrated form of self-employment – being a writer. My interest in this form of work is because it may be assumed to capture the essence of working for oneself: it involves having control over one's own time. This cherished ambition of having temporal control is a repeated mantra across different forms of self-employment in more advanced economies. For example, Sharma's research with gig economy workers highlights their willingness to trade employment security for time freedom and being able to choose when to work.[40] My own previous collaborative research on young entrepreneurs, found that one of the most striking features of the commitment of these young people was the desire to have control over their own lives, even though this meant having to devote most of their time to their business venture.[41] Their commitment was not realised through temporal self-control; instead they had to keep going and to invest themselves, rather than capital, in their projects. These young entrepreneurs were not, for the most part, seeking to join the new rich and secure temporal freedom through the exploitation of others. Instead, they were interweaving self-identity with entrepreneurial ambition.[42] Being able to maximise time, whether by choosing when or where to work or by throwing oneself into the temporal intensity of a new venture, defines the temporalities of self-enterprise.

---

[37]ONS (2020).
[38]OECD (2020).
[39]Pofeldt (2020).
[40]Sharma (2017).
[41]Holdsworth and Mendonça (2020, pp. 103–123).
[42]Bröckling (2015).

In this section on working for oneself, I consider how these two endorsed temporal traits – freedom and maximisation – are experienced by writers. Temporal freedom is popularly assumed to be a defining characteristic of creative work. The popular imagination concerning creative freedom fuels fascination with how time is organised to consolidate contradictions between freedom from external timetables and the requirement to be productive. Creative work is scrutinised to exemplify the potential of working outside the constraints of bureaucracy and the capacity for hard work. Yet the temporality of creative work is particularly paradoxical. As Lutz perceptively points out in his review of slacker film culture in the USA, many of the individuals whose cultural work extolls slacker culture are workaholics themselves.[43] There is a particular popular fascination with how hard writers, artists, musicians and film makers work, which is matched with a perplexity regarding the lack of productivity of artists whose creativity is condensed into a single piece of work.[44]

A Writer's Day

I have been able to take advantage of public fascination with the temporal organisation of creative workers to analyse how opportunities for self-defined temporal habits facilitate and/or jar with expectations of productivity. Between 16 April 2016 and 13 January 2018, *The Guardian* commissioned 86 writers (of fiction, biography, history, philosophy and poetry), one bookseller and one illustrator to write about 'My writing day'.[45] The series comprises 87 short descriptions of a day in the life of the contributors. With the exception of one author, they all write in English, and most live in the UK or the USA. The division by gender is almost balanced (46 male and 42 female contributors). Only one of the accounts is written as a time-structured diary; the rest are time-narrated, and clock times are used sparingly, if at all. Time is narrated through the sequencing of activities and events. These articles were published in a national newspaper and are polished pieces of writing; indeed, it is often possible to recognise the writing style of the contributor. Contributions are often humorous and self-deprecating; there is a general consensus that writers should not be too precious about writing. Hilary Mantel is adamant that being a writer is a 'job like any other'.[46] These accounts are not systematic accounts of a day, and some contributors write about their ideal routine rather than what they experience. These contributions are performative and, as Rose Tremain reminds the reader, 'writers can lie about everything'.[47]

---

[43]Lutz (2006).

[44]One of the most celebrated writers who only had one book published during her lifetime is Harper Lee; see Cep (2019).

[45]This series can be found at https://www.theguardian.com/books/series/my-writing-day

[46]Mantel, H. (2016). My writing day: Hilary Mantel. *The Guardian*, April 16. Retrieved from https://www.theguardian.com/books/2016/apr/16/hilary-mantel-my-writing-day.

[47]Tremain, R. (2016). Rose Tremain: truth, insomnia and waiting for inspiration in Norwich John Lewis. *The Guardian*, May 28. Retrieved from: https://www.theguardian.com/books/2016/may/28/my-writing-day-rose-tremain.

Routines. Whether any routines and rituals are necessary is discussed throughout the contributions and there is no agreement about this. Jonathan Safran Foer suggests that while writing does not require anything, a 'feeling of necessity goes a long way'.[48] For some writers who have developed routines and rituals over time, these become integral to the task of writing. Permanence is a feature; the late Judith Kerr worked in the same house for over 55 years[49] and Michael Bond wrote every day for over 50 years and 30 years in the same house respectively.[50] Rituals start at the beginning of the day. Breakfast is often predictable – Geoff Dyer goes to the same café for breakfast with his wife every morning – and physically moving to a working space, even if it is in the same house, is acknowledged.[51] There are fewer rituals at the end of the day, though writers often purposely do something different after finishing work: go for a swim, meet friends or colleagues or go out for a meal/to the cinema or theatre. Starts and ends are, therefore, managed by using space rather than noting clock time.

Almost all contributors write in the morning, confirming self-help authors' endorsement of morning routines. However, the writing in the morning can be a practice that develops over time. Authors often have to begin their writing careers in conjunction with other work. Writing outside standard hours of work is often the only way in which an unpublished author can write. For some, the hours that are worked during these initial stages are simply carried over to full-time writing. Roddy Doyle writes from 9 a.m. to 6 p.m., the same hours he worked as a teacher.[52] While almost all writers state that the morning is their preferred time to work, some recognise that morning routines are the only way of combining being a writer with other responsibilities and commitments. Kamila Shamsie is a reformed night owl, not out of choice but because her 'life requires both solitude and sociability' and the only way she can sustain the latter is through how she engages with the former.[53]

---

[48]Foer, J. S. (2016). Jonathan Safran Foer: 'I don't have writer's block, but am a chronic sufferer of "Jonathan block"', *The Guardian*, August 27. Retrieved from: https://www. theguardian.com/books/2016/aug/27/my-writing-day-jonathan-safran-foer.

[49]Kerr, J. (2017). Judith Kerr: 'I'm still surprised at the success of The Tiger Who Came to Tea'. *The Guardian*, November 25. Retrieved from: https://www.theguardian. com/books/2017/nov/25/judith-kerr-my-writing-day.

[50]Bond, M. (2016). Michael Bond: 'I'm at my desk by 9am. I even write on Christmas Day'. *The Guardian*, December 24. Retrieved from: https://www.theguardian.com/ books/2016/dec/24/michael-bond-writing-day-paddington-bear.

[51]Dyer, G. (2017). Geoff Dyer: 'At the first sign of sleepiness I commit absolutely to a nap … I lie down and force myself'. *The Guardian*, May 20. Retrieved from: https:// www.theguardian.com/books/2017/may/20/geoff-dyer-my-writing-day.

[52]Doyle, R. (2017). Roddy Doyle: my work is fuelled by music, mitching and mugs of green tea. *The Guardian*, September 9. Retrieved from: https://www.theguardian.com/ books/2017/sep/09/roddy-doyle-writing-day-smile-novel.

[53]Shamsie, K. (2017). Kamila Shamsie: you can't avoid talking about your relationship with the internet. *The Guardian*, September 16. Retrieved from: https://www.theguard-ian.com/books/2017/sep/16/my-writing-day-kamila-shamsie.

Though routines dominate, writing is acknowledged to be difficult as well as enjoyable. Procrastination is inevitable and can be the fun part of writing; Sebastian Faulks, for example, describes the pleasure of unproductive research visits.[54] Other authors are more consumed by the guilt and frustrations of being a writer. Yaa Gyasi compares her writing to digging a well: sometimes she digs 200 ft down but does not find any water. Other days fall into a rhythm and she is no longer aware that she is writing.[55] Reactions to distractions can be classified in two ways: embrace them or try to minimise them. Douglas Coupland changed his routine from 'AM clock-based passivity' to unpredictability and now does his best writing on planes.[56] Other writers use linear time as a way of reducing distractions, for example, Val McDermid writes in 20-minute bursts.[57] The trick of not moving or doing something else until something is produced (a certain number of words, a time span or a small achievement) is used by many contributors. This can then be followed by a distracting treat.

There is a general awareness of other authors' methods of writing, particularly celebrated ones, and Ernest Hemingway's systematic approach to writing in the morning is referenced. Will Self claims to write in 'Conrads', defined as 800 words a day and named for the target that 'the master wrote daily'.[58] Over time, the number of 'Conrads' he writes each day has diminished and he now works at 1.25. Self's droll division of writing into 'Conrads' hints at the ambivalence that most authors have towards daily targets. Targets are not a way of organising writing, because for most writers this is too goal orientated and distracts from the actuality of just writing. What targets provide is a sense of value and justification that a day's work has been completed, and this can assuage the guilt that some writers feel about devoting their productive time to what is seen by many as a very introspective activity.

Space.   Time to write is identified with writing space, and most of the detail in these accounts is about where writers write and the technologies that they use. The majority of writers concur with Allen's insistence on the unity of working space. Authors have a preferred writing space, and usually they are slightly

---

[54]Faulks, S. (2016). Sebastian Faulks: 'I used to pull the curtains and put in earplugs, but what kind of life is that?'. *The Guardian*, July 16. Retrieved from: https://www.theguardian.com/books/2016/jul/16/my-writing-day-sebastian-faulks.

[55]Gyasi, Y. (2017). Yaa Gyasi: 'I write a sentence. I delete it. I wonder if it's too early for lunch'. *The Guardian*, October 28. Retrieved from: https://www.theguardian.com/books/2017/oct/28/yaa-gyasi-my-writing-day.

[56]Coupland, D. (2016). Douglas Coupland: 'I'm actually at my happiest when I'm writing on a plane'. *The Guardian*, October 8. Retrieved from: https://www.theguardian.com/books/2016/oct/08/my-writing-day-douglas-coupland.

[57]McDermid, V. (2016). Val McDermid: 'Left to our own devices, writers adopt the habits of a hermit crab'. *The Guardian*, September 3. Retrieved from: https://www.theguardian.com/books/2016/sep/03/val-mcdermid-my-writing-day.

[58]Self, W. (20160. Will Self: 'I write first thing, when I can suspend disbelief in the act of making things up'. *The Guardian*, June 18. Retrieved from https://www.theguardian.com/books/2016/jun/18/my-writing-day-will-self.

segregated from living spaces. Echoing Gaston Bachelard's *Poetics of Space*, attics are popular places to write in, as are sheds and garages.[59] In contrast to seeking isolation in an attic, writers may choose to write in a public space, though more choose libraries than cafés. Spaces such as libraries are simultaneously public and private and combine the requirement for isolation and sociability. A few writers have studios in a separate location. The difficult task of writing needs to be done, and for some this is exaggerated by their uncomfortable working space. Deborah Levy works in a shed that is 'freezing in the winter and sweltering in the summer'.[60] There is, therefore, no agreement on what a writing space should be, and some writers break with Allen's productivity method by adopting hot-desking strategies rather than sticking to one space.[61] It is simply a question of what works. For some this has to be consistent, but for others it is varied.

Many authors embrace untidy writing spaces. There is considerable detail about the objects that writers surround themselves with, often books, which may be either sources of inspiration or representations of a talisman. Phillip Pullman describes the objects that he has in his study in particular detail but says nothing about the act of writing. He acknowledges that this stuff constitutes a necessary distraction; it is impossible to spend all day writing.[62] A striking theme is that authors do not necessarily seek to maximise productivity through ergonomic practices. Pullman's desk is covered with an ancient kilim, which, although it looks nice, is not a practical surface to write on, so he places a green cutting mat, usually used in craft, on top. Other writers use old computers, often because they cannot be connected to the Internet, but also because inefficiency can foster creativity. The detailed attention given to space is also given to the technology that is used for writing, which varies: computers, typewriters and pen and paper. There is no definitive way of writing; authors have diverse assemblages of technologies that facilitate their craft. These may be precise, for example, Pullman writes using Montblanc ballpoint pens, or chaotic, for example, Andrew Michael Hurley tells himself that clear desks are 'sterile'.[63]

It is not just the immediate writing space that writers need to attend to. Locality can also be important. West London is a popular location, being particularly green and affording walks along the River Thames. This location confirms the wealth and status of some contributors. Views from attic windows are cherished.

---

[59]Bachelard (1958/1969).

[60]Levy, D. (2016). Deborah Levy: 'I have grown to love my writing shed in every season'. *The Guardian*, October 1. Retrieved from https://www.theguardian.com/books/2016/oct/01/deborah-levy-my-writing-day.

[61]Allen (2015).

[62]Pullman, P. (2017). Philip Pullman: 'I use coloured pencils to show which key I'm writing in – D minor, at the moment'. *The Guardian*, December 23. Retrieved from: https://www.theguardian.com/books/2017/dec/23/philip-pullman-writing-day-coloured-pencils.

[63]Hurley, A.M. (2017). Andrew Michael Hurley: 'Some days I don't look up until my wife texts to tell me to eat'. *The Guardian*, October 21. Retrieved from: https://www.theguardian.com/books/2017/oct/21/andrew-michael-hurley-my-writing-day.

Authors unable to afford these affluent localities write in more stark environments, such as basements with no views. Locality can also distract from writing: Petina Gappah does not live in her native Zimbabwe as she found it impossible to establish a writing practice in Zimbabwean unpredictable temporalities. She now lives in Berlin.[64]

Finally, being a successful writer cannot be achieved through isolation; John McGregor thinks that if he lived life as a hermit, he would probably have nothing to write about.[65] Writers are involved in a continual coordination of activities to create and sustain intimate and professional relationships.

Being A Writer

These brief synopses of working days illustrate that in the absence of organisational structure, writers have to establish their own. Where and when these structures are located varies; there are no rules for curating the creative working day. On balance, writers endorse morning routines in a defined space, though this is not unanimous. The consistent feature of a writing day is an author's commitment to self-discipline and repetition. Even if the output is very different each day, their attitude towards writing is consistent (even for those authors who rely on more chaotic inspiration). These accounts also subtly underscore the fallacy that one can have control over one's own time. Temporal freedom is unachievable because writers, like everyone else, have to respond to others: publishers, readers, promoters, etc. Being an author is not just about writing but is also about the curation of the writer's identity. Writers have to engage in projectised working networks; it is not sufficient to simply write, and earning a living as a writer is not an antidote to meaningless busyness. Writers do outsource activities and their working day is immersed in networks of interdependencies with workers in the hospitality trade and libraries and other writers and artists. What is missing in these accounts is probably what most readers really want to know: how do they write? But the successful completion of a novel is too subjective and elusive an activity to be distilled into a formal set of practices. In place of this, authors provide detail about the spatial and temporal organisation of writing. They have more to say about the frustration and guilt of their craft than about its satisfying elements. The moral requirement to justify work, which this newspaper series investigates for its readers, ultimately leads to dissatisfaction in how work is carried out, even for those deemed fortunate enough to have the opportunity for self-expression.

---

[64]Gappah, P. (2016). Petina Gappah: 'I was a lawyer, but I forced myself to write before I went to work'. *The Guardian*, December 3. Retrieved from: https://www.theguardian.com/books/2016/dec/03/petina-gappah-my-writing-day.
[65]McGregor, J. (2018). Jon McGregor: 'I have never been asked how I juggle writing and fatherhood'. *The Guardian*, January 6. Retrieved from: https://www.theguardian.com/books/2018/jan/06/jon-mcgregor-my-writing-day.

Summary

My initial interest in busyness was sparked from overhearing colleagues' comments about struggling because they had too much to do. However, following this initial curiosity to try and understand why busyness has taken over working life is not straightforward. For some workers at the apex of accelerating global capitalism, the structural forces that demand speed and commitment are transparent; however, busyness is not simply a matter of speed. Busyness revolves around judgements concerning time, productivity and the uneven distribution of responsibilities. It is more useful to think about busyness as the interception of competing ethics of how work should be organised and experienced rather than the outcome of linear social and cultural change.

While work-related busyness is necessarily diverse, it is possible to identify broader organisational trends and unifying experiences. The most obvious, and one that is concomitant with interpretations of individualisation, is that all workers have to assimilate responsibilities and cannot rely on organisational structures to facilitate these or ensure that they are distributed evenly. Thus, workers face personal challenges when responding to relentless, competing demands, though how these are materialised in time and space is different for different people. Competing interests can be de-territorialised, as in project work, or bounded by the precision of time and space, as in care work. In more structured or hierarchical employment, acceleration is more muted, as competing requests can be distributed across the organisation. However, in hierarchical systems, the moral justification of this distribution can be challenged, and the feelings of time pressure may be linked with whether or not the distribution of tasks is viewed as fair and reasonable. Across diverse organisational structures, workers' willingness and ability to recalibrate time in response to competing demands varies. Responses can be structural, as the ability to delegate or take on more responsibilities depends on employees' positions within an organisation. In the case studies, temporal recalibration also reproduced gendered orientations towards inter-dependency and expectations that women are more willing to take on additional responsibilities. One MOA correspondent neatly captures this gender difference: 'a man at his desk is at work. A woman at her desk is available to all the world'.[66] In other words, while the expectation that a person will exercise self-responsibility might characterise many forms of work in the twenty-first century, what this means for how busyness is experienced is varied. It might revolve around anxieties about managing ongoing competing interests in teams of multiple co-workers; the challenges of working in assemblages of technologies and (non-)human beings that do not correspond with bounded temporal and spatial boundaries; or the frustration that not all co-workers are equally committed to fulfilling responsibilities.

The organisation of work is central to understanding busyness, and this applies equally to those who do not work for other people. While working outside an

---

[66]MOA correspondent M6082, Autumn 2017 Directive Part 1:. *One-Day Diary: Organising and Experiencing Time.*

organisation might free up individual time, it does not mitigate responsibilities and the interdependencies of working life. The coordination of activity when working on one's own is an individual concern that requires as much attention as the activity to be performed. Therefore, although writers have the freedom to choose when and where to work, there is little flexibility to change these parameters. Rather than confirming Veblen's distinction between exploit and industry, writers are industrious in their orientation towards creative work. Writers are not immune to periods of frenetic inactivity and may use busy habits to block the overwhelming pressure to be productive, but they can also feel guilty about periods of procrastination. The incessant need to keep on going and to be busy because of the aspiration that creativity will blossom from industry remains inescapable. Busyness, therefore, is not just an outcome of having too much to do and too many people to respond to; it is also, perversely, a way of managing competing responsibilities.

Chapter 6

Family Time

This is Family

At Christmas in 2018, the holiday company Center Parcs[1] launched its advertising campaign for 2019 with the theme 'This is family'.[2] The TV campaign comprised three films about the fictional Parson family, Dave (Dad), Jo (Mum) and Sam (Big Sister). The fourth member, Sam's younger brother, does not have his own film but features in the films narrated by the other three members. The format of the films is the same: they all begin with the narrator stating I am Dave/Jo/Sam Parson and summarising who they are during the week. Dave is a grumpy, worried worker; Jo operates as half machine, constantly wrangling with people to get things done; and Sam is a moody teenager who gets blamed for most things and complains that her brother is a brat. During their weekend at Center Parcs, they each have the opportunity to be someone different to these versions of themselves and to do something different. Over the weekend, they are no longer Dave, Jo or Sam; they become Dad/Mum/Big Sister, respectively. They go on bike rides, water slides and zip wires together, and by spending time with each other, they become 'family'. The promotion of a holiday as providing the space and time for families to spend quality time together is a mainstay of holiday promotion,[3] and the Center Parcs films are not breaking any new ground in using images of family members having fun. However, these films take this motif further; the message is that Dave, Jo and Sam are so busy multitasking responsibilities and obligations during the week that they do not have time to be the family they want to be or think they should be. Their weekend away is not just about having a good time and enjoying the company of family. Time that is free from their weekly duties gives them the opportunity to perform their idealised family roles. The roles of Mum, Dad and Big Sister are not simply acquired through the positional status of being a mother,

---

[1]Center Parcs run short-break holiday villaes in England and Ireland. Retrieved from https://en.wikipedia.org/wiki/Center_Parcs_UK_and_Ireland. Accessed on September 4, 2020.
[2]The campaign was designed by VMLY&R. Retrieved from https://www.vmlyr.com/en-gb/united-kingdom/work/family. Accessed on September 4, 2020.
[3]Hall and Holdsworth (2016, pp. 284–302).

The Social Life of Busyness, 113–132
Copyright © 2021 by Clare Holdsworth
Published under exclusive licence by Emerald Publishing Limited
doi:10.1108/978-1-78743-698-520211007

father or sibling. These roles require time and space away from everyday domestic routines to be enacted and to enrich the potential of doing family together.

These short advertising films capture a popular lament of contemporary busyness – that it gets in the way of family life. The messy, chaotic character of busyness jars with the expectation of balance and the management of responsibilities in discrete times and spaces. In this chapter on family time, I consider how the ideal of balance is narrated in accounts of family time. I am less interested in considering how balance can be achieved against the pull of busyness but rather in examining how the ideal of balance versus busyness frames both the families we live by and the families we live with. The chapter begins with a review of the principles of work–life balance (WLB) and empirically investigates this using the UK Timescapes Work and Family Lives study.

WLB

The Parson family monologues explicitly refer to the busyness of everyday life impeding doing and being family. The weekend away is an opportunity to rebalance the one-sidedness of everyday life. The films succeed as an advertising campaign by appealing to shared concerns about the imbalance between work and family life. The need to make time for family and establish a balance between (non-)domestic responsibilities drives academic research, self-help books on time management and cultural interpretations of the temporal and popular interest in this topic. The desire to have a better family life through the effective balancing of responsibilities can be seen everywhere, from homilies that decorate the office and/or home[4] to institutional human resources policies and the corporate promotion of 'family-friendly' policies.[5]

Working Balance

This ascendancy of WLB as the main temporal challenge of contemporary working lives is often interpreted as a new area of concern, though this is a misrepresentation. According to Suzan Lewis, Richenda Gambles and Rhona Rapoport,[6] although WLB as a social construct is a product of Western societies in recent decades,[7] the problem of managing paid work alongside other aspects of life is not a recent phenomenon. The question to consider is not whether the ascendancy of WLB is due to long-term temporal change (i.e. we are all busier now); rather, how the metaphor of balance has come to dominate interpretations of time should be examined. Lewis, Gambles and Rapoport[8] explain the dominance of balance

---

[4]Examples of homilies include 'No one ever wished they spent more time at work on their death bed'.
[5]Edwards and Wajcman (2005).
[6]Lewis, Gambles, and Rapoport (2007, pp. 360–373).
[7]Fleetwood (2007, pp. 387–400).
[8]Lewis et al. (2007).

in relation to two factors. The first is the increase in women's paid employment outside the home. As I discussed in Chapter 3, the consistent finding in time use studies confirms that this has not been compensated for by an equal decline in domestic responsibilities, and women are more likely to report multitasking than men. Second, as the case studies of work-related busyness explored, political and social endorsements of the delegation of responsibility from the institution to the individual emphasise an expectation that people should work out their own solutions, albeit within a broader institutional framework of flexible working. This type of delegation of individual responsibility assumes that people have an infinite capacity to respond to multiple requests. Flexible working is endorsed as the preferred solution to negotiating competing work and domestic responsibilities. Flexibility overhauls assumptions about the physical demarcation between work space and domestic space.[9] This process of spatial compression is facilitated by technology and the ongoing creation of social norms regarding using technology to 'work' in different spaces.[10] In this way, WLB and flexibility are made possible by the social disembedding of relations from local contexts.[11] This trend has clearly been accelerated during Covid-19 lockdowns, and the sudden switch to home working has been facilitated by technologies and norms that were already being established.

This ascendancy of WLB needs qualification. Balance has come to the fore because of changes in women's lives, though Sally Alexander's observation of the dominance of middle class experiences in her history of women's work is relevant here.[12] Statements and statistics about increases in women's employment outside the home in the latter half of the twentieth century capture what has happened to middle class women in professional occupations. This middle class bias reflects the interests and experiences of those writing this history. I discussed in Chapter 3 how Schulte neatly captures this in her description of attending the 2010 International Association for Time Use and encountering busy, frantic female researchers obsessed with temporal overload.[13] As Tracey Warren has argued, for working class women, the balance of family life revolves as much around economic challenges as temporal ones.[14] It is not having enough money that causes more anxiety and hardship. And securing sufficient financial resources is a time-consuming business, from the temporal demands of having to claim state benefits to working multiple insecure jobs and accessing networks of material and emotional support.[15] Despite this observation, the assumption that the overwhelming problem facing workers in the twenty-first century is that they have too much

---

[9]Gregg (2011).

[10]Wajcman (2015).

[11]Tietze and Musson (2002).

[12]Alexander (1983).

[13]Schulte (2014).

[14]Warren (2015, pp. 691–717).

[15]For empirical studies of the temporalities of poverty/austerity in two very different time periods, see Hall (2019) and Sarsby (1988).

work rather than too little frames both research and policy. Yet, particularly since the global economic crisis of 2008, the challenges of economic precarity cannot be ignored.[16] Moreover, evidence about the impact of Covid-19 lockdowns confirms that women are experiencing more extreme economic hardship than men.[17]

The everyday realities of juggling money rather than time are not only unevenly distributed by social class; they are also embedded in place.[18] Precarity is more than being on the wrong side of the forces of acceleration and the disembedding of social relations; it engenders very different experiences of time and space that are assumed in broader narratives of social and economic change. Warren's conclusion is that the concept of WLB does not need to be dropped as much as reworked to be more inclusive of economic well-being. The drawback here is that slackening the conceptual tightness of WLB so that it is not just about time may make it less useful as a concept that can tie together both empirical research and employment policy.

Family Balance

If WLB fails to grasp inequalities concerning what is happening at work, it is equally blinkered when it comes to family and intimacy. This is precisely because it is premised on the assumption that employment-related and domestic activities are separated, albeit a separation that has blurred in recent years. WLB is written about from the perspective of work, even if the point is to make the case that there is more to life than work.[19] WLB research and policy starts by asking questions about working time and extrapolating this to family life.[20] Family is a destination, a black box that people return to when the working day is done. As I discussed in Chapter 4, this assumption is repeated in self-help literature, particularly books authored by men. For example, McKeown's statement that one of the main benefits of adopting his essentialist approach to life is having more time to go trampolining with his children,[21] and Babauta's achievement after embracing *The Power of Less* is 'raising and making time for six beautiful kids'.[22] However, dissatisfaction with WLB does not just stem from what happens at work. To return to the Parson family, their monologues about everyday life are equally about dissatisfaction with work and the exhaustion of everyday family life that is not simply experienced through fun activities and affirmative relationships.

In academic literature, the distribution of labour is often between scholars who write about work and those who focus on family life. Starting from a space between work and family receives less attention and is empirically more challenging to capture. There are, though, important exceptions. Bissell's empirically

---

[16]Standing (2011).
[17]World Economic Forum (2020).
[18] Hall (2019).
[19]Lewis et al. (2007).
[20]Dex and Bond (2005, pp. 627–637).
[21]McKeown (2014).
[22]Babauta (2009, p. xi).

rich study of long-distance commuting in Sydney, Australia, conceptualises commuting as a thread that ties the interplay of work and intimacy.[23] From a simple WLB perspective, commuting gets in the way. If the aim of a balanced life is to maximise work productivity and time with family, commuting is an unnecessary distraction. We saw in the analysis of time points in the MOA diaries in Chapter 3 that the morning rush is a pinch point for temporal intensity. Bissell, however, develops geographers' interest in the emotions and rhythms of mobility and in encounters with it to move on from treating commuting as a simple act of getting from A to B.[24] For Bissell, commuting is not necessarily efficient or a daily trial to be endured but a necessary thread of everyday life that simultaneously ties and separates work and family. Rather than being rendered obsolete by Covid-19 lockdowns, this observation about the significance of commuting is reinforced through debates about the need to rethink this practice in a post-pandemic society rather than doing away with it altogether.[25] My point here is that while commuting is clearly a specific spatial manifestation linking work and home, the ambiguity that emerges from treating it as more than a simple transport issue concerning getting to work gets at the essential and broader concerns of family time.

Family Practices

Rather than treating family as a destination and boxing family life into an unexamined space, the concept of WLB could be extended to resonate with family practices literature. This approach interprets family activities not simply as stuff that families do but as embodied, emotional and normative practices.[26] Family practices are not neutral; they engender affect, for example, feeling harried[27] or exhausted.[28] These practices also co-constitute moral identities, such as whether the distribution of activities is fair and whether family members are pulling their weight. In this way, family is co-constituted through practices because these involve doing things together and in doing so frame the quality and moral evaluations of relationships. As earlier research on British families by Janet Finch and Jennifer Mason established, family responsibilities are not given, that is, individuals do not simply fulfil family roles as defined by genealogical positions (i.e. being a mother, father, son, daughter, grandparent, etc.).[29] Rather, responsibilities are conditional and moral positions within family are developed through these negotiations. Personal life is, as Carol Smart writes, embedded in diverse links and bonds with family members, friends and neighbourhoods that can be supportive[30]

---

[23]Bissell (2018).
[24]See, for example, Cresswell (2006).
[25]See, for example, Sohn (2020).
[26]Morgan (2011) and Smart (2007).
[27]Southerton (2020).
[28]Straughan, Bissell, and Gorman-Murray (2020, 201–216).
[29]Finch and Mason (1993).
[30]Jarvis (1999, pp. 225–247).

or restrictive in equal measure.[31] Assuming the ascendancy of the disembedding of social relations is counter to the tenacity of these links. Family does not simply exist as a self-contained vessel that can be segregated from broader social relations, such as those formed through work and in communities.

Thus, WLB applies equally to what happens within families as well as to what is done to families. The busyness of family life, as the Parson family monologues exemplify, is about the interactions and emotions of family practices just as much as about the bleeding of external responsibilities into the domestic sphere. If there is a value to examining the balance of the temporality of family life, it might exist in examining how balance is used to frame the negotiations of family practices and responsibilities rather than in detailing how balance can be achieved. In other words, it is more germane to consider how the ideal of balance is used as a narrative tool to make sense of the complexity of everyday practices and to reveal its pinch points and related frustrations concerning time, financial and spatial resources.

Work and Family Lives

My analysis of busyness and family time investigates the dynamic synthesis of time and responsibilities rather than identifying solutions for achieving WLB. I am particularly interested in the interplay between work and time and the sentiments that family life needs to be organised to make work life possible and that, equally, work needs to be organised to maximise the potential for family life. To investigate this further, I searched for secondary qualitative data on the topic of family time. In keeping with my methodological ethics, which involve, ideally, not taking up the time of other people to study busyness, I required data to repurpose instead of gathering new data.

Study Design

The Work and Family Lives data set from the Economic and Social Research Council's Timescapes archive in the UK fits this purpose.[32] These data were

---

[31]Diane Leonard's pioneering study of courtship and marriage in South Wales describes how mothers could adopt strategies to 'spoil and keep close' to limit the aspirations of older children to move on: Leonard (1980).

[32]This data set is designed to interrogate the interplay between family and work time; it is restrictive in its definition of family: parent(s) with dependent children. While most of the literature and popular assumptions about WLB assume that this is a concern for parents with young children, it is not only parents who have commitments beyond work. However, in the limited space, I have to discuss the dynamics of family time, I do not consider the dynamics of work/commitment configurations over the life-course. My intention is not to investigate the reality of family time, but its interpretation and the generic themes that are narrated in accounts of family and work may be relevant to other intimate configurations. That is, individuals with caring responsibilities for elderly parents or adult children are faced with similar concerns about resolving caring responsibilities to make life possible, though the details of the spatial and temporal requirements of care will be different for different people.

deposited by researchers from the Centre for Research on Families and Relationships at the University of Edinburgh.[33] The data set comprises interviews with 13 families living in southern Scotland and the data were collected in three waves from 2007 to 2010.[34] Family members were interviewed separately at waves one and three, with a joint family interview at wave two. Not all family members participated in the interviews, but mothers from all families took part. Interviews were carried out with six partnered (married or cohabiting) and five non-partnered (single, divorced or separated) mothers. None of the interviewees were or had been in same-sex relationships. Of the seven present fathers, five took part in the study. All mothers worked (seven full-time and six part-time). Of the five fathers interviewed, two worked full-time, one part-time and two were retired (early and medical retirement). Children from eleven of the families took part, though the child interviews were not carried out with all of the children who were talked about in the interviews. Some were too young, some lived away and some did not want to participate. All respondents were interviewed at wave one and three, and eight families were interviewed collectively at wave two.

Analysis Strategy

The Work and Family Lives project was designed to follow the families over time to reveal how they adapted to changes associated with the granular detail of life-course events as well as more definitive and celebrated transitions (such as leaving home, moving in together). In wave one of the study, family members who took part were interviewed separately. Interviews had a semi-structured format. For example, each interview with a parent starts with the same question: what is it like being a mother/father? The interviewer has certain topics to cover in each interview and she explores how family relationships and practices are co-constituted through the ebb and flow of childcare, parental employment, family health and leisure activities. Although I do not have the interview template that was used, it is possible to follow the general themes as these are repeated throughout the interviews. Wave two comprises family interviews with participants who took part in wave one. These family interviews included activities to facilitate family discussions. I find these interviews difficult to analyse; my interpretation after reading them is that they contain a lot of shouting and people talking over each other. What these interviews do capture is the noisy temporality of family life. In other words, they give an insight into family time rather than how family members talk about time. The final interviews provided an opportunity to explore changes that had happened since wave one. Some of these are fascinating, such as the story

---

[33]Cunningham-Burley, Jamieson, and Harden (2011).
[34]Fourteen families took part in the project. The Timescapes archive available for secondary analysis comprises interviews relating to 13 families. The archive is also missing one father interview. My classification of mothers' partnership status is based on the presence of a partner, not marital status. One of the lone parents is married (separated from her husband).

of a father who had set himself up as a self-employed consultant at the time of wave one. The subsequent interviews follow how his hopes and financial position changed over the three years (he had to keep postponing his ambition to pay himself a salary). I wanted to know whether he stuck at trying to make the business work or whether he gave up and looked for a salaried position, though this was not resolved by wave three. What is more accessible in the wave three interviews is how these carry forward the stories from wave one, thus, revealing the intransience and stubbornness of family life. It is the repetition of the narratives in waves one and three that are as revealing as any accounts of change.

One of the advantages of repurposing data is that it can bring new insight to primary data through engaging with how the data were originally collected.[35] The difference between repurposing the family and working time data and using the Mass Observation Archive diaries is that other than the topic of time pressure, there is very little external direction of the diaries. MOA correspondents could choose to answer the directive as requested or write a diary with no reference to the detailed questions suggested by the archive. In the Work and Family Lives survey, the interchange between etic (external or interviewer-led) and emic (internal or family-led) themes during the interview is discernible, though what is more interesting is how the narratives of family life are co-produced by the researcher and the participant over and above the specific detail that is being asked about. For example, a particular question from the interviewer can influence the orientation of the interview. I, therefore, needed to adapt an analysis strategy that is not polarised between etic and emic themes. Rather than distinguishing between external and internal themes, I have adapted Gillis's differentiation between the family we live by (the family that does the symbolic work that represent us as the people we like to think we are) and that which we live with (the more self-interested and often disruptive family that is fragmented and indeterminate).[36] The analysis distinguishes between the accounts of family time that accord with the symbolic family lived by and the everyday family that participants live with.

Families We Live By

The symbolic family that participants live by is balanced. All parental interviews in wave one begin with the question 'What is it like being a mother/father?'. Not surprisingly, the unanimous response is both affirmative and heroic: parenting is the most rewarding experience but is concurrently challenging and/or frustrating. These responses are to be expected. It is reasonable to assume that voluntary participants in a project on work and family time will express positive emotions about parenting. However, these benefits have to be set against the difficulty of getting parenting right. Starting with this generalised question implicitly invites parents to reflect on the competing demands and conflicting emotions of family life. The sovereignty of balance is assumed by both interviewer and interviewee.

---

[35]Tarrant and Hughes (2020, pp. 101–118).
[36]Gillis (1997).

Moreover, the very act of sitting down and talking with parents provides the opportunity to articulate balance as the resolution of responsibilities rather than an active state.[37] Balancing caring and employment responsibilities is not something that can achieved in the present as this would require continual streaming of competing activities.[38] The ideal of WLB is not to perform simultaneous activities but to ensure evenness and equality through the sequencing of activities. Thus, achieving balance is realised through the synthesis of the present into the past or future. WLB is a retrospective and/or hopeful judgement that defines the families that are lived by.

In and Out of Balance

Parental narratives of balance ebb and flow rhythmically through the interviews; narratives capture balance, but then it falls away again. The following extract from Gillian's interview begins with an affirmation of balance. Gillian can achieve balance because of supportive neighbours and employers and her avowal not to cross the temporal and spatial boundaries of work and home. She has used these networks to achieve balance. But then her doubts creep in. Her conviction that she does not bring work home from the office falters as she acknowledges her need to get on with things and leave her son to watch TV. Gillian's guilt about 'abandoning' her son is reconciled with the hopeful future promise of card games:

> Not really, I think probably because I actually enjoy my work as well will probably help, I mean, I think if I didn't enjoy my work, I would maybe wish that I could do less hours or for the same money or, things like that, you know, where people tend to work because they have to well, I mean, I know I have to work but to actually have a job that you enjoy doing and my employer is pretty good as well, not only support wise but, you know, I'm on flexi time so I can do a half hour lunch and come home early or, you know, if he's away, because sometimes my friend'll pick him up and say right well I'm taking him tonight so I'll maybe work on a couple of hours so, actually all in all I've probably got quite a good balance, I try not to bring work home, sometimes it's inevitable, you know, if I'm particularly busy or I've had to leave to go and pick my son up and I've not managed to get something finished, that I know has to be finished, I can actually come home and I've got a computer upstairs which actually links in to my office, so I can go straight in through the connection onto my office PC and actually

---

[37]The interviews implicitly confirm the unanimous verdict of time use gurus and researchers that multitasking is best avoided.

[38]Laura Vanderkam's writing is particularly insightful about the limits of multitasking: when it is unavoidable (such as taking children along on activities that do not directly concern them) and how outsourcing (such as hiring a sitter) can be used to limit it.

work as if I was in the office and get access to all the files, I try not to do that too often to be honest, but it's just, you know, general coming back, you know, you've got washing to do and sometimes I think well I'm just kind of leaving my son to watch the telly or to do his homework himself because I've got to do the other things, you know, tomorrow is bucket[39] day, so while the tea was on I was going around the house emptying all the buckets tonight and he was just sitting watching telly and sometimes you think ... not that you're abandoning them but, you know, you feel that you could probably do something else during that time, but the buckets aren't going to empty themselves, you know. So it's just, you have to balance it all out, you know, obviously homework's a priority, sometimes we'll sit and play cards or, you know, we like doing this Sudoku and stuff so, we sit and do them or... (*Gillian Nicholson, non-partnered mother, works full-time*)[40]

Guilt and Exhaustion

Gillian's journey from the certainty of being in balance to the guilt of abandonment illustrates the illusiveness of WLB. Her reflections on being in balance segue into the unevenness of family life and the rhythm of balance gives way to the arhythmical sensation of instability. While most narratives do come back to the achievement of balance and unevenness is not a final outcome; the judgement about whether parents get it 'right' can never be absolute or affirmative. This lack of certainty about balance engenders expressions of guilt.[41] Parental guilt associated with imbalance is omnipresent in the interviews alongside the expectation of being in balance:

> I do love being a parent, but I do quite often feel guilty about not spending enough time, not doing enough with him. (*Debra Grieve, partnered mother, works full-time*)[42]

> But I do still sometimes feel guilty that I don't have the time that I would like to have with him. (*Sally Shaw, partnered mother, works full-time*)[43]

---

[39]Buckets are household bins.

[40]The Timescapes Archive. (2020). Work and family lives: Gillian Nicholson – wave one 2008. Leeds: University of Leeds and Timescapes.

[41]Parental guilt can be associated with adherence to expectations of 'good enough' parenting; it is not simply an internal response but is also influenced by political, institutional and cultural discourses and practices. See, for example, Collins (2020), Lawler (2000), Sullivan (2015, pp. 284–298) and Sutherland (2010, pp. 310–321).

[42]The Timescapes Archive. (2020). Work and family lives: Debra Grieve – wave one 2008. Leeds: University of Leeds and Timescapes.

[43]The Timescapes Archive. (2020). Work and family lives: Sally Shaw – wave one 2007. Leeds: University of Leeds and Timescapes.

So you have an awful lot of guilt that there's a whole day passed that you're not with your children. (*Nicci Rankin, non-partnered mother, works part-time*)[44]

So you do feel quite guilty about saying, you know, this week I've got to do something this weekend. (*Graham Reid, partnered father, works part-time*)[45]

Guilt about not being in balance is checked by two observations, though. The first, which is Gillian's starting point in the previous extract, is that work is just as important as fulfilling family responsibilities. Work is both a financial and a moral necessity, and trying to meet both work- and family-related responsibilities is beneficial for individuals' well-being:

So, I do like the social interaction at work, the challenge of being at work, cos you get to use your brain a lot more at work than possibly you do at home. (*Emma Philipps, non-partnered mother, works full-time*)[46]

On the plus side it's sometimes quite nice to go to work. You can get away from it all and just be able to have an adult conversation and do something for yourself, so it's a two-way kind of a ... I don't know. It's difficult sometimes. (*Jan Ritchie, partnered mother, works part-time*)[47]

A second qualification of the necessity of balance is recognising that it is simply not possible to tie everything down in reticular family relationships. The conditional and endless nature of personal life require letting some things go and submitting to the discord of the families we live by. Debra, for example, reflects on how she strives to be in control while recognising that this can never be achieved, and she has to give up on the ideal of fine-tuning her family life:

Absolutely. It's a pressure. It's a pressure, I don't [pause]. I don't like it because I, because I – I mean I am a self-confessed, bit of a control freak. And I hate it because I don't feel like anything's in control. I don't feel like my life's in control. I feel like I'm in control of my life to a degree, but you can't be totally in control of

---

[44]The Timescapes Archive. (2020). Work and family lives: Nicci Rankin – wave one 2009. Leeds: University of Leeds and Timescapes.
[45]The Timescapes Archive. (2020). Work and family lives: Graham Reid – wave one 2008. Leeds: University of Leeds and Timescapes.
[46]The Timescapes Archive. (2020). Work and family lives: Emma Philipps – wave one 2008. Leeds: University of Leeds and Timescapes.
[47]The Timescapes Archive. (2020). Work and family lives: Jan Ritchie – wave one 2008. Leeds: University of Leeds and Timescapes.

your life when you live in a family. Because you've got, you've got to consider everyone within the family. (*Debra Grieve, partnered mother, works full-time*)[48]

While Debra recognises that she cannot perfectly orchestrate family routines and practices, her inability to be in balance is exhausting:

It's emotionally draining, it's not just the going out and working it's the worrying and the guilt and the lack of sleep. (*Debra Grieve, partnered mother, works full-time*)[49]

Feeling exhausted is not just associated with the rush of getting things done but also with not achieving balance, or not doing things. Parents invest emotional work in trying to be in balance. Feeling guilty about not doing enough (at work, at home or both) is draining. Exhaustion cannot simply be attributed to the volume of work (however, defined) that has to be done. It is equally associated with the inability to complete everything and a sense of failure because of not being in balance. The balanced family that parents live by is a heroic aspiration that generates feelings of guilt and exhaustion rather than simply a given. It is always just out of reach.

Balance in Retrospect

Pivoting between balance and guilt can be resolved retrospectively. Looking back, parents can summarise the family they live by as having been formed serendipitously, not strategically and purposefully. Being able to meet responsibilities is attributed to good fortune:

Obviously if I got paid a bit more I wouldn't maybe have to work such long hours. I think I'm fortunate in my job that, you know, it is flexible. If I work in an evening then I have these hours to take off at another time. (*Julia Fisher, partnered mother, works part-time*)[50]

[W]hen I've been phoned to come in to school and because of the way I work and because of my role at work I can just say 'I'm going', you know, that's it and again I know that's really privileged because I can do that and so I do feel very fortunate that

[48]The Timescapes Archive. (2020) Work and family lives: Debra Grieve – wave one 2008. Leeds: University of Leeds and Timescapes.

[49]The Timescapes Archive. (2020). Work and family lives: Debra Grieve – wave one 2008. Leeds: University of Leeds and Timescapes.

[50]The Timescapes Archive. (2020). Work and family lives: Julia Fisher – wave one 2008. Leeds: University of Leeds and Timescapes.

I can although I'm, I don't know, maybe I'm just bloody minded but I could imagine for some people who don't have that sort of security or aren't high enough up a ladder at work, you can't just say 'well I'm going, my child's not well', you know, they'd have to phone around, they'd have to get relatives whereas, you know, I can just say 'I'm sorry, you know, that's it'. (*Sheila Watson, partnered mother, works part-time*)[51]

A serendipitous sense of balance is also realised through comparisons with generalised, less fortunate others. If parents feel they are getting it right, more or less, they are conscious of how easy this could fall apart and reason about this through the assumed difficulties that other families face. The good fortune of achieving WLB can suddenly change. Associating balance with luck also reduces the need to acknowledge structural factors and downplays the significance of social identities of class, ethnicity, gender and sexuality in achieving WLB.

Families We Live With

Parental accounts in the data set of the families we live by oscillate around the impossibility of not being in balance and the guilt of not spending more time at home. Their accounts of the families we live with reverse this direction of flow, or at least correct the assumption that the quest for balance can only be sought by focussing on the organisation of non-domestic tasks. In the family we live by, work needs to be organised to make family life possible; in the family we live with, family life needs to be organised to make work possible. It is not only work that bleeds into family time; personal issues are also taken to work.[52]

Family Time

The family interviews carried out in wave two give an insight into family time. The transcripts of these interviews reveal that everyone talks in short bursts, though occasionally a parent may dominate the conversation. These interviews capture the chaotic time of family and the tensions created by responding to multiple familial requests and responsibilities rather than the detail of what is talked about. For example, the Christie family comprise parents Fiona and John and their three daughters, and the following extract details their response to being asked to talk about what they did the previous weekend.

---

[51]The Timescapes Archive. (2020). Work and family lives: Sheila Watson – wave one 2007. Leeds: University of Leeds and Timescapes.
[52]Emily Rose's research on personal communications at work identifies the benefits of these communications but also employees' strategies to control these and manage the boundaries between work and home: Rose (2013, pp. 694–710).

Daughter 1:   What did we do?

Interviewer: Last weekend.

Fiona: Well you had your choir concert.

Daughter 1:   Oh yeah I had my concert on Sunday. I've had three
                concerts in the last, Sunday, Monday and Tuesday, so.

Daughter 2:   I had swimming.

Fiona: That's right.

Interviewer: Oh right that's quite busy.

Daughter 1:   Yeah.

Fiona: The choir concert was great wasn't it? It was really
                good.

Daughter 3:   I didn't really do anything.

John: And you had your march for nativity during the
                week, I don't know if that's included for last weekend.

Fiona: That was last, it was the weekend, yeah.

Daughter 1:   I know, but.

Fiona: I had a night out with the girls from the street.

Interviewer: Oh right.

Fiona: And... yeah so that was a good night. Not a good
                Sunday but [Laughs].

Daughter 2:   We went shopping didn't we?

Fiona: Went shopping in [nearby city]. So that was good, we
                enjoyed that and went and had hot chocolate and...

Interviewer: Was that on the Saturday?

Fiona: Yeah aha. So that was fun.

Daughter 1:   What was the best and worst things about it?

John: We went to the pictures.[53]

Fiona is the main narrator in the interview (supported by John), and it is reasonable to assume that her direction of the interview reflects her organisation of family time, including time for herself. Fiona's balancing of responsibilities

[53]The Timescapes Archive. (2020) Work and family lives: Christie family – wave two 2008. Leeds: University of Leeds and Timescapes.

is not simply about managing work and family time – we can see how it imbues the smaller details of everyday life and her assertion that these smaller details are important as they are 'good' activities to do.

Routines

Not surprisingly, the busiest times of day in the family we live with are morning and evening routines:

> Probably all this juggling. We stick to a very strict routine in the mornings, cos we have to leave here by eight. So we leave here at eight, I abandon them at half past eight in the morning at school ... [laugh]. (*Emma Philipps, non-partnered mother, works full-time*)[54]

> In the morning, I take Calum so far and then he walks the rest of the way. And then I have to drive round and either park and then walk Anna round to school or if I can, get into the ... she's got a sort of drop-off area in front of her school, so if I can drop her off there. And that takes me up to about quarter to 9, and then I drive on and I'm there for about 20 past usually .... And it's the same at the other end. I finish at quarter past 5, and then I get home and pick up the kids. Well it used to be from an after school club but I've now got somebody coming to the house after school, so how that will work I'm not quite sure, so hopefully it should make things a little bit easier. When I come in they will have done their homework. (*Jan Ritchie, partnered mother, works part-time*)[55]

These parental interviews confirm what we have already encountered in the analysis of clock time in the MOA diaries, which is that the organisation of family life at the beginning and end of the work day requires careful attention to clock time. The orchestration of different schedules intensifies the busyness of these daily routines.[56]

Accounts of leaving and returning home resonate in the families that we live with. These are not just a matter of internal family organisation. The need to be on time is driven by external timetables.[57] Staying on time can be calibrated through observations of other people's routines. Neighbours leave the house at similar times, and these observations coordinate routine in addition to deference to clock time:

---

[54]The Timescapes Archive. (2020). Work and family lives: Emma Phillips – wave one 2008. Leeds: University of Leeds and Timescapes.

[55]The Timescapes Archive. (2020). Work and family lives: Jan Ritchie – wave one 2008. Leeds: University of Leeds and Timescapes.

[56]For an empirical account of juggling activities at the beginning and the end of the day, see Thompson (1996, pp. 388–407).

[57]Schwanen (2006).

Half past eight's usually the set time for going out the door. We've got a neighbour over the way and she's always leaving in the car at half past eight so we're meeting, waving as I'm walking down and she's leaving to go to a different school. (*John Christie, partnered father, retired*)[58]

Notions of being on time are necessarily collective. People can only be late for someone else or something (e.g. a train journey). Temporal routines and the rhythms of the family we live with are not just contained within the domestic sphere; they are coordinated across different spaces and are simultaneously internal and external.[59]

Moral Positions

Routines co-constitute family identities and moral positions. Some children, for example, are quite compliant, but others require more encouragement to get ready and do what is required, such as getting ready to go to school in the morning or doing homework in the afternoon. The following extract from Archie Ritchie's interview captures the unexceptional detail of family routines and how this repetition consolidates moral identities within the family and notions of being good or not good:

What time did we get up yesterday? Jan got up first, yeah, so that was a bad thing for a start [laughs]. She got up at about ten past and I got up at about twenty past and I just got up and I can't remember what happened yesterday morning apart from the fact that I got Anna dressed because I've started to dress her in a morning because she's so bloody slow at getting everything done. And she's like me, I was exactly like that, I used to fall asleep in front of the fire in the morning I was so bad, I actually started going to bed … it was like I used to go to bed in my school clothes. I used to put my pyjamas on over my school clothes so I could stay in bed longer in the morning so she's kind of like that. But Jan's not like that at all and she gets really frustrated by Anna being like that so I've started to help her in the morning to try and get her up. Calum's great he just jumps out and puts his things on and heads downstairs and switches the telly on or whatever. So that's the way it happened and I ended up doing less work yesterday morning than I would have done normally because I was up the rest of the week. I was up first and I had the shower and I get Anna up and get Calum up and then do

---

[58]The Timescapes Archive. (2020). Work and family lives: John Christie – wave one 2008. Leeds: University of Leeds and Timescapes.
[59]Elaine Stratford's work on rhythmic geographies explores the micropolitics of everyday mobilities and how rhythms segue between biological, psychological and social realms. Stratford (2015).

Daniel and give him his breakfast. So whatever she told you is lies! But yesterday I was not as on the ball with that, I just got Anna up and I took Calum to school about half eight. But I think Jan was a bit peeved off with me because I hadn't got up and done as much as I might do so she got me to get Daniel into his snow-suit and then his wee jacket and I was getting a bit humpy about it because I had to get off but you know I could tell she was annoyed with me and I thought, ah sod you but … so that's what happened from that point of view. (*Archie Ritchie, partnered father, works full-time*)[60]

Routines are not just about getting everyone out of the house; they are constitutive of family relationships and responsibilities. Archie and Jan acknowledge the difference in the behaviours of their two older children and share responsibilities according to their tolerance of each child's behaviour. Their account illustrates how temporal morality is a component of family practices and that routines do not just coordinate bodies in time and space, they also interweave with moral identities and individual orientation towards the coordination of time-space. Some people are on time, others are always in a rush. These identities are not fixed. Some children, such as Charlotte, experience morning routines in two houses, her father's and her mother's. Charlotte has to get used to being late with her father and on time with her mum:

Charlotte: And at our dad's house, we're just late. So we have to rush in, so we walk all the round to the top end, it's closed and we have to walk all the way right round to the office. But at our mum's house, we just run up and then we shall either go in or play.

Interviewer: Mm-hm. And what do you prefer? Do you prefer being there early or being late?

Charlotte: I prefer being early 'cause you can chill out a little bit wi' your friends before you have to walk in. (*Charlotte Phillips, age 9 at time of interview*)[61]

Space

Children are perceptive about before- and after-school routines. I discern a difference in how children frame routines compared to their parents. Children's accounts provide more spatial detail of the orchestration of family life, as opposed to the times at which things happen. This does not mean that children are unobservant

---

[60]The Timescapes Archive. (2020). Work and family lives: Archie Ritchie – wave one 2008. Leeds: University of Leeds and Timescapes.
[61]The Timescapes Archive. (2020) Work and family lives: Charlotte Phillips – wave one 2008. Leeds: University of Leeds and Timescapes.

of time, for example, they might note the time they get up each morning – or are expected to get up. However, their orientation towards routine is articulated more through the spatial sequencing of events, as Jack describes regarding his Tuesday evening routine:

> Well the busiest day we ever have in the week is a Tuesday. Even though my mum's not working, we've got three things on during the day, no two things on in the day, no yeah three. My sister's got two things on the same day, it's Yogabugs,[62] it's an after school club, then Rainbows.[63] And after Yogabugs she has to rush straight to Rainbows and I have to go straight to choir but they start the same time so my mum's got somebody called Emma and we pick up, she picks up Katie, her name's Katie, that's Emma's daughter and we take her to choir, then my mum takes Evie, rushes to Rainbows and then somebody called Anna Fergus who's in my class, her mother takes Evie back home to us. (*Jack Erskine, age 8 at time of interview*)[64]

There is less detail in children's account of morning routines, as less stuff happens (children get up, get dressed, have breakfast, leave the house). They are alert to parental expectations of timeliness and the order of things, though:

> What happens is a big rush. It's like, 'Have you packed you school bag?' 'Yep'. 'Get your jacket on'. 'Okay'. 'Get your shoes on', but usually a lot quicker. In fact Charlotte's usually slow at that. And we have to feed the rabbits. (*Hannah Phillips, age 10 at time of interview*)[65]

Refreshing Habits

Routines define the family we live with, but they require refreshing. Habits are not simply taken-for-granted behaviours as constant disruption to this 'taken-for-granted' world requires ongoing adaptation and reform of habits.[66] Predictable sequencing of activities (even if not done on time) can stymie family relationships. If there is no friction in routine, the boredom of repetition is tedious and exhausting:

> A lot of domestic drudge, it just becomes monotonous. There's only so many times you can clean the kitchen floor of spaghetti bolognese or – you know, it's just routine, routine, routine. And

---

[62]Children's yoga classes.

[63]Rainbows is the programme for the youngest age group of the Girlguiding organisation in the UK.

[64]The Timescapes Archive. (2020). Work and family lives: Jack Erskine – wave one 2008. Leeds: University of Leeds and Timescapes.

[65]The Timescapes Archive. (2020). Work and family lives: Hannah Phillips – wave one 2008. Leeds: University of Leeds and Timescapes.

[66]Crossley (2013, pp. 136-161).

sometimes I can get a bit lost in the routine and forget to feel – that maybe I'm too busy with the routine sometimes to – maybe I miss some of the mummy moments, I think. (*Rachel Erskine, non-partnered mother, works part-time*)[67]

Rachel's solution to the monotony of domestic routine is to introduce a new 'fun' routine:

And I just was so aware I was getting so drawn into the downward spiral. And I could see them just – they sort of – not cowered when I came in the room, but there was a kind of concerned look on their faces, like, 'What's she wanting now? What's she going to shout about now or…' and so I instigated Friday night disco night. And we had a disco ball and put all the lights out and then everybody got to choose two tracks of their own choosing. And we had some very dodgy discos. (*Rachel Erskine, non-partnered mother, works part-time*)[68]

This routine 'guaranteed half hour of fun' was difficult to sustain. Rachel and her children moved to a new house, the disco ball broke, and Friday night disco night became a routine of the past. Her inability to sustain fun became another thing for Rachel to feel guilty about.

Technology

One final observation about the data is the lack of reference to technology; when it is mentioned, it tends to be as an aspect of the background of family practices.[69] For example, television is acknowledged as a means for doing nothing together or as a babysitting device. Technology is discussed when it does not work, such as problems with transport or when domestic appliances break down. For example, Gail Adams gets up early to put her washing on, as her machine is not working properly and the water is flowing down the garden path, not the drain. She does not want her neighbours to see this but cannot afford to get the machine fixed. Domestic technology might save time, but, as in Gail's situation, it is not necessarily used in a time-efficient way. To repeat Wajcman's perspective, social norms are produced through the use of technology; they are not directed by it.[70]

---

[67]The Timescapes Archive. (2020). Work and family lives: Rachel Erskine – wave one 2008. Leeds: University of Leeds and Timescapes.

[68]The Timescapes Archive. (2020) .Work and family lives: Rachel Erskine – wave one 2008. Leeds: University of Leeds and Timescapes.

[69]The data were collected before the mass uptake of smartphones (the first iPhone was released in 2007, the year of the first interviews), and it is reasonable to assume that family use of technology has changed since these data were collected. However, the same observation holds for the MOA diaries, which were written in the smart phone era but also contain relatively few mentions of how technology influences the timing of everyday life.

[70]Wajcman (2015).

Summary

Accounts of acceleration do not for the most part consider if family life has speeded up. There are two reasons for this; first, acceleration is assumed to be a sociocultural process rooted in economic, political and technological domains; second, these accounts prioritise the individual over relational contexts. A popular extrapolation of this interpretation of the social locations of acceleration is that family provides respite from speed and a space where accelerated domains can be held in check. This dichotomous interpretation is not validated in sociological and geographical studies of family and work practices that emphasise the erosion of physical demarcations between work and domestic spaces. Following the principles of WLB, this dissolution has for the most part been considered in the direction from work to family and the need to keep work in check. However, as endorsed by Center Parc's snapshots of the Parson family, achieving a balance between work and family is multidirectional; work bleeds into intimate life and vice versa. Moreover, balance is not just a function of time; it applies equally to economic resources and the necessary interlinkages between time and money in family life.

In this analysis of family time, balance is a guiding narrative principle, one that is used to make sense of the families we live by. These narratives are not stories with definitive beginnings, ends and consistent threads; they recall memories and recast them into the present and future. Balance is not a present state; instead, it justifies the past and moves people forward into the future with the possibility that they can achieve equilibrium while they negotiate competing responsibilities. The narrative of balance allows for inconsistencies, failures and disappointments. If something is not right at one point in time, it can be compensated for in other ways, such as having Friday night disco nights to make up for everyday drudgery and tensions. In the families we live with, busyness can be orchestrated and anticipated and becomes ordinary and mundane, including the repetition of elements such as morning routines, domestic chores and ongoing practices of care. Everyone has their role to play in moving towards a balanced family life, and different positions can consolidate family responsibilities and identities, such as the child or parent who is 'good' at getting up in the morning and not making everyone else late. Narratives of balance are also made possible by embedded relations with family members and the wider community – these groups form the support that is drawn upon to make everyday life possible. The busyness of family life is not just about tensions between work and domestic spheres; it is played out in broader social life and consolidates social relations. If balance is a state to move towards or imagine in the past, it revolves around the activity of family practices and the ongoing mental chatter about getting it right. Judgements about work and family time being in or out of balance are not static. They are, to repeat Bissell's definition,[71] thinking habits that enliven the family we live with and bring it closer to the family we would like to live by. In short, family is busyness.

---

[71]Bissell (2011).

Chapter 7

Free Time

24/7: A Wake-up Call for Our Non-stop World

In 2011, the Canadian writer and artist Douglas Copeland initiated a project called *Slogans for the 21st Century*. This project originally comprised 148 slogans printed in bold text on brightly coloured paper. The collection has been exhibited at different locations and Copeland has continued to add news slogans. In 2019, Copeland's work was featured in an exhibition titled *24/7 A Wake-Up Call for Our Non-Stop World* at Somerset House in London,[1] inspired by the book of the same name by the art historian and essayist Jonathan Crary.[2] The narrative of Copeland's art incorporates the premise of Crary's book that late capitalism's obsession with 24-hour consumption and production disrupts and shrinks sleep. In addition, 24-hour production and consumption diminish discretionary control over time and intensify the exhaustion of feeling that there is not enough time. Two slogans adroitly capture these sentiments: 'I Miss Time' and 'I Want my Time Back'. This reading of the demise of me-time brought about through the intensity of commitments, mobility and consumption offers a different perspective on the temporal condition of late modern societies from accounts which identify a lack of connection as the primary cause of contemporary social dysfunction.[3] These interpretations may start from similar positions, especially in their critique of over-reliance on virtual communication, but end up with different remedies: having more time for oneself or engaging in more and diverse connections.

'I want my time back' is a statement that resonates with popular sentiment. The demise of discretionary time is frequently cited as the corrosive pinch point of contemporary busyness. While browsing social media around the themes of time and busyness, I have often encountered declarations that people should be more self-centred about how to spend time, to put themselves first rather than

---

[1]Cook (2019).
[2]Crary (2014).
[3]See, for example, Turkle (2011).

The Social Life of Busyness, 133–150
Copyright © 2021 by Clare Holdsworth
Published under exclusive licence by Emerald Publishing Limited
doi:10.1108/978-1-78743-698-520211010

the demands of others.[4] Defining and capturing me-time is interwoven into the preceding chapters: self-help books offer the search for and capture of me-time as a corrective for time pressure, while narratives of work and family responsibilities reflect how these restrict opportunities to have time for oneself. Lack of free time is not just a personal issue. The liberal theorist Julie Rose argues that a just society must guarantee all citizens their fair share of free time.[5] Michelle Shir-Wise suggests that free time is not 'an empty space to be filled by actors as they wish'; it is shaped by cultural forces that interweave notions of freedom, authenticity and choice.[6]

Academic segregation of labour allocates the analysis of free time to the study of leisure. This literature focusses on structured recreational activities, hobbies, entertainment and tourism.[7] Leisure denotes a particular type of activity rather than its relational or moral status. In this chapter, I do not focus on the concept of leisure as an activity that is distinct from work and family commitments. Instead, I consider the possibility of having free time and its limits as having time for oneself rather than a particular type of activity. For example, in Chapter 3, I discussed the journalist Brigid Schulte's rejection of her weekly yoga session being classified as leisure. She does not view this activity as free time as it is something that she feels she has to do, rather than an affirmative choice. Furthermore, the analysis of family time in the preceding chapter details the busyness of families coordinating children's after-school leisure activities. This dissonance between freedom and leisure is debated by leisure scholars particularly in relation to the commodification of leisure.[8] My starting point is to consider the possibility of having free time rather than how this might be experienced through a specific focus on leisure.

Copeland's slogans are more than end points; they express yearning for what might be possible, and the possibility of me-time is as important as its realisation. In discourses of busyness, me-time is not simply time unfettered by external responsibilities; it is therapeutic time that can mend the strain of everyday time squeeze. The morality of yearning for me-time is that putting oneself first is not a selfish act but a necessary one to resist being overwhelmed by demands on one's time. In this chapter, I consider the challenges involved in expecting free time to deliver time for oneself and the inevitable tensions with responsibilities for other people, as well as the therapeutic benefits associated with free time. To develop this relational and therapeutic interpretation of free time, this chapter begins with an examination of freedom and the positive psychology concept of flow, which is

---

[4]Initially I tried to follow and capture #busy on Twitter, but these data were too general and diverse as #busy is often used to advertise shops and services. For example, restaurants use #busy to encourage customers to book a table (because the restaurant is busy) or to alert customers that tables are available.
[5]Rose (2016).
[6]Shir-Wise (2019a, p. 1669).
[7]See, for example, Roberts (2006) and Rojek (1999).
[8]Carr (2017, pp. 137–151).

associated with therapeutic activities. Empirically, this study of freedom and flow is explored through my own experiences of therapeutic me-time gained through sewing and crochet and teaching these activities to others.

Freedom

Positive Freedom

Defining freedom is a mainstay of Western philosophical debates,[9] and a conventional starting point is Isaiah Berlin's distinction between freedom from (negative) and freedom to (positive).[10] This division considers whether freedom is understood as escaping oppression – the freedom not to live as a slave and to have no coercions or restrictions; or the opportunity to do and be, to have control over one's life and to choose what to do and when to do it. Claims that discretionary time is needed appeal to both interpretations of freedom: freedom from the temporal demands of assemblages of power and technology and the importance of being able to make choices about how to spend time. However, the emphasis on choice concerning how to allocate and spend time that is captured in the sentiment of me-time is particularly central to positive notions of freedom. Positive freedom requires self-determination, that is, the ability for individuals to control their own destiny and interests. If busyness is at the fault lines of competing responsibilities, then it is also a manifestation of the limits of positive freedom: we are too busy doing things for other people rather than for ourselves.

If temporal freedom is an expression of positive freedom, there is a subtle but important distinction to make between having time for leisure so that we can live the good life and having time to do good.[11] Discussions about busyness and the demise of me-time often conflate these two perspectives – that leading the good life is necessary for individual well-being,[12] which in turn is a public good. However, the existence of individual freedom for leisure time is not necessarily a public good. Take, for example, the opportunity to engage in therapeutic tourist experiences. In his book *Time and How to Spend It: The 7 Rules for Richer, Happier Days*,[13] James Wallman promotes the therapeutic benefits of the Japanese practice of shinrin-yoku (forest bathing), which requires spending meditative time in

---

[9]See, for example, Gray (1991).

[10]Berlin (1969/2002).

[11]Rose (2016).

[12]For the purposes of this discussion of free time, I approach well-being as a dynamic and intersubjective entity rather than a thing in itself; it is a structure of feeling that is moved towards rather than an objective state that can be measured; see Ahmed (2010).

[13]Wallman's thesis promotes the benefits of experiences. In the 'experience economy', these are marketed as memorable and personalised activities that are 'rich with sensations, created within the customer': Pine and Gillmore (1999, p. 12). This promotion of marketised experiences does not simply consider the importance of leisure time as distinctive from work time but emphasises the vitalist elements of me-time.

forests for well-being. This practice is particularly associated with the isolated Japanese Island of Yukashima. One-fifth of Yukashima is registered as a World Natural Heritage Site, and its wet climate and geology support a unique ecology that is recognised as particularly meditative. Wallman accedes that forest bathing is a marketing genius as the practice is little more than common sense, albeit one that has been proven to be beneficial in medical research.[14] The point to make about forest bathing is that one person's right to meditate in a forest may impact on others. It is reasonable to assume that the tranquillity of forest bathing relies on solitude, or at least the absence of crowds. Yukashima's unique ecology is not suited to mass tourism. Although the island is isolated and not overrun by visitors, the impact of overcrowding is an important issue in other more accessible therapeutic natural spaces. For example, in the USA, the problem of overcrowding in the National Parks is well documented and the challenge of promoting human access while protecting the natural environment is a key concern in the management of the parks.[15] If too many people choose to participate in forest bathing at the same time and location, what does this mean for the experience of bathers and the impact on the forest? Does some people's freedom to indulge in forest bathing have precedence over that of others, and who decides who gets to take part in these activities?

A simple manifestation of the necessity of free time does not negate our responsibilities to others. It is not a simple question of demarcating time without responsibilities and being cut off from the needs of others. Put another way, positive freedom allows the possibility of self-realisation, but this should not end with the self.[16] While free time might be used to refine what Foucault terms technologies of the self, these techniques are sculptured by and with other people and the same applies to experiences of free time.[17] The duality of this self means that to care for oneself is to simultaneously pay attention to the self and others.

---

[14]There is considerable discussion of the benefits of forest bathing in popular media; see, for example, Fitzgerald (2019).

[15]For a discussion of these challenges of over-tourism in US national parks, see Starr (2019).

[16]In her detailed empirical account of free time, Michelle Shir-Wise (2019b) discusses the ongoing dynamics between free time and the self and presents the 'social self' as a component of this. I suggest that when trying to make sense of busyness and free time, it is necessary to move on from treating the social as a part of the self and to interrogate the ongoing dualism between the self and others.

[17]For example, Foucault adroitly explores the relational qualities of the self in his later writings. He expresses an interest in understanding 'the interaction between oneself and others and in the technologies of individual domination' rather than the technologies of power and dominion, which he was previously preoccupied with; see Foucault (1982). These technologies of the self are 'not something invented by the individual himself [sic]. They are models that he finds in his culture and are proposed, suggested, imposed upon him' quoted in Kelly (2013, p. 517).

Community and Immunity

The conceptual challenge of making sense of free time revolves around the dualism between the self and others, as doing something for oneself does not infer the absence of other interests. I have found the writings of the philosopher Roberto Esposito on the duality between community and immunity a useful thinking device to make sense of the relational qualities of me-time.[18] The usefulness of Esposito's thinking lies in how he holds together the competing pulls of community and immunity. For Esposito, community turns the individual inside out, exposing us to the other. Immunity is the reverse: 'it returns individuals to themselves, encloses them once again in their skin'.[19] Esposito does not interpret community as an entity that is constructed through rights or human action. In other words, although we might talk colloquially about building community – in the sense of an active community as a thing to be built – this is not Esposito's interpretation. Academic studies of community are replete with the values associated with it, but to Esposito community simply is; it is the condition 'of our complete existence'.[20] He maintains that we have always existed in common. His reading of community does not identify it with common belonging but with the idea that members 'are bound instead by the duty of reciprocal gift' or the 'munus'.[21] According to Esposito, community threatens the unity of the individual with this perpetual approach that oscillates around the obligations of the munus. Rather than offering the comfort of belonging, this interpretation of community is threatening because it expresses loss and/or removal. In other words, community threatens the possibility of a stable, unique self.

Esposito's interpretation of community makes analytical sense when conjoined with his interpretation of immunity. Immunisation is a general response to this threat to the individual. It is 'a kind of progressive interiorization of exteriority', a process through which individuals can severe 'all contact with the outside'.[22] This paradigmatic clash between community and immunity is inevitable. He writes:

> If the former [community] binds individuals to something that pushes them beyond themselves, then the latter [immunity] reconstructs their identity by protecting them from a risky contiguity with the other, relieving them of every obligation toward the other and enclosing them once again in the shell of their own subjectivity.[23]

Esposito does not develop these two paradigmatic concepts as abstracts; his argument is that the interplay between community and immunity is not fixed.

---

[18]Esposito's writings about community and immunity are particularly pertinent in the aftermath of the Covid-19 pandemic; see, for example, Wyllie (2020).
[19]Esposito (2013, p. 49).
[20]Esposito (2013, p. 11).
[21]Esposito (2013, p. 49).
[22]Esposito (2013, p. 41).
[23]Esposito (2013, p. 49).

The drive towards immunity will necessarily be held in check. He argues that late modernity is defined by the immunity paradigm that seeks to delimit the self and community and to simultaneously include and exclude. The risk of this direction of social change is that although immunity is necessary, if it is driven too far then we risk losing the meaning of our existence. That is, we may lose touch with the obligation to others – to the exteriority of the self.

The significance of this interpretation of the relationship between the self and community is that it turns the quest for me-time from a statement about temporality in late modernity (and from the assumption that in the past there was more discretionary time) to an expression of the ongoing conflict between the self and others, between immunity and community. Esposito argues that the immunity paradigm dominates late modernity but that it is not a condition that is specific to this time. There is no exact existential threat to me-time compared with the position in other historical periods. My suggestion is that Esposito's interpretation of the tension between immunity and community and how these are played out in favour of immunisation at the expense of community is a useful way of understanding preoccupations with the demise of free time and how it can be reclaimed. This reclaiming would not appear as the manifestation of the self but would take place precisely at the interface between the desire to retreat inwards and the wish to fulfil obligations to others.

Flow

The promise of free time is not simply about the possibility or avoiding responsibilities or the inability to do so; it is also bound up with expectations of well-being and happiness. To return to the example of forest bathing, having the opportunity to spend time in this way is endorsed because of its positive outcomes. Forest bathing is a good, not simply because it prioritises the self but because it is good for the self. An interrogation of free time needs, therefore, to consider its therapeutic potential. Unravelling associations between free time and well-being or happiness is not straightforward, though. In her thoughtful theoretical interrogation of *The Promise of Happiness*, the feminist theorist Sara Ahmed acknowledges the elusive quality of happiness and its potential to be all things to all people.[24] She does, however, identify a useful starting point: happiness is not a destination. Ahmed argues instead that it is the possibility of happiness that resonates with narratives of (un)happiness. The possibility of happiness retains the ideal that it is something that we can move towards rather than a discernible thing that can be acquired and distributed. This is a second problem with the assumption about the benefits of forest bathing; it relies on a teleological logic which says that the outcome of forest bathing defines the activity itself. Put another way, if forest bathing is carried out to enhance well-being, this is not the same as taking time to enjoy being in a forest. If forest bathing is a marketing triumph, this has been achieved through selling its benefits rather than simply via the activity itself.

---

[24]Ahmed (2010).

This subtle but important difference between the relative importance of means and ends can usefully be applied to the therapeutic qualities of me-time.[25] This shift from detailing outcomes to understanding intention and the actuality of experience reveals an important idea that has developed in the field of positive psychology: the concept of flow.

Experience Sample Method

Mihaly Csikszentmihalyi's formative research on flow and his contribution to the field of positive psychology and the study of happiness define how these activities are understood.[26] Csikszentmihalyi's research permeates popular literature, so the benefits of 'flow' are no longer a matter of academic research. The originality of his contribution does not just concern what he learnt about happiness; it is also about how he studied it. Csikszentmihalyi and his colleagues developed an empirical methodology known as the experience sample method.[27] This method is straightforward; it involves providing participants with pagers so that they can be contacted remotely and randomly during the day. When contacted by the pager, participants are asked to complete a self-reported questionnaire about their experience at that moment in time. This relatively straightforward method has a temporal advantage over face-to-face scientific research, as data using the experience sample method are collected in the present rather than retrospectively. Another advantage of this method is that it can be carried out with a large sample of participants to ensure ecological validity of conventional diary approaches, which are, necessarily, carried out with small samples. This method reveals a consistent finding about happiness and the everyday. Times when participants are focussed on a task are when they are more likely to self-report positive emotions. The clarity of Csikszentmihalyi's finding is that the best moments are not times when people are relaxed; they 'usually occur if a person's body or mind is stretched to its limits in a voluntary effort to accomplish something difficult and worthwhile'.[28]

Experiencing Flow

The flow element of a flow activity is not about the activity itself but about how the activity is carried out. Flow activities can be found in listening and playing music or computer games, physical exercise, work, family practices and leisure activities. Anyone can achieve flow, though some people find it easier to grasp than others. Csikszentmihalyi's response to this contemporary problem, that is, people do not necessarily do what is good for them (although are often aware of what this could be), is that there is an internal condition that facilitates flow.

---

[25]I have already discussed non-teleological interpretations of means and ends in relation to the work of John Dewy in chapter four and its relevance to *Getting Things Done*.
[26]Csikszentmihalyi (1990/2008).
[27]Larson and Csikszentmihalyi (2014, pp. 21–34).
[28]Csikszentmihalyi (1990/2008, p. 3).

He describes this condition as the autotelic personality, which he associates with the ability to transform ordinary experiences into flow, a practice he claims that all individuals can improve.

The simplicity of this finding makes flow a very useful concept to work with, though interrogating what flow is and, more importantly, how it can be achieved is less straightforward. Csikszentmihalyi defines components of enjoyment that respondents mention at least once when defining a positive experience. These elements are as follows[29]:

- Concentrating on tasks that can be completed. Activities should not be mindless or pointless, nor too abstract to have no clear intention.
- To be able to concentrate. This requires temporal focus and reliance on selective actions or skills.
- Having clear goals. The ability to concentrate and stay focussed is facilitated by a clarity of intention and goals that can be achieved over different timescales.
- Getting immediate feedback. Feedback gives reassurance that goals have been, or can be, achieved.
- Deep but effortless enjoyment. Flow requires the merging of action and awareness; it is reached through spontaneous action rather than deliberate and planned engagement.
- The transformation of time. In flow, time does not pass in the same way as at other times. Flow adheres to internal rhythms rather than clock time.
- Having control over one's actions. The essence of flow is that it engenders disregard for the possibility or fear of losing control. This is not achieved by maximising control over what one is doing but through constricting the margins of error or failure.
- Concern for the self disappears during flow but is stronger after a flow activity. In flow, the sense of the individualised self is muted through the loss of self-consciousness of the relational self – where and who we are and what others might think of us. There is no room for self-scrutiny, which is displaced by intense concentration.

Flow and the Self

Flow activities do not constitute all these features and can be achieved through a selection of these attributes. What is consistent about flow is the implication for the interpretation of the self. According to the theory of flow, the development of the self is achieved by containing the self. Csikszentmihalyi quotes a climber describing flow:

> When things become automatic, it's like an egoless thing, in a way. Somehow the right thing is done without you ever thinking about it or doing anything at all …. It just happens.[30]

---

[29]Csikszentmihalyi (1990/2008, pp. 71–93).
[30]Csikszentmihalyi (1990/2008, pp. 62–63).

Csikszentmihalyi's interpretation of the self presupposes an ongoing circulatory system flowing between psychic energy and the self. Psychic energy is directed by the self, but the self in turn is 'the sum of contents of consciousness and the structure of its goals'.[31] In this way, 'attention shapes the self, and in turn is shaped by it'.[32] This feedback interpretation of the self identifies the benefits of the control of consciousness and the threats of disorder. The normal state of mind is chaos – it is an ongoing dialogue between attention and the self. The effect of flow is to create order and to ensure the direction of psychic energy.

Flow is about orientation towards activity, not the activity itself. And the orientation is about supressing the self to develop the self. The challenge of knowing oneself, of having conscious control, is achieved through being able to set the self aside and to direct attention to goals and intentions. However, while the achievement of flow requires clear goals, the goal of achieving flow is not one of these. I interpret this as meaning that the activity must have an endpoint. Flow needs to reach a climax or end but this endpoint cannot be enhancing well-being and happiness. As Ahmed notes, happiness is not a destination that is reached through flow. This is a slippage that appears in lay interpretations of flow. The intention cannot be to achieve flow but to climb a rockface, practice the piano, complete a level on a computer game or focus on a task at work. We do not engage in tasks to achieve flow; it comes about through our focus on activities. In this way, flow can be interpreted as a non-teleological experience, because intentions orientate the activity (the means), not the beneficial outcome of this activity (the end).

In the empirical study presented in this chapter, I consider what we can learn from theories of freedom and flow to respond to Copeland's plea for me-time. This is a me-time that does not shut out the other and does not dive into an immunised world; it embraces obligations to others and the assemblage of material stuff that make this possible. And it is orientated towards the possibility of happiness through the realisation of flow rather than being obsessed with the acquisition of predefined outcomes. I explore this challenge through my own orientation towards free time and my attempts to engender flow activities for other people.

Crafting Free Time

To explore the dimensions of free time that incorporate having responsibilities towards others and its therapeutic potential, my empirical examination considers the potential of craft. Because I am studying craft as a practice of free time, I am interested in the dimensions of making time and space for craft and how these have to be negotiated with others and within the confines of domestic and other spaces.[33] This analysis develops my own autoethnographic use of sewing and crochet and includes the findings from a participatory research project, carried out with colleagues at the Keele University and the University of Manchester, on

---

[31]Csikszentmihalyi (1990/2008, p. 34).
[32]Csikszentmihalyi (1990/2008, p. 34).
[33]Medley-Rath (2016, pp. 58–72).

teaching crochet as a practice of self-care.[34] Focussing on the activity of doing a specific craft provides an empirical example of the relational framing of me-time and its therapeutic qualities. The possibility that craft is a practice of self-care has received much empirical attention in recent years, with studies demonstrating the therapeutic benefits of doing specific craft activities.[35] These studies highlight the intersubjectivity of craft, as it simultaneously returns one to oneself while redefining or creating new relationships with others. Thus, craft activities provide a 'bodily means of focussing attention outwards',[36] and in doing so draw attention to the intrinsic/extrinsic interface of flow activities. I use these empirical case studies of doing and learning crochet to explore the contours of me-time and its therapeutic potential. This includes the practical and emotional calibrations of making time for oneself; how crafting as me-time interweaves relationships and care; and communal endorsements of taking time out for oneself.

My account of using free time is especially aligned with learning skills more than simply doing craft, as I have sought to teach others how to learn crochet as a practice of self-care. Using me-time to learn a new skill is publicly endorsed as a strategy for improving well-being, yet detail about the benefits of learning is more elusive.[37] My orientation to learning an embodied craft practice develops a phenomenological interpretation of what we can do with our bodies, as I have had to learn how to prioritise embodied practice over mental organisation to teach crochet. This teaching method was inspired by reading David Sudnow's detailed account of learning to improvise jazz piano, which perfectly captures the importance of letting the body take control.[38] Improvised Jazz piano is not defined by having a specific goal, because there is no musical score to follow. Sudnow defines jazz as 'particular ways of moving from place to place'.[39] Becoming proficient in improvised jazz piano requires an intuitive understanding of the fundamental facts of song structure. Sudnow did not master jazz piano by learning to improvise (the mind knowing how to play) but through the embodied skills of playing chords and scales (the hands knowing how to play). Mastering improvisation sup-

---

[34]The participatory research was carried out in collaboration with Tamsin Fisher, Lisa Dikomitis (Keele University) and Sarah Marie Hall (University of Manchester) and was supported by a North West Social Science DTP award for Tamsin Fisher's PhD research on Learning and Wellbeing and a Collaborative Innovation Grant awarded by Methods North West. Both awards were funded by the UK Economic and Social Research Council. Ethics approval was granted by Keele University's Ethics Committee.

[35]See, for example, Burt and Atkinson (2012), Brooks, Ngan Ta, Townsend, and Backman (2019), Dickie (2011) and Kenning (2015).

[36]Bunn (2020, p. 55).

[37]In the UK, guidance from the National Health Service lists learning something new as one of five steps to mental well-being. This advice is based on research that demonstrates the benefits of learning, though this research is not clearly evidenced and the empirical evidence on the benefits of learning a new skill, rather than taking part in an activity, is not transparent. See Aked, Marks, Cordon, and Thompson (2008).

[38]Sudnow (2001). See also Lea (2009, pp. 465–474).

[39]Sudnow (2001, p. 127).

presses the 'I that plans' and the 'mind that aims ahead'; instead, it is the knowing jazz hand that performs.[40] I am not suggesting that learning crochet involves the same intensity as learning to improvise jazz piano; however, Sudnow's immersive phenomenological method can be applied to less intensive techniques. This requires an important amendment to the theory of flow that would include the idea that immersive practice does not simply stimulate mental concentration to channel psychic energy; it also frees the body to learn and do.

Crochet and (Self-) Care

I have always enjoyed dressmaking and have made clothes and curtains since learning to use a sewing machine at school. Dressmaking meets the requirements of a flow activity.[41] It requires focus; there are clear goals and immediate feedback; a dressmaker has control over the activity (though mistakes occur, they can be undone); and time certainly flows differently – usually dressmaking takes much longer than you think it is going to. It is not, though, a spontaneous activity; it requires defined and bounded space (a room or part of a room with at least a table and an ironing board) and demarcated time. Dressmaking is an intimate activity; it is not easy to do for other people as it requires transgressing embodied boundaries through fitting. It is not static; a dressmaker spends as much time at an ironing board or countertop piecing seams together and pressing them as at the machine itself. The end product of dressmaking is achieved through the intimate relationship between the sewer and machine. Machines are not simply tools; a dressmaker sews with a machine rather than simply uses it. So although dressmaking is a flow activity, there are limitations to how, when and why it is carried out. I only sew at weekends, usually a Sunday afternoon when all other responsibilities are completed or at least can be put to one side and I can take the time and space for myself.

These spatial and temporal constraints limited the time that I could spend sewing. That is why I learnt to crochet – to have an activity that I could take with me and do in different spaces at diverse times, particularly in the evenings after work and family obligations are completed. Fortunately, I learnt quickly, and my evening routine soon assimilated a couple of hours' work on this new craft. Unlike dressmaking, crochet is a craft that can easily be done for other people. Although personal items can be crocheted, blankets especially are an intimate gift symbolising care and comfort, but these are not specific to the contours of the body. I soon realised that the satisfaction of crochet was, more so than dressmaking, its potential for creating a gift for others.

Crochet and Flow. Crochet's capacity to be a flow activity is different to that of dressmaking. It requires less focus; you can watch television or listen to music/ an audiobook at the same time. My preference is to have sound in the background when crocheting. There are moments of intense concentration (usually counting

---

[40]Dreyfus (2001, p. x).
[41]For discussions of the social and personal aspects of sewing, see Hall and Jayne (2016) and Martindale and McKinney (2020).

stitches), but these are interjected with moments of quasi-automatic repetition. When I sew, I might put some music on, but often do not bother as sewing is a more internalised experience than crocheting. The stillness of crochet is balanced by the slight distraction of external noise. This stillness also alerts the body to its immediate environment. I had to adapt my crochet 'station' on my living room sofa: I purchased a daylight lamp to crochet under; replaced the legs on my sofa so that my feet touched the ground when I sit up straight and started to use a cushion to slightly elevate my feet; and invested in a pair of headphones to block out the noise of my family if required. I purchased a pair of old-fashioned bifocal glasses to wear specifically for crocheting. Comfort, posture, light and noise are not simply background components; they are integral to the activity itself.

Therefore, flow is, as Pauliina Rautio writes, a 'feeling of union with the environment'.[42] In social psychology interpretations, the performance of skill downplays the role of material surroundings and non-human agents. From this perspective, the self is internalised and focussed on the control of consciousness and is assumed to have control over the surroundings and artefacts through which flow is achieved. My experience of crochet leads me to concur with Rautio that we need to attend to the assemblage of material, human and non-human agents that co-constitute the environment of flow. The flow of crochet is not simply about being in tune with the environment; it intensifies awareness of material objects and sensual interactions with these. It is simultaneously introverted and extraverted, and awareness is not simply directed to the control of consciousness but also to the external conditions which co-constitute the practice of crochet.[43] Interpreting the flow of crochet as the interception between the self and the external environment redirects the interpretation of flow realised through mental control towards being the assimilation of the self, the environment and (non-)human beings.

Crocheting for Others.   Another aspect of crochet that is pertinent to this reading is its form as a gift to others. The goal of crochet is not just to make something, to finish a blanket or shawl; the intention involves who this is for. Unlike dressmaking, it is easier for crochet to be a gift as it does not require co-presence – dressmaking at some stage requires a fit. Crocheting objects for others allows friendship and care and the responsibilities one has towards others to be expressed at a distance. However, the intended recipient of the crocheted object is integral to its practice; thinking about and deciding on this are more than a simple afterthought.

My realisation that crochet has the potential to express obligations to and responsibilities for others intensified in 2019, just under a year after I first picked up a crochet hook following my sister's and partner's cancer diagnoses. The day after my sister's diagnosis, I drove to a craft shop to purchase yarn to make her a blanket. I needed to do something to care for her and myself. Over the next year, I made four blankets, the first for my sister, the second for my daughter, the third for myself and

---

[42]Rautio (2013, pp. 394–408).
[43]Stephanie Bunn details the intersubjectivity of crafting in her examination of different therapeutic applications of basket weaving; see Bunn (2020).

the fourth for my mother. During a year spent waiting in hospital treatment rooms and carrying out caring tasks in other people's houses, having an activity I could take with me and do at any time was invaluable. Even when I was caught within the inevitable intransience of care, I could be doing something. As Baraitser states, care requires a temporality that interweaves through tropes of waiting, staying, maintaining, repeating and delaying.[44] Having something to do and a purpose beyond the repetition of care (i.e. finishing a blanket and giving it to someone I cared for) facilitates accepting the inevitably that some times have to be endured. Making the blankets was more than a respite that was needed to nullify the emotional and practical challenges of responding to multiple caring responsibilities; it also allowed me not to care. At times, I was as frustrated, bored and fed up with making blankets as I was with the prolonged temporality of treatment and recovery.

My obsession with making these large, time-consuming material artefacts involved more than simply having something to do; it provided an anchor between the competing desires to retreat inwards away from responsibilities and the external commitment to obligation and care. The blankets expressed the impossibility of having me-time that was cut off from external responsibilities. Crocheting the blankets provided a form of flow and a practice of self-care that was very much crafted within the fused tangle of the caring commitments of everyday life. Thus, my interpretation of how I use crochet for self-care concurs with Esposito's community–immunity paradigm rather than a yearning for me-time. Time that can be spent doing something for myself cannot be carved out by rejecting my obligations to others. Ultimately, the time that I take for myself is not in opposition to my responsibilities but continues to acknowledge these.

Teaching Crochet

As well as studying my own use of crochet, I have also been involved in collaborative workshops that teach crochet to others as a potential practice of self-care. During my attempts to teach crochet, I learnt as much about the challenges of teaching an embodied skill as about the benefits of learning.

From the Workshop to a Person-centred Practice.   I have already discussed how my orientation towards teaching was influenced by Sudnow's phenomenological self-examination of learning jazz piano. This approach was also provoked by our (colleagues from Keele and Manchester universities) first failed attempt to teach crochet. Initially, we adopted a workshop model and standard pedagogic practices of teaching in universities.[45] We identified intended learning outcomes concerning what was to be achieved in the workshop (introduction to basic crochet stitches, the qualities of different types of yarn and details for how to make a basic 'granny square'), and this was to be supported by handouts detailing the organisation of the workshop and instructions on how to crochet. We carefully organised the spatial layout of the workshop, with each place denoted by a hook, yarn and hand-

---

[44]Baraitser (2017).
[45]The first workshop was organised by Tamsin Fisher at Keele University.

out, and set defined start and end times for the activity. I stood at one end of the table and demonstrated each stage, moving around the table in an anti-clockwise rotation to respond to individual participants' requests for help. But no one learnt anything in this workshop. We were all exhausted; the participants were frustrated because they had not learnt anything and I was exhausted because I had spent two hours running around in circles trying to respond to everyone doing something slightly different. We forgot everything that we had planned to tell participants about patterns, yarns and hooks. All of our planning was wasted and we were all exhausted by achieving nothing. The lesson I learnt from this experience was that I needed to suppress the 'I that plans' to free up my hands to be able to do.

Teaching an activity that could be done during me-time required a rethink, including less focus on bounded temporal and spatial organisation and a simpler endorsement of the assemblage of materials, space and time to teach effectively. I had the opportunity to put this approach into practice in a series of informal Friday 'Crafternoons' organised by Keele University Student Union.[46] The format was simple: every Friday afternoon in the 'living room' space of the student union refectory, we would facilitate a craft, and every other Friday this craft was crochet.[47] These informal, drop-in sessions organised in an open space with people walking past or sitting around chatting and eating provided a very different format for spending me-time compared with the formal workshops. In particular, organising these activities on an open drop-in basis facilitated person-centred learning, as we could respond to the specific requests of participants and their own knowledge about crochet.[48] The potential to spend time learning from each other was also an essential appeal of the crochet sessions. Our intention was to facilitate a community of practice so that students could support each other to find the time and learn to do craft.[49]

---

[46]These sessions were the inspiration of Charlotte Burke, a student activities coordinator at Keele University Student Union. Charlotte is a keen crafter and crochet enthusiast and wanted to share her enthusiasm with students. The crochet crafternoons were facilitated by Charlotte and myself. Tamsin Fisher took part and observed the sessions.
[47]We took part in 11 crochet sessions and two sewing sessions between October 2019 and March 2020. We also observed six sessions on other craft-related topics. In total, 75 people, including five members of staff (academic and professional services) benefitted from these sessions. Of these participants, eight were male, one identified as trans female and one identified as gender neutral. Seventeen participants attended two or more sessions that were observed. We were not able to monitor participants' ethnicity, though we noted that all of the sessions attracted a diverse group of students, confounding our expectation that craft is a predominately 'white' practice.
[48]In educational settings, a person-centred approach has been developed to ensure that the requirements of students with disabilities or special educational needs are central to the delivery of education; see, for example, Sanderson, Goodwin, and Kinsella (n.d.).
[49]See Wenger (1998). This community was not immune from the 'idiosyncratic and always performative nature of learning', Amin and Roberts (2008, p. 353). The dynamics of the group changed over the course of each session; I became more aware of diverse opinions being expressed towards the end and how some members dominated the practice more than others.

Procrastination, Waiting and Rhythm.   Crafternoons were a gentle invitation to take time out rather than the formal request of a workshop. Staff and students who came along joked about the procrastination involved in deciding to spend a few hours doing crochet; there were always essays to write or work to be done. The crafternoons were a communal endorsement that making time for oneself is important. In this sense, the time spent on the crochet crafternoons was as important as the practice of crochet. These afternoons were examples of how Helen Holmes writes about time for the self, that is, the time spent doing something is an inherent part of practice.[50] It mattered that others were spending time in the same way, and, because the activity was run by the student union, this period of me-time was not an individual indulgence but officially sanctioned.[51] Having an open space was more conducive than having an organised and bounded space to learning and spending time for oneself. The space itself was not particularly comfortable, though. The space in the student union was lit with green lights, which made it difficult to see the yarn. The crafternoon table was a wooden rustic bench that looked 'crafty' but became incrusted with food and yarn over the year. The wooden benches that we sat on gave very little support. This discomfort became a feature of the crafternoons; participants were not simply lost in the activity but were also acutely aware of their immediate environment. If students achieved flow in learning crochet, this heightened their environmental sensibilities rather than shut out their surroundings.

My attitude to teaching crochet also changed. Rather than organise what I needed to teach, I simply waited with yarn and hooks for students who wanted to come along and learn; I had no plans, no outcomes, no written instructions. I learnt that to teach crochet I needed to be still: to sit next to students, watch them and guide their hands. Sometimes I had to touch their hands to correct them or use my voice and apologetically point out that a student was doing it wrong. I encouraged students to make stiches look like stitches so that the slow steps of learning were happening. Some participants did learn and returned for further advice to develop their practices. Two early attendees became teachers themselves and a couple more completed projects, such as stuffed toys. However, for others the frustration of not being able to do basic stitches, so tangible outcomes of practice were too far in the distance to be realised, suppressed the initial attraction of having some me-time. The frustrations of not being able to do, not seeing progress being made and feeling that no outcome is possible can be too much. My role as a teacher was not to organise and direct this, but to be responsive and facilitate the hands to learn.

The activity of learning did not stop abruptly, because the sessions did not end precisely on time. To recall Linda's experience as a speech therapist, there was no obvious end to these encounters; it was often down to the facilitators to

---

[50]Holmes (2018).
[51]The most popular crafternoon involved making pom-pom hedgehogs, a straightforward activity that all participants could accomplish in a short period of time, and the quality of the end product was inconsequential.

proactively divert attention from the present learning to future practice. We ended sessions by offering resources – yarn and a hook – so that participants could continue learning at home. There was also a discernible temporal rhythm to the crafternoons. The first hour was distinguished by silence (and sometimes singing) as participants focussed on crochet. In the second hour, stitches started to come together and the atmosphere changed. Conversations become louder, plans for the weekend, future craft projects and career plans were discussed. The internalising of the initial intention to learn and/or to practice segued into external engagement with fellow crafters. Plans to do more shared activities, such as visiting a local yarn store, were discussed more than once. These plans never materialised, but the possibility of extending the community of crafting to more structured, external activities mattered more than realising these opportunities.

The Possibility of Me-Time

Yearning for me-time inverts popular interpretations of busyness – not being busy for other people but being busy for oneself. Thus, getting one's time back does not require a suppression of busyness but rather doing busyness differently: keeping busy for oneself rather than running around segueing discrete and oppositional responsibilities. This approach to interpreting free time with respect to busyness can be seen as analogous to the popularity of the slow movement in response to acceleration: not to stop doing, but to do things differently.[52] The busyness of free time can be a time for consolidating the duality of caring for the self and others as well as about relinquishing responsibilities for and obligations to others. This fits with my experiences of free time and my attempts to coordinate this for others, which unsettled my aspiration that me-time is a simple expression of positive freedom. I do not just crochet for myself, but with and for other people.

If me-time is defined as enabling time for activities that do not involve having any responsibilities, it is still defined by them. Rather than valuing me-time as an expression of the internalised self, it is more useful to think about having time for oneself as the ongoing resolution between having obligations to others and the internalisation of technologies of the self. Free time cannot be carved out in spite of obligations, but the tacit affordance of others accommodates time for oneself. I suggest that the crafternoons offered the possibility of me-time through the obligations involved in belonging to a community, in particular gifting the option of spending time doing a craft activity as a break from the requirements of study and work. Participants in the crafternoons welcomed the communal sanction of procrastination. The guilt linked to procrastination was still present in the crafternoons, but spending a couple of hours during the day not working or studying was justified because it was shared with others. Although it might be assumed that spending an afternoon doing crochet is valued because it is not wasting time, that is not what mattered. Some attendees did very little; not everyone applied themselves

---

[52]The slow movement offers an alternative to the fetishising of speed; see, for example, Honoré (2004) and Sunin (2012).

to the crafts, and participants could simply sit and watch. The requirement to do was not integral to these drop-in sessions. More than being about craft, the craft-ernoon sessions were public expressions of free time, casually witnessed by others gathered in the student union building.

For those who did choose to craft, the option of spending me-time making things for other people was frequently acknowledged. Indeed, making objects for friends and family was a common motivation for learning to crochet. It should be noted, though, that while the possibility of making things for others is a celebrated component of crafting,[53] crafters can choose *not* to make. Making for others can be an idealised expression of relationships that are worked on in isolation. Crafting provides a bounded and controlled expression of responsibilities in contrast to the chaotic and messy experiences of everyday life.

If me-time can be a respite from the relentless activity of accelerated society, again this is not necessarily realised by shutting out external requests and stimuli. The flow of an activity such as crochet is achieved through the repetition of embodied practice rather than the dominance of the planning mind. This immersion is experienced through the assemblage of material and human and non-human agents. Rather than focussing inwards, the concentration of flow can heighten the sense of being in union with the environment. Moreover, if flow is goal orientated, it is not directed towards a more distant end but to the immediacy of the means that can be completed in the present time.

Summary

'I am yearning for me-time' would be an appropriate slogan for the twenty-first century, but it works as a slogan rather than a social remedy that can readily be put into practice. The issue of yearning for me-time can be interpreted as a temporal expression of wanting positive freedom, that is, wanting the time for personal development. However, the paradox of me-time is that it cannot be achieved as a solo project; it depends on the tacit and active affordances of others. Me-time as care for oneself cannot be easily disentangled from care with and for others. Thus, our desire to maximising free time nullifies the obligations that we have as members of communities, so this can only ever be a temporary respite. A more sustainable orientation towards free time can be realised through engaging with the internalising pull of immunity and the reciprocal duty of community. Rather than me-time being a realisable temporal expression that is distinctive from time dedicated to external commitments, it is more useful to think about the possibility of having time for oneself, what this might mean and how it can be moved towards through engaging with other people and responsibilities rather than shutting them out.

Solutions to resolving the dialectical paradoxes of me-time will vary. I have chosen to study the practice of craft as an expression of me-time because it is a practice that is readily available to me and it is how I choose to demarcate

---

[53]Gauntlet (2018).

and spend much of my free time. Another reason for interrogating craft as an expression for me-time was because I would also have had the opportunity to interrogate how we can learn new skills as a tactic of self-care. My focus on craft illustrates how the therapeutic benefits of free time are not found in self-isolation or by abandoning responsibilities but through intersubjective immersion in activities, or the possibility of flow. The flow of craft not only intensifies unity with the environment but it is also facilitated by and with others. Sharing me-time with others by doing an activity together or simply acknowledging its time and space underscores the relational qualities of free time. Getting my time back might require shutting out the incessant stimulus of 24-hour living, but, equally, it also depends on ongoing negotiation of communal relationships and support and resisting the urge to immunise ourselves from the outside world.

Chapter 8

The Social Lives of Busyness

In the introduction to his 2015 book *The Burnout Society*, Byung-Chul Han summarises the defining condition of the twenty-first century society: '[d]espite widespread fear of an influenza epidemic, we are not living in a viral age'.[1] This claim that we no longer live in fear of bacteria or viruses in the twenty-first century is fundamental to his interpretation of burnout and the ascendancy of the possibility that we *can* do things rather than that we *should* do things. While it is unfair to judge Han's theorisation of burnout with the benefit of hindsight, his conviction about the demise of viral infection and what this infers for social conditions has rapidly become obsolete. The year 2020 will be remembered as a time when everyday life became conditioned by restrictions to limit the spread of coronavirus (the ascendancy of *cannot* over *can*) that fundamentally unsettled the overarching direction of theoretical projects to define and explain the twenty-first century. In this final chapter to conclude my investigation into the social life of busyness, I do not intend to follow Han with an alternative interpretation of the social condition of the twenty-first century. The shock of the Covid-19 pandemic has radically undermined the possibility of singularly defining social conditions and the direction of change.[2] My conclusion is quite simple: busyness has and will always be with us in different forms. It is, however, possible to identify shared narratives about busyness that speak to interpretations of responsibilities we have to ourselves and to others. The intensification of busyness in the twenty-first century condenses the delegation of responsibilities to individuals with little guidance on how to resolve these, so leading to feelings of injustice that this displacement of responsibilities is uneven. In this concluding chapter, I synthesise the empirical material and analysis with reference to the past, present and future of busyness. The last section necessarily reflects on the future of busyness during and beyond the Covid-19 pandemic.

---

[1]Han (2015, p. 1).

[2]The political commentator Robert Colvile is equally certain about the future of time in the twenty-first century. Although he does not discuss pandemics, he dismisses the possibility that the force of acceleration could be blown off course by economic crises or environmental collapse. Colvile (2016).

The Social Life of Busyness, 151–157
Copyright © 2021 by Clare Holdsworth
Published under exclusive licence by Emerald Publishing Limited
doi:10.1108/978-1-78743-698-520211011

Past

When we think about the past, busyness is invariably eliminated. This is evident in popular and academic narratives of social change as well as in personal accounts of everyday life. If busyness is the pinch point of juggling responsibilities, it cannot be revisited. The synthesis of the present and the future into the past settles the question of what should be done or who should do it. This is at the core of Allen's methodology for getting things done; what matters is ensuring that as many activities as possible can be completed. Moving the synthesis of activities into the past improves productivity and well-being. However, the appeal of being able to streamline busyness into an effective system of getting things done is elusive, especially outside the confined spaces of organisations. Instead of having the satisfaction of completion, we are left with guilt concerning what has not been achieved and the balance of competing responsibilities remains unresolved, as the analysis of the Work and Family Lives data set reveals. The past lives of busyness do not just provide a utopian view of an unhurried and leisurely life; they are also bound up with anxieties about unresolved responsibilities.

Experiences of busyness are not independent of the processes of social change. Throughout the empirical material considered in this book, the relevance of increasing individualisation and personal responsibility cannot be ignored, though, at the same time, these trends also need to be held in check. Empirical data on both work and family time reveal the significance of managing responsibilities in everyday life and frustrations about how this is changing, and responsibility is increasingly being delegated to the individual. However, the analysis of temporal rhythm makes the obvious, though still important, point that references to time are used to coordinate collective synchronisation as much as individual prioritisation. Busyness, and its frustrations, come about because responsibilities are not individual but shared, and this collaboration has to be coordinated in time and space. Everyday family and working lives are lived through messy and entangled ties of interpersonal relationships and responsibilities, and resolving these is busy work. Responding to multiple responsibilities undermines expectations about getting things done, as much of what needs to be done is circular as well as linear. Thus, the responsibilities of everyday life cannot be readily ticked off and synthesised into the past. Moreover, the distribution of these resolutions remains uneven, and longitudinal analysis of time use reveals the persistence of inequalities, especially by gender. In other words, we can identify both continuity and change in experiences of busyness.

Present

Busyness is popularly interpreted as a fault of the present, specifically preoccupations with the now. Busyness defies the synthesis of the present into the past or the future; instead, it oscillates around the mental chatter about what needs to be done but has not yet been completed. This mental chatter about busyness is rehearsed and repeated. Busyness can be known in advance: the conflict of different morning routines of household members; the frustrations linked to the desire to be on time for work or school; or balancing competing responsibilities at home and at work. Habits anticipate the pinch points of temporal squeeze rather than resolve them precisely because they are unavoidable, especially during morning routines. Knowing about being busy and being busy joins embodied practices and mental processes; busyness is experienced as intensive activity *and* thought.

Temporal intensity cannot be simply interpreted as the speeding up of everyday life. It is about responding to multiple requests. What needs to be done in the moment is not a matter of prioritisation but an assemblage of people, technologies and space that make getting things done possible. Busyness in the present implicitly involves managing space and other people and is not just about how time is used. Thus, as the analysis of one-day diaries has shown, different organisational structures generate diverse experiences of temporal pressure. Working in a hierarchical organisation is, therefore, associated with different temporal pinch points to being involved in project work or in employment that requires precise temporal and spatial coordination, such as healthcare work. Even working on one's own does not negate the need to pay attention to other people as well as material things and spaces. It follows that frustrations about domestic or work responsibilities cannot be resolved by following internalised processes; people, technologies and spaces are needed.

Despite empirical evidence pointing to the relational context of busyness, techniques for time management in self-help literature offer solutions that isolate people from each other. Instead of engaging with relational challenges, much of the advice in self-help parodies one-dimensional relationships that inevitably reproduce cultural gender norms. Moreover, the ambition of self-help, which is to perfect the self, is contradictory, as the potential of external, collective advice on how to curate self-knowledge will always fall short. The end result of this paradoxical endorsement of prescriptive methods of self-development is that these texts are characterised by repetition and busyness in terms of the techniques and resources they make available.

Busyness in the present can also be therapeutic through facilitating flow. Doing something without paying attention to synthesising this activity into the past (getting it done) or future (moving towards future goals) can enable a present focus that is required for the state of flow. However, therapeutic busyness should not involve shutting out external responsibilities associated with its more dystopic expressions. Rather, therapeutic activities can provide an alternative practice for assimilating responsibilities and duties to care for others. Keeping busy might be a strategy for self-care but it is one that can be enabled and supported by others.

Future

One aspiration for the future of busyness is for a more equal distribution of responsibilities, and, thus, also time, between ourselves and others. Frustrations about busyness, whether at work or at home, are often caused by the feeling that others are not pulling their weight, leading to a sense of unfairness about unreasonable encroachments into free time. However, one of the conundrums of time studies is that it is not possible to isolate the determinants of overwork and excessive responsibilities. It is, therefore, equally challenging to propose possible remedies. Those that are available, such as self-help texts, emphasise individual solutions rather than collective ones. Moreover, collective remedies that are proposed, such as shortening the working week, necessarily have to make universal assumptions about the cause of overwork rather than acknowledging the unevenness of busyness.

My analysis of the diversity of the social lives of busyness does not readily lend itself to solutions to the question that I started with: why has busyness become a social issue? My main interest in studying busyness was to interrogate the assumptions we make about being busy rather than to provide solutions. However, one outcome of studying busyness is that I can use this empirical detail to identify possible solutions to being overwhelmed by being busy, and I tentatively offer the following suggestions:

- Much of everyday busyness is anticipated. This expectation can be a source of anxiety but equally we develop habits to deal with this. Changing habits that anticipate busyness is a key message of self-help. There can be benefits to rethinking automatic responses to ongoing commitments. However, rethinking our responses to temporal pinch points will not be achieved by focussing on the end result of balanced responsibilities but through more intermediate changes. Thus, it might be more helpful to develop new habits that accommodate different ways of reconciling commitments, such as letting teenage children sleep in later on a weekday; organising a daily commute to maximise time with family members; or building new routines to liven up family nights.
- If there is one piece of advice that I have learnt from reading self-help books, it is that time management is a red herring. Rather than investing employees' time and organisational resources in time management courses, it might make more sense to focus on how responsibilities are delegated and distributed within organisational structures. This process of organisational investigation should include considering the practice of delegation and how it is received and managed; in other words, the distribution of tasks in different directions within organisations should be looked at. Moreover, time management courses could be replaced with courses on 'how to make the most of space' (this is essentially a key point of Allen's productivity method).
- Responding to multiple responsibilities necessarily creates tensions between what can be achieved in a certain moment and what others expect you to do. On balance, attempts to prioritise responsibilities should ideally involve what you can actually do at a particular time rather than a judgement about other people's priorities. This requires self-awareness of the rhythms of work and when activities can be scheduled, but it will only work if other people also respect your own temporal prioritisation. These are the everyday tensions of family life, but they are also present at work.
- I am not convinced by universal schemes that aim to make the most of time and the assumption that condensing the time in which activities are done should be mandated in the twenty-first century. Shifting to a four-day week has been demonstrated to work for many people, but it will not work for everyone (and

those for whom it does work are likely to be in more secure employment situations). There are two valid limitations to universal temporal policies. First, they make assumptions about work as a cultural practice and ignore its diversity; workers in people-facing jobs such as those working in healthcare and sales or customer service assistants will not necessarily become more productive if they have a shorter working week. Second, they assume that condensing work facilitates negotiating competing responsibilities, but this depends on what these responsibilities are. For some people, stretching out the time available for work might be more efficient or appropriate (i.e. working more than four days, but shorter days). However, the advantage of universal policy change is that it removes the responsibility of resolving how to get work time right from individuals, which policies for workplace flexibility essentially do. One lesson that can be carried forward from campaigns for a shorter working week are that resolutions to lessen the temporal pressures need to be collective, not top down or left to individuals to resolve.

- Managing relationships can take more time than doing stuff, yet the shift to projectised working encourages the former. This observation also applies to personal life, and we need to recognise the necessity of investing time in maintaining relationships through non-productive acts of caring. Rather than assuming that productivity and well-being across domestic and work settings are achieved through streamlining or obliterating non-productive activity, it could be more beneficial to consider how investing time in developing and sustaining relationships is necessary for efficient productivity.
- Instead of starting from the assumption that work dictates family life, any suggested resolution to the stress of busyness needs to acknowledge the obvious point that personal life also needs to be arranged to make work possible. If the notion of work–life balance is to have any relevance, this relates to how the possibility of balance can be moved towards in all dimensions of public and personal life, not to how this can be achieved through organising work. This is a significant challenge and one that cannot be done without personal and public recognition of the uneven distribution of responsibilities between men and women. I hope that by drawing attention to the persistence of gendered experiences of time, this analysis can contribute to ensuring that the relevance of gender in studies of time is not rendered obsolete.[3]
- The desire for more me-time might be counterproductive if it is only considered as a project of the self. If busyness has come about as a problem because of the concentration of responsibilities, then its resolution can be reached by acknowledging these rather than dismissing them. One obvious way in which this can be done is recognising that me-time is something we can grant to others. This might sound like a convenient homily, but sometimes we do have to accept that busyness is not just about ourselves – other people's busyness is equally important.

---

[3]For example, in his influential text *Social Acceleration*, Rosa (2013) claims that the process of acceleration is experienced equally by men and women.

Busyness in a Pandemic

Writing about the future of busyness in 2020 cannot avoid considering how everyday life has been radically restricted by the Covid-19 pandemic. At its onset in March 2020, my initial reaction was essentially an extrapolation of Han's interpretation of burnout, that is, Covid-19 would wipe out busyness as we were being forced to stay in our homes. My assumption that social responses to the novel disease would put the brakes on everyday life was exacerbated by being cut off from the chatter about busyness at work that had originally inspired this project. However, busyness was not dissipated by the necessary lockdowns of the pandemic; instead it was bifurcated. Responsibilities were redrawn; some people had the responsibility of keeping essential services going, whereas others had to remain at home. Shutting down schools resulted in more entrenched gender divisions in childcare in the home. Carers for family members were cut off from external support and had to continue to care on their own. Thus, the quality of busyness changed and shifted towards a less negotiated time pressure; those under the most stress had little choice but to get on with what they had to do. In contrast, for others, the stretching out of free time in lockdown was difficult to fill with meaningful activities. If there is a universal temporal experience of lockdowns it is that we all have come to recognise the necessity, and sometimes the difficulty, of acceding to the endurance of time.[4] However, it soon became obvious that the pandemic was not heralding a new social order but was exaggerating and intensifying existing inequalities and unevenness. Ultimately, the pandemic has underscored the pervasiveness of economic inequalities, and as unemployment increases, worries about temporal overload are being replaced with the fundamental concern about having sufficient income.

The temporalities of the pandemic contradict those assumed to dominate the Twenty-first century society. Not only has the pace of everyday life slowed down but societies and economies are described as going backwards. Financial losses, from those of a nation state to those of a household, have reversed recent years of economic progress. Rather than moving forward into the future the restrictions of life during a pandemic have brought about a reversal into past. The fear of social and economic retreat contrasts with nostalgic interpretations of past times. The past that the pandemic recalls is not a past that we would choose to return to. It is one that is riddled with inequalities of gender, class and race rather than being full of rest and fairness. The pandemic also radically reframes the future. In recent years, the future has been identified by social scientists as a meaningful topic for analysis, as it is ever-present in everyday and political life.[5] The pandemic does not diminish the importance of thinking about the future, but it does radically alter how this might be done. We have had to adjust to everyday life in the absence of plans and submit to the possibility that any plans that are made might be radically changed with little notice. Ironically, this unsettling of

---

[4]Baraitser (2017).
[5]Urry (2016).

the synthesis of temporality into past and future has intensified individual and collective commitment to keeping busy. We can see this in the increased popularity of baking, craft and do-it-yourself activities during the pandemic, as well as in political appeals to eat out and shop, to keep the economy going. The therapeutic and economic benefits of busyness have become more prominent as we adjust to how the pandemic reshapes the synthesis of temporality.

The impacts of the pandemic on work are unavoidable and are predicted to outlive the intensity of Covid-19 itself. Employment is being restructured by the economic shocks of the pandemic; some workers have more to do but many have less, and mass unemployment is inevitable, particularly for the young and over-50s. For those working in professional occupations, the assumption that working from home will remain is unavoidable, ushering in radical changes to the spatial and temporal organisations of some forms of work. Workers who have quickly had to adjust to working at home might be unimpressed with Allen's advice that a home desk should be unique and not shared with others. Retaining the airtight boundaries of work that Allen advocates is simply not possible in overcrowded domestic spaces. Moreover, his reluctance to recommend hot- or hotel-desking is obsolete as more workers expect to manage blended working spaces at home and in the office. What does remain is his insistence that we need to pay close attention to how these multiple spaces are managed. The challenges of spatial organisation when working from home can also be confounded by the absence of everyday encounters beyond the desk that characterise the busyness of work. The monotony of Julie's home work might be less intensive than that of others, though it captures the problem of segueing between productive and non-productive activities. The incidental busyness of work is more than unnecessary noise, because, just like other habits of busyness, it keeps us away from incessant requests from others and the ongoing delegation of responsibility.

My initial interpretation that busyness would no longer be a social issue with the advent of Covid-19 dissipated during the first few months of the pandemic. Busyness has been relocated, though. Oliver Burkeman chose Times Square in New York to start his 2017 investigation of being busy, but in 2020, he might have chosen an intensive care ward in a hospital, a family kitchen coordinating working from home and home schooling, or a distribution centre sending out packages of items ordered online. At the start of this project, I identified the White Rabbit running away from Alice as a figurative expression of busyness; in 2020, Lewis Carroll's depiction of the Red Queen running as fast as she can to stay in one place might be more apposite.[6] Both the spatial and the temporal conditions of busyness appear to have been shortened and condensed. Rather than being overwhelmed by busyness as we grapple with the fear of returning to an unappealing past and the inability to plan for the future, it is busyness that holds us in place against the shock of a global pandemic.

---

[6]Carroll (1872).

Appendix

Publications Included in Scoping Study of Longitudinal Time-Use Analysis.

No.	Authors	Year of Publication	Title	Journal/Website
1	Mullan, K and Wajcman, J.	2019	Have mobile devices changed working patterns in the 21st century? A time-diary analysis of work extension in the UK	*Work, Employment and Society, 33*(1), 3–20
2	Lamote de Grignon Pérez et al.	2019	Sleep differences in the UK between 1974 and 2015: Insights from detailed time diaries	*Journal of Sleep Research,* https://doi.org/10.1111/jsr.12753
3	Etile, F. and Plessez, M.	2018	Women's employment and the decline of home cooking: Evidence from France, 1985–2010	*Review of Economics of the Household, 16,* 939–970
4	Fernandez-Lozano, I.	2018	Finding time for children. Fatherhood, jobs and available time in Spain, 2003–10	*Revista Internacional De Sociología, 76*(3), e104.
5	Lenhart, O	2018	More than just the adoption of Western Capitalism? Time use changes in East Germany following reunification	*Journal of Labor Research, 39,* 306–328
6	Mullan, K.	2018	Technology and children's screen-based activities in the UK: The story of the Millennium so far	*Child Indicators Research, 11,* 1781–1800
7	Mullan, K.	2018	A child's day: Trends in time use in the UK from 1975 to 2015	*The British Journal of Sociology,* https://doi.org/10.1111/1468-4446.12369
8	Neilson, J. and Stanfors, M.	2018	Time alone or time together: Trends and trade-off between dual earner couples, Sweden 1990–2010	*Journal of Marriage and the Family, 80*(1), 80–98

No.	Authors	Year of Publication	Title	Journal/Website
9	Sullivan, O. and Gershuny, J.	2018	Speed up society? Evidence from UK 2000 and 2015 time use diary surveys	*Sociology, 52*(1), 20–38
10	Taillie, L. S.	2018	Who's cooking? Trends in US home food preparation by gender, education and race/ethnicity from 2003 to 2016	*Nutrition Journal, 17*, 41
11	Vihelmson, B, Elder, E., and Thulin, E.	2018	What did we do when the Internet wasn't around? Variation in free-time activities among three young-adult cohorts from 1990/1991, 2000/2001 and 2010/2011	*New Media and Society, 20*(8), 2898–2916
12	Kim, J. W. and Jin, K.	2017	A study on unpaid work time of Korean married men: Time use survey from 1999 to 2014 data	Retrieved from https://www.kci.go.kr/kciportal/main.kci
13	Kim, O. -S.	2017	Changes in adolescents' time use and time famine: Focussing on the differences between 2004 and 2010	*Journal of Family Resource Management, 21*(4), 35–59
14	Klunder, N. and Meirer-Grawe, U.	2017	Everyday food routines and division of labour in two-parent households – A quantitative analysis based on the German representative time use survey 2012/3 and 2001/02	*Zeitschrifte Fur Familienforschung – Journal of Family Research, 29*(2), 179–201
15	Leech, J. A.	2017	Changes in sleep duration and recreational screen time among Canadians, 1998–2010	*Journal of Sleep Research, 26*(2), 202–209
16	Schulz, F. and Engelhardt-Wolfer, H.	2017	The development, education stratification and decomposition of mothers' and fathers' childcare time in Germany. An update for 2001–2013	*Zeitschrifte Fur Familienforschung – Journal of Family Research*, https://doi.org/10.3224/zff.v2913.02

17	Zuzanek, J.	2017	What happened to the society of leisure? Of the gap between the 'haves' and the 'have nots' (Canadian time use and well-being trends)	*Social Indicators Research, 130,* 27–38
18	Genadek, K. R. Flood, S. M., and Roman, J. G.	2016	Trends in spouses' shared time in the United States, 1965–2012	Demography, *53*(6),1801–1820
19	Gershuny, J. and Harms, T. A.	2016	Housework now takes much less time: 85 Years of US rural women's time use.	*Social Forces, 95*(7), 503–524
20	Dotti Sani, G. M. and Treas, J.	2016	Educational gradients in parents' child-care time across countries 1965–2012	*Journal of Marriage and the Family, 78*(4), 1083–1096
21	Glorieux, I. et al.	2015	Evolutions in time-use and division of labour of men and women	*Papers in Political Economy,* htt ps:-/doi.org/10.4000/ interventionseconomiques.2568
22	Hofferth, S. and Lee, Y.	2015	Family structure and trends in US fathers' time with children, 2003–2013	*Family Science, 6*(1), 318–329
23	Han, J. and Koo, J.	2013	Persistence or change? Patterns of work schedules in Korea, 1990–2010	*Korean Journal of Sociology, 47*(6), 69–82
24	Procher, V. and Vance, C.	2013	Who does the shopping? Evidence of German time use from 1996 to 2009	*Transportation Research Record, 2357*(1), 125–133
25	Smith, L. P, Ng, S. W., and Popkin, B. M.	2013	Trends in US home food preparation and consumption: Analysis of national nutrition surveys and time use studies from 1965–1966 to 2007–08	*Nutrition Journal, 12,* 45
26	Van der Ploeg, H. P. et al.	2013	Non-occupational sedentary behaviors population changes in the Netherlands, 1975–2005	*American Journal of Preventative Medicine, 44*(4), 382–387

No.	Authors	Year of Publication	Title	Journal/Website
27	Chau, J. Y. et al	2012	Temporal trends in non-occupational sedentary behaviours from Australian time use surveys 1992, 1997 and 2006	*International Journal of Behavioral Nutrition and Physical Activity, 9*, 76)
28	Gimenez-Natal, J. I. and Sevilla, A.	2012	Trends in time allocation: A cross-country analysis	*European Economic Review, 56*(6), 1338–1359
29	Sevilla, A., Gimenez-Nadal, J. I., and Gershuny, J.	2012	Leisure Inequality in the US: 1965–2003	*Demography, 49*(3), 939–964
30	Craig, L., Mullan, K., and Blaxland, M.	2010	Parenthood, policy and work–family time in Australia 1992–2006	*Work, Employment and Society, 24*(1), 27–45
31	Hook, J. L.	2010	Gender inequality in the Welfare state: Sex segregation in housework, 1965–2003	*American Journal of Sociology, 115*(5), 1480–1523
32	Kuroda, S.	2010	Do Japanese work shorter hours than before? Measuring trends in market work and leisure using 1976–2006 Japanese time-use survey	*Journal of the Japanese and International Economies, 24*(4), 481–502
33	Voorpostel, M., van der Lippe, T., and Gershuny, J.	2010	Spending time together—Changes over four decades in leisure time spent with a spouse	*Journal of Leisure Research, 42*(2), 243–265
34	Zick, C. D. and Stevens, R. B.	2010	Trends in Americans' food-related time use: 1975–2006	*Public Health Nutrition, 13*(7), 1064–1072
35	Mestdag, I. and Glorieux, I.	2009	Change and stability in commensality patterns: A comparative analysis of Belgium time-use data from 1966, 1999 and 2004.	*The Sociological Review, 57*(4), 703–726

36	Gershuny, J.	2005	Busyness as the badge of honour for the new superordinate working class.	*Social Research, 72*(2), 287–314
37	Sayer, L. C.	2005	Gender, time and inequality: Trends in women's and men's paid work, unpaid work and free time	*Social Forces, 84*(1), 285–303
38	Zander, U., Meirer-Graewe, U., and Moeser, A.	2005	Change in time use for daily eating and household work activities in Germany	*International Journal of Human Ecology, 6*(2), 37–49
39	Sullivan, O.	2000	The division of domestic labour: Twenty years of change?	*Sociology, 34*(3), 437–456
40	Bittman, M.	1998	The land of the lost long weekend: Trends in free-time among working-age Australians 1974–1992	*Society and Leisure, 21*(2), 353–378
41	Bittman, M.	1993	Australians changing use of time, 1974–1987	*Social Indicators Research, 30*, 91–108

Bibliography

Adam, A. (1995). *Timewatch: The social analysis of time*. Cambridge: Polity Press.

Adam, B. (1990). *Time and social theory*. London: Polity Press.

Adam, B. (2004). *Time*. Cambridge: Polity Press.

Ahmed, S. (2010). *The promise of happiness*. Durham, NC: Duke University Press.

Aked, J., Marks, N., Cordon, C., & Thompson, S. (2008). *Five ways to wellbeing; communicating the evidence*. London: New Economics Foundation. Retrieved from https://neweconomics.org/2008/10/five-ways-to-wellbeing

Alexander, S. (1983). *Women's work in nineteenth-century London: A study of the years 1820–50*. London: Journeyman.

Alice-in-Wonderland.net. (n.d.). White Rabbit character description. Retrieved from http://www.alice-in-wonderland.net/resources/analysis/character-descriptions/white-rabbit/

Allcott G. (2014/2016). *Productivity Ninja: Worry less, achieve more, love what you do*. London: Icon Books Ltd.

Allen. D. (2015). *Getting things done: The art of stress free productivity* (revised ed.). London: Piatkus.

Amin, A., & Roberts, J. (2008). Knowing in action: Beyond communities of practice. *Research Policy, 37*(2), 353–369.

Antonopolous, R., & Hirway, I. (Eds.). (2010). *Unpaid work and the economy: Gender, time use and poverty in developing countries*. London: Palgrave Macmillan.

Atkinson. S. (2011). Scales of care and responsibility: Debating the surgically globalised body. *Social & Cultural Geography, 12*(6), 623–637.

Babauta, L. (2009). *The power of less: The 6 essential productivity principles that will change your life*. London: Hay House.

Bachelard, G. (1958/1969). *The poetics of space*. [M. Jolas, Trans.]. Boston, MA: Beacon Press.

Baraitser, L. (2017). *Enduring time*. London: Bloomsbury.

Bastian, M. (2017). Liberating clocks: Developing a critical horology to rethink the potential of clock time. *New Formations: A Journal of Culture/Theory/Politics, 92*, 41–55.

Bastian, M., Baraitser, L., Flexer, M. J., Hom, A. R., & Salisbury, L. (2020). Introduction: The social life of time. *Time & Society, 29*(2), 289–296.

Batchelor, D. (2000). *Chromophobia*. London: Reaktion Books.

Beck, U., & Beck-Gernsheim, E. (2002). *Individualisation: Institutionalized individualism and its social and political consequences*. London: Sage.

Berg, M., & Seeber, B. K. (2016). *The slow professor*. Toronto: University of Toronto Press.

Bergmann, W. (1992). The problem of time in sociology. *Time & Society, 1*(1), 81–134.

Bergson, H. (2004). *Matter and memory*. [N. Margaret Paul & W. Scott Palmer, Trans.]. Mineola, NY: Dover.

Berlin, I. (1969/2002). Two concepts of liberty. In II. Hardy (Ed.), *Liberty* (pp.166–217). Oxford: Oxford University Press.

Bissell, D. (2011). Thinking habits for uncertain subjects: Movement, stillness, susceptibility. *Environment and Planning A, 43*(11), 2649–2665.

Bissell, D. (2018). *Transit life: How commuting is transforming our cities*. Cambridge, MA: MIT Press.

Bittman, M. (1998). The land of the lost long weekend? Trends in free time among working age Australians, 1974–1992. *Leisure and Society*, *21*(2), 353–378.

Bittman, M., & Wajcman, J. (2000). The rush hour: The character of leisure time and gender equity. *Social Forces*, *79*(1), 165–189.

Blyth, C. (2017). *On time: Finding your pace in a world addicted to fast.* London: William Collins.

Boltanski, L., & Chiapello, E. (2005). *The new spirit of capitalism.* London: Verso.

Bourdieu, P. (1992). *The logic of practice.* [R. Nice, Trans.]. Cambridge: Polity Press.

Bowlby, S. (2012). Recognising the time–space dimensions of care: Caringscapes and carescapes. *Environment and Planning A*, *44*(9), 2101–2118.

Briggs, J. (2015). *All day long: A portrait of Britain at work.* London: Serpent's Tail.

Bröckling, U. (2015). *The entrepreneurial self: Fabricating a new type of subject.* London: Sage.

Brooks, L., Ngan Ta, K.-H., Townsend, A. F., & Backman, C. L. (2019). "I just love it": Avid knitters describe health and well-being through occupation. *Canadian Journal of Occupational Therapy*, *86*(2), 114–124.

Bunn, S. (2020). Basket-work, well-being and recovery: The story from Scotland. *Craft Research*, *11*(1), 39–56.

Burkeman, O. (2017). Oliver Burkeman is busy. Retrieved from https://www.bbc.co.uk/programmes/b07w1dpx/episodes/player

Burt, E. L., & Atkinson, J. (2012). The relationship between quilting and wellbeing. *Journal of Public Health*, *34*(1), 54–59.

Butler, J. (2004). *Precarious life: The powers of mourning and violence.* London: Verso.

Carr, N. (2017). Re-thinking the relation between leisure and freedom. *Annals of Leisure Research*, *20*(2), 137–151.

Carroll, L. (1865). *Alice's adventures in Wonderland.* London: Macmillan & Co.

Carroll, L. (1872). *Through the looking-glass, and what Alice found there.* London: Macmillan & Co.

Castells, M. (2010). *The rise of the networked society* (2nd ed.). Oxford: Wiley-Blackwell.

Cep, C. (2019). *Furious hours: Murder, fraud and the last trail of Harper Lee.* London: William Heinemann.

Charmes. J. (2015). *Time use across the world: Findings of a world compilation of time use surveys.* New York, NY: UNDP Human Development Report Office. Retrieved from http://www.hdr.undp.org/sites/default/files/charmes_hdr_2015_final.pdf

Chenu, A., Lesnard, L., & Jacobs, A. (2006). Time use surveys: A review of their aims, methods, and results. *European Journal of Sociology*, *47*(3), 335–359.

Cherry, S. (2008). The ontology of a self-help book: A paradox of its own existence. *Social Semiotics*, *18*(3), 337–348.

Choiceadmin. (n.d.). How much time do your staff waste waiting for the kettle to boil? Retrieved from https://www.choicerefreshments.co.uk/staff-time-lost-boiling-kettle/

Clausen, C. (1993). How to join the middle classes: With the help of Dr Smiles and Mrs Beeton. *American Scholar*, *62*(3), 403–418.

Clement, J. (2020). Daily social media usage worldwide 2012–2019. *Statista*, February 26. Retrieved from https://www.statista.com/statistics/433871/daily-social-media-usage-worldwide/

Collins, C. (2021). Is maternal guilt a cross-national experience? *Qualitative Sociology 44*, 1–29. doi:10.1007/s11133-020-09451-2

Colvile, R. (2016). *The great acceleration: How the world is getting faster, faster.* London: Bloomsbury.

Cook, S. (Ed.). (2019). *24/7: A wake-up call for our non-stop world.* London: Somerset House Trust.

Corrigan, P. (2006). Doing nothing. In S. Hall & T. Jeffersen (Eds.), *Resistance through ritual: Youth subcultures in post-war Britain* (pp. 84–87). London: Routledge.

Crabbe, T. (2014/2015). *Busy: How to thrive in a world of too much.* London: Piatkus.

Craig, L., Mullan, K., & Blaxland, M. (2010). Parenthood, policy and work-family time in Australia 1992–2006. *Work, Employment and Society, 24*(1), 27–45.

Crary, J. (2014). *24/7: Late capitalism and the ends of sleep.* London: Verso.

Cresswell, T. (2006). *On the move: Mobility in the modern western world.* London: Routledge.

Crossley, N. (2013). Habit and habitus. *Body & Society, 19*(2–3), 136–161.

Csikszentmihalyi, M. (1990/2008). *Flow: The psychology of optimal experience.* London: Harper Perennial Modern Classics.

Cunningham-Burley, S., Jamieson, L., & Harden, J. (2011). *Work and family lives dataset.* Leeds: University of Leeds, Timescapes Archive. Retrieved from https://timescapes-archive.leeds.ac.uk/timescapes/

Cuzzocrea, V. (2019). Moratorium or waithood? Forms of time-taking and the changing shape of youth. *Time & Society, 28*(2), 567–586.

Davies, W. (2014). *The limits of neoliberalism: Authority, sovereignty and the logic of competition.* London: Sage.

de la Bellacasa, M. P. (2012). "Nothing comes without its world": Thinking with care. *Sociological Review, 60*(2), 197–216.

Deleuze, G. (1992). Postscript on the societies of control. *October, 59*(Winter), 3–7.

Deleuze, G., & Guattari, F. (2004). *A thousand plateaus* (B. Massumi, Trans.). London: Continuum.

Design Boom (n.d.). In conversation with Christian Marclay about 'The Clock' screening at TATE Modern. Retrieved from https://www.designboom.com/art/conversation-christian-marclay-the-clock-tate-modern-11-23-2018/

Dewey, J. (1922). *Human nature and conduct: An introduction to social psychology.* New York, NY: Henry Holt and Company.

Dex, S., & Bond, S. (2005). Measuring work–life balance and its covariates. *Work, Employment and Society, 19*(3), 627–637.

Dickie, V. A. (2011). Experiencing therapy through doing: Making quilts. *OTJR: Occupation, Participation and Health, 31*(4), 209–215.

Dorling, D. (2014/2019). *Inequality and the 1%.* London: Verso.

Dreyfus, H. L. (2001). Foreword. In D. Sudnow (Ed.). *Ways of the hand, ways of the hand: A rewritten account* (pp. ix–xiii). Cambridge, MA: MIT Press.

Du Gay, P. (2017). 'A pause in the impatience of things': Notes on formal organisation, the bureaucratic ethos and speed. In J. Wajcman & N. Dodd (Eds.), *The sociology of speed: Digital, organizational, and social temporalities* (pp. 86–101). Oxford: Oxford University Press.

Du Gay, P., & Morgan, G. (2013). Understanding capitalism: Crises, legitimacy, and change through the prism of *The New Spirit of Capitalism.* In P. Du Gay & G. Morgan (Eds.), *New spirits of capitalism* (pp. 1–42). Oxford: Oxford University Press.

Edwards, P., & Wajcman, J. (2005). *The politics of working life.* Oxford: Oxford University Press.

Elden, S. (2005). Missing the point: Globalization, deterritorialization and the space of the world. *Transactions of the Institute of British Geographers, 30*(1), 8–19.

Elrod. H. (2017). *The miracle morning: The 6 habits that will transform your life before 8 am.* London: Hodder & Stoughton.

Erikson, I., & Mazmanian, M. (2017). Bending time to a new end: Investigating the idea of temporal entrepreneurship. In J. Wajcman & N. Dodd (Eds.), *The sociology of speed: Digital, organizational, and social temporalities* (pp. 152–168). Oxford: Oxford University Press.

Esposito, R. (2013). *Terms of the political: Community, immunity and biopolitics.* [R. Noel Welch, Trans.]. New York, NY: Fordham University Press.

Etilé, F., & Plessz, M. (2018). Women's employment and the decline of home cooking: Evidence from France, 1985–2010. *Review of Economics of the Household, 16*(4), 939–970.

Ferriss, T. (2007/2011). *The 4-hour work week: Escape the 9–5, live anywhere and join the new rich.* London: Penguin Random House.

Finch, J., & Mason, J. (1993). *Negotiating family responsibilities.* London: Routledge.

Fitzgerald, S. (2019). What is forest-bathing and how does it help. *National Geographic,* October 21. Retrieved from https://www.nationalgeographic.co.uk/environment-and-conservation/2019/10/what-forest-bathing-and-how-does-it-help

Fleetwood, S. (2007). Why work–life balance now? *International Journal of Human Resource Management, 18*(3), 387–400.

Florida, R. (2005). *Cities and the creative class.* New York, NY: Routledge.

Folbre, N., & Bittman, M. (Eds.). (2004). *Family time: The social organisation of care.* London: Routledge.

Foucault, M. (1982). Technologies of the self: Lectures at the University of Vermont October 1982. Retrieved from https://foucault.info/documents/foucault.technolo-giesOfSelf.en/

Foucault, M. (2008). *The birth of biopolitics: Lectures at the Collège de France, 1978–79.* [G. Burchell, Trans.]. Basingstoke: Palgrave.

Fraser, N. (1994). After the family wage. *Political Theory, 22*(4), 591–618.

Frayne, D. (2015). *The refusal of work: The theory and practice of resistance to work.* London: Zed Books.

Frazis, H., & Stewart, J. (2007). Where does the time go? Concepts and measurement in the American time use survey. In E. R. Berndt & C. R. Hulten (Eds.), *Hard-to-measure goods and services: Essays in Honor of Zvi Griliches* (pp. 73–97). Chicago, IL: National Bureau of Economic Research.

Freeman, E. (2010). *Time binds: Queer temporalities, queer histories.* Durham, NC: Duke University Press.

Gauntlet, D. (2018). *Making is connecting: The social meaning of creativity from DIY and Knitting to Youtube and Web 2.0* (2nd ed.). Cambridge: Polity Press.

Genadek, K. R., Flood, S. M., & Garcia Roman, J. (2016). Trends in spouses' shared time in the United States, 1965–2012. *Demography, 53*(6), 1801–1820.

Gershuny, J. (2000). *Changing times: Work and leisure in postindustrial society.* Oxford: Oxford University Press.

Gershuny, J. (2005). Busyness as the badge of honor for the new superordinate working class. *Social Research, 72,* 287–314.

Gershuny, J., & Harms, T. A. (2016). Housework now takes much less time: 85 Years of US rural women's time use. *Social Forces, 95*(2), 1–22.

Gershuny, J., & Sullivan, O. (2019). *What we really do all day: Insights from the centre for time use research.* London: Penguin.

Ghosh, P. (2019). History and theory in Max Weber's "Protestant Ethic". *Global Intellectual History, 4*(2), 121–155.

Giddens, A. (1991). *Modernity and self-identity. Self and society in the late modern age.* Cambridge: Polity Press.

Gillis, J. R. (1997). *A world of their own making: A history of myth and ritual in family life.* Oxford: Oxford University Press.

Gimenez-Nadal, J. I., & Sevilla, A. (2012). Trends in time allocation: A cross-country analysis. *European Economic Review, 56*(6), 1338–1359.

Glennie, P., & Thrift, N. (2009). *Shaping the day: A history of timekeeping in England and Wales 1300–1800.* Oxford: Oxford University Press.

Graeber, D. (2019). *Bullshit jobs: The rise of pointless work, and what we can do about it.* New York, NY: Simon & Schuster.

Gray, T. (1991). *Freedom.* Basingstoke: Macmillan.

Greenhalgh, T., Thorne, S., & Malterud, K. (2018). Time to challenge the spurious hierarchy of systematic over narrative reviews? *European Journal of Clinical Investigation, 48*(6), e12931.

Gregg, M. (2011). *Work's intimacy*. London: Polity Press.

Gregg, M. (2018). *Counterproductive: Time management in the knowledge economy*. Durham, NC: Duke University Press.

Griffiths, J. (2004). *A sideways look at time*. New York, NY: Penguin.

Griffiths, M. (1995) *Feminism and the self: The web of identity*. London: Routledge.

Hägerstrand, T. (1970). What about people in regional science? *Papers of the Regional Science Association, 24*, 7–21.

Hall, K. (2010). *A chronology of Filofax*. Retrieved from https://www.philofaxy.com/files/filofax-chronology.pdf. Accessed on September 17, 2015.

Hall, S. M. (2019). *Everyday life in Austerity: Family, friends and intimate relations*. Cham: Palgrave Macmillan.

Hall, S. M., & Holdsworth, C. (2016). Family practices, holiday and the everyday. *Mobilities. 11*(2), 284–302.

Hall, S. M., & Jayne, M. (2016). Make, mend and befriend: Geographies of austerity, crafting and friendship in contemporary cultures of dressmaking in the UK. *Gender, Place and Culture, 23*(2), 216–234.

Hammermesh, D. S. (2018). *Spending time: The most valuable resource*. Oxford: Oxford University Press.

Han, B.-C. (2015). *The burnout society*. Palo Alto, CA: Stanford University Press.

Harvey, D. (1990). *The condition of postmodernity: An enquiry into the origins of cultural change*. Oxford: Blackwell.

Hassan, R. (2009). *Empires of speed: Time and the acceleration of politics and society*. Leiden: Brill.

Hazleden, R. (2003). Love yourself. *Journal of Sociology, 39*(4), 413–428.

Heidigger, M. (1962). *Being and time*. [J. Macquarrie & E. Robinson, Trans.]. Oxford: Blackwell.

Hofferth, S., & Lee, Y. (2015). Family structure and trends in US fathers' time with children, 2003–2013. *Family Science, 6*(1), 318–329.

Holdsworth, C. (2019). Families and flow: The temporalities of everyday family practices. In L. Murray, L. McDonnell, T. Hinton-Smith, N. Ferreira, & K. Walsh (Eds.), *Families in motion: Ebbing and flowing through space and time* (pp. 155–176). Bingley: Emerald.

Holdsworth, C. (2020a). The paradoxical habits of busyness and the complexity of intimate time-space. *Social and Cultural Geography*. doi:10.1080/14649365.2020.176916

Holdsworth, C. (2020b). Gendered temporalities of everyday family practices: An analysis of Anglo-American self-help literature on 'busyness'. *Gender Place and Culture, 27*(5), 677–694.

Holdsworth, C., & Mendonça, M. (2020). Young entrepreneurs and non-teleological temporality in Portugal and the UK. *Time & Society, 29*(1), 103–123.

Holmes, H. (2018). Self-time: The importance of temporal experience within practice. *Time & Society, 27*(2), 176–194.

Honoré, C. (2005). *In praise of slow: How a worldwide movement is challenging the cult of speed*. London: Orion Books.

Hook, J. L. (2010). Gender inequality in the welfare state: Sex segregation in housework, 1965–2003. *American Journal of Sociology, 115*(5), 1480–1523.

Hoy, D. C. (2012). *The time of our lives: A critical history of temporality*. Cambridge, MA: MIT Press.

Hsieh, H.-F., & Shannon, S. E. (2005). Three approaches to qualitative content analysis. *Qualitative Health Research, 15*(9), 1277–1288.

Husserl, E. (1964). *The phenomenology of internal time consciousness*. (M. Heidegger, Ed. & J. S. Churchill, Trans.). The Hague: Martinus Nijoff.

Jarvis, H. (1999). The tangled webs we weave: Household strategies to co-ordinate home and work. *Work, Employment and Society, 13*(2), 225–247.

Jeffrey, C. (2010). *Timepass: Youth, class and the politics of waiting in India*. Palo Alto, CA: Stanford University Press.

Jenks, C. (1996). *Childhood*. London: Routledge.

Jones, J. (2011). Time flies at the Venice Biennale. *The Guardian*, June 7. Retrieved from https://www.theguardian.com/artanddesign/jonathanjonesblog/2011/jun/07/time-venice-biennale-marclay-fischer

Keller, G., & Papasan, J. (2013). *The one thing: The surprisingly simple truth behind extraordinary results*. London: John Murray.

Kelly, M. G. E. (2013). Foucault, subjectivity, and technologies of the self. In C. Falzon, T. O'Leary, & J. Sawicki (Eds.), *A companion to Foucault* (pp. 510–525). Oxford: Blackwell.

Kenning, G. (2015). "Fiddling with threads": Craft-based textile activities and positive well-being. *Textile – The Journal of Cloth & Culture, 13*(1), 50–65.

Keynes, J. M. (1932). Economic possibilities for our grandchildren (1930). In L. Pecchi & G. Piga (Eds.), *Revisiting Keynes: Economic possibilities for our grandchildren* (pp. 17–26). Cambridge, MA: MIT Press.

Klünder, N., & Meier-Gräwe, U. (2017). Essalltag Und Arbeitsteilung von Eltern in Paarbeziehungen – Eine Quantitative Analyse Auf Basis Der Repräsentativen Zeitverwendungsdaten 2012/13 Und 2001/02. *Zeitschrift Fur Familienforschung, 29*(2), 179–201.

Knapp, J., & Zeratsky, J. (2018). *Make time: How to focus on what matters every day.* London: Bantam Press.

Kondo, M. (2011). *The life-changing magic of tidying*. [C. Hirano, Trans.]. London: Penguin Random House.

Kristeva, J., Jardine, A., & Blake, H. (1981). Women's time. *Signs, 7*(1), 13–35.

Kubicek, B., Korunka, C., & Ulferts, H. (2013). Acceleration in the care of older adults: New demands as predictors of employee burnout and engagement. *Journal of Advanced Nursing, 69*(7), 1525–1538.

La Rosa, J. (2018). The $10 billion self-improvement market adjusts to a new generation. *Market Research.com*. Retrieved from https://blog.marketresearch.com/the-10-billion-self-improvement-market-adjusts-to-a-new-generation

Lahad, K. (2017). *A table for one; A critical reading of singlehood, gender and time*. Manchester: Manchester University Press.

Lamote de Grignon Pérez, J., Gershuny, J., Foster, R., & De Vos, M. (2019). Sleep differences in the UK between 1974 and 2015: Insights from detailed time diaries. *Journal of Sleep Research, 28*(1), e12753.

Larson, R., & Csikszentmihalyi, M. (2014). The experience sampling method. In A. Daniel (Ed.), *Flow and the foundations of positive psychology: The collected works of Mihaly Csikszentmihalyi* (pp. 21–34). Heidelberg: Springer Netherlands.

Laverty, P. (2019). *Sorry we missed you*. Pontefract: Route.

Lawler, S. (2000). *Mothering the self: Mothers, daughters, subjects*. London: Routledge.

Lea, J. (2009). Becoming skilled: The cultural and corporeal geographies of teaching and learning Thai yoga massage. *Geoforum, 40*(3), 465–474.

Leech, J. A. (2017). Changes in sleep duration and recreational screen time among Canadians, 1998–2010. *Journal of Sleep Research, 26*(2), 202–209.

Lefax. (1928). 1928 Catalogue and radio log. Retrieved from https://philofaxy.blogspot.com/2019/01/lefax-radio-log-and-catalogue-1928.html

Lefebvre, H. (2004). *Rhythm analysis: Space, time and everyday life* (p. 74). [S. Elden & G. Moore, Trans.]. London: Continuum.

Lenhart, O. (2018). More than just the adoption of western capitalism? Time use changes in East Germany following reunification. *Journal of Labor Research, 39*(3), 306–328.

Leonard, D. (1980). *Sex and generation: Study of courtships and weddings*. London: Tavistock.

Lewis, S., Gambles, R., & Rapoport, R. (2007). The constraints of a "work–life balance" approach: An international perspective. *International Journal of Human Resource Management, 18*(3), 360–373.

Lucherini, M. (2017). Diabetes and an inescapable (auto)ethnography. *Area*, *49*(4), 429–435.

Lutz, T. (2006). *Doing nothing: A history of loafers, loungers, slackers and bums in America*. New York, NY: Farrar, Strauss and Giroux.

Marshall, G. (2012). *21 Ways to manage the stuff that sucks up your time*. High Point, NC: Discover Books.

Martindale, A., & McKinney, E. (2020). Self-sewn identity: How female home sewers use garment sewing to control self-presentation. *Journal of Consumer Culture, 20*(4), 564–577.

Massey, D. (1994) *Space, place and gender*. Minneapolis, MN: University of Minnesota Press.

May, J., & Thrift, N. (2001). Introduction. In J. May & N. Thrift (Eds.), *Timespace: Geographies of temporality* (pp. 1–46). London: Routledge.

McGee, M. (2005). *Self-help, Inc. Makeover culture in American Life*. Oxford: Oxford University Press.

Mckeown. G. (2014). *Essentialism: The disciplined pursuit of less*. London: Virgin Books.

Medley-Rath, S. (2016). "If you want to do it, you will have the time": Combining family, work, and leisure among scrapbookers. *Journal of the Indiana Academy of the Social Sciences, 19*(1). Retrieved from https://digitalcommons.butler.edu/jiass/vol19/iss1/8/

Merriman, P. (2019). Molar and molecular mobilities: The politics of perceptible and imperceptible movements. *Environment and Planning D: Society and Space, 37*(1), 65–82.

Moch, L. P. (2003). *Moving Europeans: Migration in Western Europe since 1650*. Bloomington, IN: Indianapolis University Press.

Morgan, D. H. J. (2011). *Rethinking family practices*. Basingstoke: Palgrave.

Mullan, K., & Wajcman, J. (2019). Have mobile devices changed working patterns in the 21st century? A time-diary analysis of work extension in the UK. *Work, Employment and Society, 33*(1), 3–20.

Mullan. K. A. (2019). A child's day: Trends in time use in the UK from 1975 to 2015. *British Journal of Sociology, 70*(3), 997–1024.

Nansen, B., Arnold, M., Gibbs, M. R., & Davis, H. (2009). Domestic orchestration. *Time & Society, 18*(2–3), 181–207.

Nowotny, H. (1994). *Time: The modern and postmodern experience*. [N. Place, Trans.]. Cambridge: Polity Press.

OECD. (2020). *Self-employment rate (Indicator)*. Retrieved from https://www.oecd-ilibrary. org/employment/self-employment-rate/indicator/english_fb58715e-en. Accessed on January 14, 2020.

Olson, E. (2015). Geography and ethics I: Waiting and urgency. *Progress in Human Geography, 39*(4), 517–526.

ONS. (2020). Coronavirus virus and self-employment in the UK. Retrieved from https://www.ons.gov.uk/employmentandlabourmarket/peopleinwork/employmentandemployeetypes/articles/coronavirusandselfemploymentintheuk/2020. Accessed on September 3, 2020.

Pang, A. S.-K. (2016). *Rest: Why you get more done when you work less*. London: Penguin.

Philofaxy. (n.d.). *For the love of Philofax*. Retrieved from https://philofaxy.blogspot.com/

Pickett, K. E., & Wilkinson, R. G. (2010). *The spirit level: Why equality is better for everyone*. London: Penguin.

Piketty, T. (2014). *Capital in the twenty-first century*. [A. Goldhammer, Trans.]. Cambridge, MA: Harvard University Press.

Pine, B. J., & Gillmore, J. H. (1999). *The experience economy: Work is theatre and every business is a stage*. Boston, MA: Harvard Business School Press.

Plummer, M. (2019). How to spend way less time on email everyday. *Harvard Business Review*, January 22. Retrieved from https://hbr.org/2019/01/how-to-spend-way-less-time-on-email-every-day

Pofeldt, E. (2020). Survey: Nearly 30% of Americans are self-employed. *Forbes*, May 30. Retrieved from https://www.forbes.com/sites/elainepofeldt/2020/05/30/survey-nearly-30-of-americans-are-self-employed/?sh=162e49602d21

Pooley, C. G. (2017). Travelling through the city: Using life writing to explore individual experiences of urban travel c1840–1940. *Mobilities*, *12*(4), 598–609.

Pooley, C. G. (2019). On the street in nineteenth-century London. *Urban History*, *48*, 211–226. https://doi.org/10.1017/S096392681900097X1–16

Price, B. (1989). Frank and Lillian Gilbreth and the manufacture and marketing of motion study, 1908–1924. *Business and economic history*, *18*, 88–98.

Rautio, P. (2013). Children who carry stones in their pockets: On autotelic material practices in everyday life. *Children's Geographies*, *11*(4), 394–408.

Riessman, C. K. (1993). *Narrative analysis*. London: Sage.

Rimke, H. M. (2000). Governing citizens through self-help literature. *Cultural Studies*, *14*(1), 61–78.

Roberts, K. (2006). *Leisure in contemporary society*. Wallingford: CABI Publishing.

Robinson, J., & Godbey, G. (1997). *Time for life: The surprising ways Americans use their time*. University Park, PA: Penn State University Press.

Rojek, C. (1999). *Decentring leisure*. London: Sage.

Rosa, H. (2013). *Social acceleration: A new theory of modernity*. New York, NY: Columbia University Press.

Rosa, H. (2017). De-synchronisation, dynamic stabilisation, dispositional squeeze: The problem of temporal mismatch. In J. Wajcman & N. Dodd (Eds.), *The sociology of speed: Digital, organizational, and social temporalities* (pp. 25–41). Oxford: Oxford University Press.

Rose, E. (2013). Access denied: Employee control of personal communications at work. *Work, Employment and Society*, *27*(4), 694–710.

Rose, J. L. (2016). *Free time*. Princeton, NJ: Princeton University Press.

Rose, N. (1999). *Powers of freedom: Reframing political thought*. Cambridge: Cambridge University Press.

Rose, N. (2007). *The politics of life itself. Biomedicine, power and subjectivity in the twenty-first century*. Princeton, NJ: Princeton University Press.

Rovelli, C. (2018). *The order of time*. London: Penguin Random House.

Sanderson, H., Goodwin, G., & Kinsella, E. (n.d.). Personalising education: A guide to using person-centred practices in school. Retrieved from http://helensanderson-associates.co.uk/wp-content/uploads/2018/05/A-guide-to-using-person-centred-practices-in-school.pdf

Sarsby, J. (1988). *Missuses and mouldrunners: An oral history of women pottery workers at work and at home*. Milton Keynes: Open University Press.

Sayer, A. (2016). *Why we can't afford the rich*. Bristol: Policy Press.

Schor, J. B. (1992). *The overworked American: The unexpected decline of leisure*. New York, NY: Basic Books.

Schulte, B. (2014). *Overwhelmed: How to work, love and play when no one has the time*. London: Bloomsbury.

Schulz, F., & Engelhardt-Wölfler, H. (2017). The development, educational stratification and decomposition of mothers' and fathers' childcare time in Germany. An update for 2001–2013. *Zeitschrift Fur Familienforschung*, *29*(3), 277–297.

Schwanen. T. (2006). On "arriving on time", but what is "on time"? *Geoforum*, *37*(6), 882–894.

Sharma, S. (2014). *In the meantime: Temporality and cultural politics*. Durham, NC: Duke University Press.

Sharma, S. (2017). Speed traps and the temporal: Of taxis, truckstops and taskrabbits. In J. Wajcman & N. Dodd (Eds.), *The sociology of speed: Digital, organizational, and social temporalities* (pp. 131–151). Oxford: Oxford University Press.

Sherr, I. (2015). The cult of productivity, and the obsession with 'getting things done. *CNET Magazine*. Retrieved from https://www.cnet.com/news/the-cult-of-productivity-and-the-obsession-with-getting-things-done/

Shir-Wise, M. (2019a). Disciplined freedom: The productive self and conspicuous busyness in "free" time. *Time and Society, 28*(4), 1668–1694.

Shir-Wise, M. (2019b). *Time, freedom and the self: The cultural construction of "Free" time*. London: Palgrave Macmillan.

Simmel, G. (2004). In D. Frisby (Ed.) & T. Bottomore & D. Frisby (Trans.), *The philosophy of money* (3rd ed.). London: Routledge.

Simonds, W. (1992). *Women and self-help culture: Reading between the lines*. New Brunswick, NJ: Rutgers University Press.

Smart, C. (2007). *Personal life.* London: Polity Press.

Smith, L. P., Ng, S. W., & Popkin, B. M. (2013). Trends in US home food preparation and consumption: Analysis of national nutrition surveys and time use studies from 1965–1966 to 2007–2008. *Nutrition Journal, 12*, 45. doi:10.1186/1475-2891-12-45

Snyder, B. H. (2013). From vigilance to busyness. *Sociological Theory, 31*(3), 243–266.

Sohn, E. (2020). Your daily commute won't ever be the same. *National Geographic*, May 18. Retrieved from https://www.nationalgeographic.co.uk/science-and-technology/2020/05/your-daily-commute-wont-ever-be-the-same

Sørensen, B. M. (2008). 'Behold, I am making all things new': The entrepreneur as savior in the age of creativity. *Scandinavian Journal of Management, 24*(2), 85–93.

Southerton, D. (2020). *Time, consumption and the co-ordination of everyday life*. London: Palgrave Macmillan.

Southerton, D., & Tomlinson, M. (2005). Pressed for time – The differential impacts of a 'time squeeze.' *Sociological Review, 53*(2), 215–239.

Southwood, I. (2011). *Non-stop inertia*. Alresford: Zero books.

Standing, G. (2011). *The Precariat: The new dangerous class*. London: Bloomsbury.

Starkar, S. (1989). *Oracle at the supermarket: The American preoccupation with self-help books*. New Brunswick, NJ: Transaction Publishers.

Starr, S. (2019). Over-tourism is stressing our national parks. Here's how visitors can help. *National Geographic*, October 4. Retrieved from https://www.nationalgeographic.com/travel/destinations/north-america/united-states/national-parks/avoid-overtourism-indiana-dunes-gateway-arch/

Stratford, E. (2015). *Geographies, mobilities, and rhythms over the life-course*. London: Routledge.

Straughan, E. R., Bissell, D., & Gorman-Murray, A. (2020). Exhausting rhythms: The intimate geopolitics of resource extraction. *Cultural Geographies, 27*(2), 201–216.

Sudnow, D. (2001). *Ways of the hand: A rewritten account* (2nd revised ed.). Cambridge, MA: MIT Press.

Sullivan, C. (2015). "Bad mum guilt": The representation of "work-life balance" in UK women's magazines. *Community, Work and Family, 18*(3), 284–298.

Sullivan, O. (2004). Changing gender practices within the household. *Gender & Society, 18*(2), 207–222.

Sullivan, O., & Gershuny, J. (2018). Speed-up society? Evidence from the UK 2000 and 2015 time use diary surveys. *Sociology, 52*(1), 20–38.

Sunin, H. (2012). *The things you can see only when you slow down*. London: Penguin.

Sutherland, J.-A. (2010). Mothering, guilt and shame. *Sociology Compass, 4*(5), 310–321.

Taillie, L. S. (2018). Who's cooking? Trends in US home food preparation by gender, education, and race/ethnicity from 2003 to 2016. *Nutrition Journal, 17*, 41. doi: 10.1186/s12937-018-0347-9

Tarrant, A., & Hughes, K. (2020). Collective qualitative secondary analysis and data-sharing: strategies, insights and challenges. In A. Tarrant & K. Hughes (Eds.), *Qualitative secondary analysis* (pp. 101–118). London: Sage.

Taylor, F. W. (1919). *The principles of scientific management*. New York, NY: Harper and Brothers.

Thompson, C. (1996). Caring consumers: Gendered consumption meanings and the juggling lifestyle. *Journal of Consumer Research, 22*(4), 388–407.

Thompson, E. P. (1967). Time, work-discipline and industrial capitalism. *Past & Present, 38*, 56–97.

Tietze, S., & Musson, G. (2002). When "work" meets "home". *Time & Society, 11*(2–3), 315–334.

Tomlinson, J. (2007). *The culture of speed: The coming of immediacy*. London: Sage.

Tracy. B. (2004/2012). *Eat that frog: Get more of the important things done today*. London: Hodder & Stoughton.

Tuckle, S. (2011). *Alone together: Why we expect more from technology and less from each other*. New York, NY: Basic Books.

Urry, J. (2000). *Sociology beyond societies: Mobilities for the twenty-first century*. London: Routledge.

Urry, J. (2016). *What is the future?* Cambridge: Polity Press.

Van Der Ploeg, H. P., Venugopal, K., Chau, J. Y., Van Poppel, M. N. M., Breedveld, K. Merom, D., & Bauman, A. E. (2013). Non-occupational sedentary behaviors population changes in the Netherlands, 1975–2005. *American Journal of Preventive Medicine, 44*(4), 382–387.

Vanderkam, L. (2018). *Off the clock: Feel less busy while getting more done*. London: Piatkus.

Vanek, J. (1974). Time spent in housework. *Scientific American, 5*(231), 116–120.

Veblem, T. (1899/2007). *The theory of the leisure class*. [Edited and with an Introduction by Martha Banta]. Oxford: Oxford University Press.

Vilhelmson, B., Elldér, E., & Thulin, E. (2018). What did we do when the internet wasn't around? Variation in free-time activities among three young-adult cohorts from 1990/1991, 2000/2001, and 2010/2011. *New Media & Society, 20*(8), 2898–2916.

Virilio, P. (2006). *Speed and politics: An essay on dromology*. Los Angeles, CA: Semiotext(e).

Voorpostel, M., Van Der Lippe, T., & Gershuny, J. (2010). Spending time together-changes over four decades in leisure time spent with a spouse. *Journal of Leisure Research, 42*(2), 243–265.

Wajcman, J. (2008). Life in the fast lane? Towards a sociology of technology and time. *British Journal of Sociology, 59*(1), 59–77.

Wajcman, J. (2015). *Pressed for time: The acceleration of life on digital capitalism*. Chicago, IL: University of Chicago Press.

Wajcman, J. (2019). The digital architecture of time management. *Science, Technology, & Human Values, 44*(2), 315–337.

Wallman, J. (2019). *Time and how to spend it: The 7 rules for richer, happier days*. London: WH Allen.

Warren, T. (2015). Work–life balance/imbalance: The dominance of the middle class and the neglect of the working class. *British Journal of Sociology, 66*(4), 691–717.

Weber, M. (1905/1930). *The Protestant ethic and the spirit of capitalism*. [T. Parsons, Trans.]. London: Routledge.

Wenger, E. (1998). *Communities of practice: Learning, meaning, and identity*. Cambridge: Cambridge University Press.

Wittman, M. (2016). *Felt time: The psychology of how we perceive time*. [E. Butler, Trans.]. Cambridge, MA: MIT Press.

Woodall, P. (2017). The data repurposing challenge: New pressures from data analytics. *Journal of Data and Information Quality, 8*(3–4), 1–4.

World Economic Forum. (2020). Hitting women hard, pandemic makes gender poverty gap wider – U.N. Retrieved from https://www.weforum.org/agenda/2020/09/covid19-women-pandemic-gender-poverty-gap-united-nations. Accessed on September 4, 2020.

Wyllie, J. (2020, April 1). Roberto Esposito: Philosopher of community and immunity? *Church Life Journal*. Retrieved from https://churchlifejournal.nd.edu/articles/roberto-esposito-philosopher-of-community-and-immunity/

Zalewski, D. (2012). The hours: How Christian Marclay created the ultimate digital mosaic. *The New Yorker*, March 5. Retrieved from https://www.newyorker.com/magazine/2012/03/12/the-hours-daniel-zalewski

Zelizer, V. A. (2012). How I became a relational economic sociologist and what does that mean? *Politics & Society*, *40*(2), 145–174, p. 147.

Zuzanek, J. (2017). What happened to the society of leisure? Of the gap between the "haves" and "have nots" (Canadian time use and well-being trends). *Social Indicators Research*, *130*(1), 27–38.

Index

Note: Page numbers followed by "*n*" indicate notes.